D1785530

Brian Hart

with Herbert Puchta and Jeff Stranks

English in Mind

* Teacher's Book 5

CAMBRIDGE
UNIVERSITY PRESS

CAMBRIDGE UNIVERSITY PRESS
Cambridge, New York, Melbourne, Madrid, Cape Town, Singapore, São Paulo, Delhi

Cambridge University Press
The Edinburgh Building, Cambridge CB2 8RU, UK

www.cambridge.org
Information on this title: www.cambridge.org/9780521708982

© Cambridge University Press 2008

This book is in copyright. Subject to statutory exception
and to the provisions of relevant collective licensing agreements,
no reproduction of any part may take place without
the written permission of Cambridge University Press.

First published in 2008

Printed in the United Kingdom at the University Press, Cambridge

A catalogue record for this publication is available from the British Library

ISBN 978-0-521-70898-2 Teacher's Book

ISBN 978-0-521-70896-8 Student's Book

ISBN 978-0-521-70897-5 Workbook with Audio CD / CD-ROM

ISBN 978-0-521-70899-9 Teacher's Resource Pack

ISBN 978-0-521-70901-9 Class Audio CDs

Cambridge University Press has no responsibility for the persistence
or accuracy of URLs for external or third-party Internet websites
referred to in this book, and does not guarantee that any content
on such websites is, or will remain, accurate or appropriate.

Contents

Writing Bank ● Pronunciation ● Speaking: extra material ● Phonetic chart ● Wordlist

Listening	Speaking	Reading	Writing
Different animal abilities	Talking about 'sixth sense' in animals and people	Animals know before Literature: *Call of the Wild*	Animal story
A book review programme	Interviews Pronunciation: sounding polite or angry	Listening with your eyes	Letter of complaint
Careers talk about advertising	Designing and presenting a marketing campaign for a product of your choice	Advertising: the logic of emotions Culture: The Ultimate Refund	Covering letter of application
Radio programme on how to cope with stress Song: *Stand My Ground*	Talking about your reactions in stressful situations	Fight or flight? Dealing with stress	Report and proposal
Two women spies	Talking about crime movies Giving a short talk based on a picture	Behind the scenes – true stories from the movies Literature: *Charlotte Gray*	A biography
Phone-in / game show: *A Likely Story*	A story or anecdote Pronunciation: stress in phrases	The rise and rise of urban legends	Newspaper article
An interview about metaphors	Discussing what inspires your own creativity	What inspires the inspirational? Culture: Inspired Buildings	Poem with metaphors and similes
Virtual holidays Song: *Virtual World*	Talking about virtual holidays	The Entropia Universe	Informal letter or email turning down an invitation
Mirroring techniques	Talking about learning through imitation	A revealing reflection Literature: *Life of Pi*	Discursive composition
Conversation about cheating in sport	Talking about sports events and athletes Short monologues Pronunciation: linking sounds	Sport in the news	Description of a sporting event (magazine)
Candidates audition for a reality TV show	Talking about superheroes Designing and presenting a group of superheroes	Superheroes – Have you got what it takes? Culture: Superheroes around the world	Film review
Teenagers talk about being on their own Song: *Message in a Bottle*	Discussing what it would be like to live completely on your own Talking about what to take to a desert island	Island diary	A leaflet
People of different ages comment on the reading text	Talking about life choices	The Battle of the Generations Literature: Two poems about ageing: *Beautiful Old Age* and *A Madrigal*	Formal letter to a magazine editor
A scientist: extending life expectancy	Conversations / discussions Pronunciation: stress and intonation	Hard talk – cosmetic surgery	Report and article
Suggesting items for the museum	Discussing objects for a People's Museum Taking part in a discussion to plan a school trip	The People's Museum Culture: Museums around the world	A note
Radio film review of *Freaky Friday* Song: *My Generation*	Discussing 'swapping places' in a family	Culture Shock	Meaningless proverbs and cinquains

Introduction

'If you can teach teenagers, you can teach anyone.' Michael Grinder

Teaching teenagers is an interesting and challenging task. A group of adolescents can be highly motivated, cooperative and fun to teach on one day, and the next day the whole group or individual students might turn out to be truly 'difficult' – the teacher might, for example, be faced with discipline problems, disruptive or provocative behaviour, a lack of motivation, or unwillingness on the students' part to do homework assigned to them.

These problems are often rooted in the significant changes that teenagers experience. The key challenge in the transition between being a child and becoming an adult is the teenager's struggle for identity – when they start to develop a distinct sense of who they are. As a result, teenagers can feel threatened, and at the same time experience overwhelming emotions. In Kieran Egan's theory,[1] this phase is known as *romantic understanding*. Teenagers in this phase frequently try to compensate for perceived threats with extremely rude behaviour, and try to 'hide' their emotions and insecurities behind a wall of extreme outward conformity.

As they grow older, teenagers enter a new phase, which Egan calls *philosophic understanding*. Here, teenagers are driven by the desire to understand the workings of hierarchies and theories. It is through their growing understanding of these systems that they begin to see how facts and details are part of a bigger picture, and the more they understand, the more their confidence grows. Generally, students now feel much less threatened by the world than younger teenagers.

When choosing the right teaching content for this age group, we should note that students' interest shifts away from 'sensational' topics towards more 'academic' areas such as philosophy, sociology, politics and psychology. This is when teenagers are fascinated by metacognition – thinking about how we think. Perhaps most importantly for us as their language teachers, this is also when young people are significantly more interested in language, an interest driven mainly by the wish to learn about and discuss more sophisticated topics.

Insights into the dynamics of these changes might help us to understand better the complex situation our students are in. However, such insights do not automatically lead to more success in teaching. We need to react to the challenges in a professional way. This includes the need to:

- select content and organise the students' learning according to their psychological needs
- create a positive learning atmosphere
- cater for differences in students' learning styles and intelligence(s), and facilitate the development of our students' study skills.

English in Mind has been written taking all these points into account. They have significantly influenced the choice of texts, artwork and design, the structure of the units, the typology of exercises, and the means by which students' study skills are facilitated and extended.

The importance of the content for success

There are a number of reasons why the choice of the right content has a crucial influence over success or failure in the teaching of adolescents. Teachers frequently observe that teenagers in the 'romantic phase' are reluctant to 'talk about themselves'. This has to do with the adolescent's need for psychological security. Consequently, the 'further away' from their own world the content of the teaching is, the more motivating and stimulating it will be for the students. Their preference for psychologically remote content goes hand in hand with a fascination with extremes and realistic details. Furthermore, students love identifying with heroes and heroines, because these idols are perceived to embody the qualities needed in order to survive in a threatening world: qualities such as courage, genius, creativity, and love. In the foreign language class, students can become fascinated with stories about heroes and heroines to which they can ascribe such qualities. *English in Mind* treats students as young adults, offering them a range of interesting topics and a balance between educational value and teenage interest and fun.

Of course, not all students grow out of the *'romantic understanding'* phase exactly when and how we may expect. This is why *English in Mind 5* contains content that still reflects the psychological needs of that phase. However, a much bigger proportion of the texts enables students to learn to understand and construct theories about how nature and society work, and to discuss social values. The content also aims to help students understand their own role as part of society and the influence that historical and social processes have on the development of the world and on their own lives.

[1] An excellent analysis of teenage development and consequences for our teaching in general can be found in the following two books by Kieran Egan. Both books have had a significant influence on the thinking behind *English in Mind*, and the development of the course:
Romantic Understanding, Routledge and Kegan Paul, New York and London, 1990.
An Imaginative Approach to Teaching, Jossey-Bass, John Wiley and Sons, Inc., San Francisco, 2005.

A positive learning atmosphere

The creation of a positive learning atmosphere largely depends on the rapport between teacher and students, and that which students have among themselves. It requires the teacher to be a genuine, empathetic listener, and to have a number of other psychological skills. *English in Mind* supports the teacher's task of creating positive learning experiences through: clear tasks; a large number of carefully designed exercises; regular opportunities for the students to check their own work; and a learning process designed to guarantee that the students will learn to express themselves both in speaking and in writing.

Learning styles and multiple intelligences

There is significant evidence that students will be better motivated, and learn more successfully, if differences in learning styles and intelligences are taken into account in the teaching-learning process.[2] The development of a number of activities in *English in Mind* has been influenced by such insights, and students also find frequent study tips that show them how they can better utilise their own resources.[3]

The methodology used in *English in Mind*

Skills: *English in Mind* uses a communicative, multi-skills approach to develop the students' foreign language abilities in an interesting and motivational way. A wide range of interesting text types is used to present authentic use of language, including magazine and newspaper clippings, interviews, narratives, songs, and extracts from English literature.

Grammar: *English in Mind* is based on a strong grammatical syllabus and takes into account students' mixed abilities by dealing with grammar in a carefully graded way, and offering additional teaching support (see below).

Vocabulary: *English in Mind* offers a systematic vocabulary syllabus including important lexical chunks for conversation.

Culture: *English in Mind* gives students insights into a number of important cross-cultural and intercultural themes. Significant cultural features of English-speaking countries are presented, and students are involved in actively reflecting on the similarities and differences between other cultures and their own.

Consolidation: Four Check your progress revision sections per level will give teachers a clear picture of their students' progress and make students aware of what they have learned. Each revision section is also accompanied by a project which gives students the opportunity to use new language in a less controlled context and allows for learner independence.

Teacher support: *English in Mind* is clearly structured and easy to teach. The Teacher's Book offers step-by-step lesson notes, background information on content, culture and language, additional teaching ideas and the tapescripts. The accompanying Teacher's Resource Pack contains photocopiable materials for further practice and extra lessons, taking into consideration the needs of mixed-ability groups by providing extra material for fast finishers or students who need more support, as well as formal tests.

Student support: *English in Mind* offers systematic support to students through: Skills Tips; classroom language; guidance in units to help with the development of classroom discourse and the students' writing; a wordlist including phonetic transcriptions (at the back of the Student's Book); and a grammar reference section (at the back of the Workbook).

English in Mind: components

Each level of the *English in Mind* series contains the following components:

- Student's Book
- Class CDs (Class Cassettes available for levels Starter – 4)
- Workbook with an accompanying Audio CD / CD-ROM
- Teacher's Book
- Teacher's Resource Pack
- Website resources
- Video and DVD for levels Starter, 1, 2 and 3

The Student's Book

Modular structure: The *English in Mind* Student's Books are organised on a modular basis – each contains four modules of four units per module. The modules have broad themes and are organised as follows: a) a two-page module opener; b) four units of six pages each; c) a two-page Check your progress section.

Module openers are two pages which allow teachers to 'set the scene' for their students, concerning both the informational content and the language content of what is to come in the module itself. This helps both to motivate the students and to provide the important 'signposting' which allows them to see where their learning is going next. The pages contain: a) a visual task in which students match topics to a selection of pictures taken from the coming units; b) a list of skills learning objectives for the module; c) a short matching task which previews the main grammar content of the coming module; and d) a simple vocabulary task, again previewing the coming content.

---

[2] See for example Eric Jensen: *Brain-Based Learning and Teaching*, Turning Point Publishing, Del Mar, CA, USA, 1995, on learning styles. An overview of the theory of multiple intelligences can be found in Howard Gardner: *Multiple Intelligences: The Theory in Practice*, Basic Books, New York, 1993.

[3] See Marion Williams and Robert L. Burden: *Psychology for Language Teachers*, Cambridge University Press, 1997 (pp. 143–162), on how the learner deals with the process of learning.

The **units** contain the following:

- an opening **reading** text
- one or two **grammar** sections
- one or two sets of **vocabulary**, sometimes followed by **pronunciation**
- **integrated speaking** and **listening skills** work
- either a **Literature in mind** text, a **Culture in mind** text, a **Speaking focus** or a **song**, followed by **writing skills** work.

The **reading texts** aim to engage and motivate the students with interesting and relevant content, and provide contextualised examples of target grammar and lexis. The texts have 'lead-in' tasks and are followed by comprehension tasks of various kinds. All the opening texts are also recorded on the Class CD, which allows teachers to follow the initial reading with a 'read and listen' phase, giving the students the invaluable opportunity of connecting the written word with the spoken version, which is especially useful for auditory learners. Alternatively, with stronger classes, teachers may decide to do one of the exercises as a listening task, with books closed.

There are one or two **Grammar** sections per unit. The emphasis throughout is on active involvement in the learning process. The examples from the texts are isolated and used as the basis for tasks, which focus students on both the concept and the form of the target grammar area. Students are then usually encouraged to find other examples and work out rules for themselves. Occasionally there are also Look boxes which highlight an important connected issue concerning the grammar area; for example, in Unit 9, work on hedging and boosting using adverbs has a Look box reminding students of adverb position. This is followed by a number of graded exercises, both receptive and productive, which allow students to begin to employ the target language in different contexts and to produce realistic language. Next, there is usually a speaking activity, aiming at further personalisation of the language.

Each unit has at least one **Vocabulary** section, with specific word fields. Again, examples from the initial text are focused on, and a lexical set is developed, with exercises for students to put the vocabulary into use. Vocabulary is frequently recycled in later texts in the unit (e.g. photostories or Culture in mind texts), and also in later units.

Pronunciation is included for every unit. There are exercises on common phoneme problems and also aspects of stress (within words, and across sentences), intonation, elision and links between sounds.

Language skills are present in every unit. There is always at least one **listening skills** activity, with listening texts of various genres; at least one (but usually several) **speaking skills** activity for fluency development; **reading skills** are taught through the opening texts and also later texts in some units, as well as the Culture in mind sections. There is always a **writing skills** task, at the end of each unit.

In level 5 of the course, each unit includes one of the following: a **Literature in mind** section (Units 1, 5, 9 and 13), a **Speaking focus** (Units 2, 6, 10 and 14), a **Culture in mind** section (Units 3, 7, 11 and 15) or a **song** (Units 4, 8, 12 and 16). The **Literature in mind** sections each present an extract from a novel in English, or poems, as an opportunity for students to access and appreciate some fine writing from different periods and in different styles. The **Speaking focus** sections give students model speaking situations accompanied by listening tasks that focus on meaning and then useful everyday language that will help students to complete a similar speaking task themselves. The **Culture in mind** reading texts provide further reading practice, and an opportunity for students to develop their knowledge and understanding of the world at large and in particular the English-speaking world. They include a very wide variety of stimulating topics: for example, consumer culture, inspirational architecture, comic superheroes from around the world, and unusual museums.

The final activity in each unit is a **writing skills** task. These provide an opportunity for students to further their control of language and to experiment in the production of tasks in a variety of genres (e.g. letters, emails, reports etc.). There are model texts for the students to aid their own writing, and exercises providing guidance in terms of content and organisation. Through the completion of the writing tasks, students, if they wish, can also build up a bank of materials, or 'portfolio', during their period of learning: this can be very useful to them as the source of a sense of clear progress and as a means of self-assessment. A 'portfolio' of work can also be shown to other people (exam bodies, parents, even future employers) as evidence of achievement in language learning. Many of the writing tasks also provide useful and relevant practice for examinations such as Cambridge ESOL FCE and CAE.

When a module of four units closes, the module ends with a two-page **Check your progress** section. Here the teacher will find exercises in the grammar and vocabulary that were presented in the module. The purpose of these (as opposed to the more formal tests offered in the Teacher's Resource Pack) is for teachers and students alike to quickly check the learning and progress made during the module just covered; they can be done in class or at home. Every exercise has a marking scheme, and students can use the marks they gain to do some simple self-assessment of their progress (a light 'task' is offered for this).

Beyond the modules and units themselves, *English in Mind* offers at the **end of each Student's Book** a further set of materials for teachers and students. These consist of:

- **Writing Bank:** six genre-specific writing pages which provide a written model with guided language and organisational analysis which students study before undertaking a similar task. The tasks range from informal and formal emails and letters, to reports and narrative compositions. They aim to help students develop their writing portfolio and exam writing techniques.
- A listing of **phonetic symbols**, for student reference.
- A **wordlist** with the core lexis of the Student's Book, with phonetic transcriptions. This is organised by unit, and within each unit heading there are the major word-fields, divided into parts of speech (verbs, nouns, adjectives, etc.). The wordlists are a feature that teachers can use in classrooms, for example to develop students' reference skills, or to indicate ways in which they themselves might organise vocabulary notebooks, and by students at home, as a useful reference and also to prepare for tests or progress checks.

The Workbook

The Workbook is a resource for both teachers and students, providing further practice in the language and skills covered in the Student's Book. It is organised unit-by-unit, following the Student's Book. Each Workbook unit has six pages, and the following contents:

Exercises: an extensive range of supporting exercises in the grammatical, lexical and phonological areas of the Student's Book unit, following the progression of the unit, so that teachers can use the exercises either during or at the end of the Student's Book unit.

Literature in mind and **Culture in mind:** extra exercises on these sections following up material in the Student's Book.

Skills in mind: these pages contain a separate skills development syllabus, which focuses on one or two main skill areas in each unit. There is also a skill tip relating to the main skill area, which the students can immediately put into action when doing the skills task(s).

Unit Check: this is a one-page check of knowledge of the key language of the unit, integrating both grammar and vocabulary in the three exercise types. The exercise types are: a) a cloze text to be completed using items given in a box; b) a sentence-level multiple choice exercise; c) a guided error correction exercise.

At the end of each Workbook, there is a **Grammar reference** section. Here, there are explanations of the main grammar topics of each unit, with examples. It can be used for reference by students at home, or the teacher might wish to refer to it in class if the students appreciate grammatical explanations.

The Workbook includes an **Audio CD / CD-ROM**, which contains both the listening material for the Workbook (listening texts and pronunciation exercises) and a CD-ROM element, containing definitions for the wordlist items with a spoken model for each one, and a range of engaging, carefully graded grammar and vocabulary, and pronunciation exercises provide further practice of language presented in each module.

The Teacher's Book

The Teacher's Book contains:

- clear, simple, practical **notes** on each unit and how to implement the exercises as effectively as possible
- complete **tapescripts** for all listening and pronunciation activities
- complete **answers** to all exercises (grammar, vocabulary, comprehension questions, etc.)
- **optional further activities**, for stronger or weaker classes, to facilitate the use of the material in mixed-ability classes
- **background notes** relating to the information content (where appropriate) of reading texts and Culture in mind pages
- **language notes** relating to grammatical areas, to assist less experienced teachers who might have concerns about the target language and how it operates (these can also be used to refer to the Workbook Grammar reference section)
- a complete **answer key** and **tapescripts** for the **Workbook**.

The Teacher's Resource Pack

This extra component, spiral bound for easy photocopying, contains the following photocopiable resources:

- an **Entry Test** which can be used for diagnostic testing or also used for remedial work
- **module tests** containing separate sections for: Grammar, Vocabulary, Everyday English, Reading, Listening (the recordings for which are on the Class CDs), Speaking and Writing. A **key** for the tests is also provided
- **photocopiable communicative activities:** one page for each unit reflecting the core grammar and/or vocabulary of the unit
- **photocopiable extra grammar exercises:** one page of four exercises for each unit, reflecting the key grammar areas of the unit
- **teaching notes** for the above.

Web resources

In addition to information about the series, the *English in Mind* website contains downloadable pages of further activities and exercises for students as well as other resources. It can be found at this part of the Cambridge University Press website:

www.cambridge.org/elt/englishinmind

Module 1
Logic and intuition

YOU WILL LEARN ABOUT ...

Ask students to look at the pictures on the page. Ask them to read through the topics in the box and check that they understand each item. You can ask them the following questions, in L1 if appropriate:

1 What is the woman holding?
2 Do you think this is true for society today?
3 What is the elephant doing?
4 Where are the people in the picture?
5 Why is the man running away in the picture?
6 What is this picture used for?

In pairs or small groups, students discuss which topic area they think each picture matches. Check the answers.

Answers
1 Women in music
2 Shopping behaviour
3 Amazing animal behaviour
4 Interview techniques
5 How humans behave in fight or flight situations
6 Advertising

YOU WILL LEARN HOW TO ...

Use grammar
Students read through the grammar points and the examples. Go through the first item with students as an example. In pairs, students now match the grammar items in their book. Check answers.

Answers
Past perfect continuous: The night before the tsunami hit, the elephants had been making strange noises.
Past perfect passive: If the city had not been evacuated, a lot of people would have been killed.
Future in the past: This time she knew she would win.
Adjective order: It won an award for the most innovative modern building.
Position of adverbs: Surprisingly, the answer was yes.
Talking about tendencies: In stressful situations my mind tends to go blank.

Use vocabulary
Write the headings on the board. Go through the items in the Student's Book and check understanding. Now ask students if they can think of one more item for the *Animal sounds* heading. Elicit some responses and add them to the list on the board. Students now do the same for the other headings. Some possibilities are:

Animal sounds: *roar, squeak*

Making decisions: *a split-second decision, dither*

Advertising: *logo, jingle*

Coping with stress: *don't overdo it, take some exercise*

1 Animal instincts

Unit overview

TOPIC: Animals – their special abilities and the sounds they make

TEXTS
Reading and listening: an article about animals' reactions to natural disasters
Listening: animal abilities
Reading and speaking: three news reports about animals
Reading: an extract from *The Call of the Wild* by Jack London
Writing: a magazine article

SPEAKING AND FUNCTIONS
Discussing the sixth sense

LANGUAGE
Grammar: past perfect continuous, past perfect simple and past perfect passive (review)
Vocabulary: animal sounds

1 Read and listen

If you set the background information as a homework research task, ask the students to tell the class what they found out.

BACKGROUND INFORMATION

The Kingdom of Thailand: lies in South-east Asia. The word Thai means *freedom* in the Thai language and is also the name of the majority ethnic group.

Tsunami: is a series of waves created when an ocean is rapidly displaced on a massive scale. Earthquakes, mass movements above or below water, volcanic eruptions and other underwater explosions all have the potential to generate a tsunami. The effects of a tsunami can range from unnoticeable to devastating. The term tsunami comes from the Japanese words meaning harbour (*tsu*) and wave (*nami*).

Sri Lanka: is an island nation in South Asia, located about 31 kilometres off the southern coast of India. It was known as Ceylon until 1972. It is home to more than 20 million people and is a multi-religious and multi-ethnic nation. Famous for the production and export of tea, coffee, rubber and coconuts, the natural beauty of Sri Lanka's tropical forests, beaches and landscape, as well as its rich cultural heritage, make it a world-famous tourist destination.

Yala National Park: is an important national park on the south-east coast of Sri Lanka. The park was badly damaged by the tsunami on 26 December 2004 but few animals died.

Japan: is an island nation in East Asia. Japan comprises over 3,000 islands and most of these are mountainous, many volcanic, including its highest peak, Mount Fuji. Japan has the world's tenth largest population, with about 128 million people. Its capital and largest city is Tokyo and the Greater Tokyo Area is the largest metropolitan area in the world, with over 30 million residents.

United States Geological Survey: was established on 3 March 1879 and provides scientific information intended to help educate the public about natural resources, natural hazards, geological data, and to help us understand the Earth. This data is used to minimise loss of life and property from natural disasters; manage water, energy and mineral resources; and enhance and protect quality of life on Earth.

Warm up

Books closed. Write the title of the unit on the board and ask students what they understand by it. What 'animal' instincts do human beings have? Ask which of our instincts remain from prehistoric days and ask for examples of how we use them today.

(a) Ask students to look at the pictures and make a list of the characteristics and abilities of elephants. Elicit some ideas and write them on the board.

(b) ◁⑴ Ask students if they remember the tsunami in Thailand in 2004. Students read the text and listen to the recording to check their answers to Exercise 1a. Before listening pre-teach difficult vocabulary: *earthquakes, trunks, chains, uphill, low frequency, electronically tagged, warning signal, tremors, evacuated.* The text includes several difficult words, but tell students only to focus on general understanding at this stage. Ask students which title they feel is most appropriate and listen to their reasons for their answers. Play the recording again, pausing as necessary to clarify any problems.

TAPESCRIPT
See the reading text on pages 6 and 7 of the Student's Book.

c 🔊 Check understanding of sentences 1–8. Students read the text and listen again in order to complete the exercise. Ask students to compare their answers in pairs before feedback in open class. Ask students to correct the false statements. Play the recording again with pauses if necessary.

Answers
2 True 3 False (they can feel vibrations, but cannot hear it) 4 False (animals can sense lots of things)
5 True 6 True 7 True 8 False (only a small portion of the population was hurt or killed)

d Read through the words and definitions, and ask students to match them. The words are in the order of the text. Check answers.

Answers
2 h 3 b 4 d 5 a 6 c 7 g 8 i 9 f

> **Discussion box**
> **Weaker classes:** Students can choose one question to discuss.
>
> **Stronger classes:** In pairs or small groups, students go through the questions in the box and discuss them.
>
> Monitor and help as necessary, encouraging students to express themselves in English and to use any vocabulary they have learned from the text. Ask pairs or groups to feedback to the class and discuss any interesting points further.

2 Grammar

Past perfect continuous, past perfect simple and past perfect passive (review)

Students covered the past perfect continuous and the past perfect passive in SB4 Unit 8 and the past perfect simple in SB3 Unit 4 and SB4 Unit 1.

If you set the background information as a homework research task, ask the students to tell the class what they found out.

> ## BACKGROUND INFORMATION
>
> *The Incredible Journey:* is a children's book by Canadian author Sheila Burnford. It was first published in 1961 and tells of the magnificent adventure shared by three domestic animals as they travel in the wilderness, searching for their masters. It reveals the suffering and stress of a difficult journey together with the loyalty and courage of the three animals.

a **Weaker classes:** If students need to be reminded of the rules of the past perfect, write the following sentences on the board:
When I arrived, the film started.
When I arrived, the film had started.

Ask students to find the example of the past perfect and ask why it is used. (It is used to describe a past event which took place before another past event. In the first example, the actions are connected or take place one directly after the other.)

Then follow the procedure for stronger classes.

Stronger classes: Look at the example sentences and focus on the verbs *had been released* and *had been making*. You may like to do this as a whole class exercise and elicit the names of the tenses used and draw attention to the forms (*had + been +* past participle; *had + been + –ing*). For sentence 1, ask: *Were gases released before or after they detected them? (Before.) Did the elephants make just one noise or a series of noises over a period of time? (A series of noises.)*

Answers
1 Past perfect passive
2 Past perfect continuous
3 Past perfect simple

> **Language note**
> Remind students that we don't describe states with continuous tenses. We use the past perfect, not the past perfect continuous, even when we focus on the length of a situation up to a particular past time, e.g. *I had owned my bicycle for three months when it was stolen* (not *… had been owning*).

b Ask students to read quickly through the text in Exercise 1b and find two more examples of both the past perfect passive and the past perfect continuous. Point out that the past perfect continuous is used to talk about a situation or activity that went on before a particular past time and finished at that time or shortly before it.

Answers
Past perfect continuous: had been behaving
Past perfect simple: had never heard
Past perfect passive: had been abandoned; had been reported; had been observed; had not been evacuated

> **Language note**
> Point out to students that the past perfect is not always necessary if the order of events is made clear by a time expression, e.g. *Before the train arrived, Sally bought a newspaper and a cup of coffee.*

c) Tell students they are going to read a review of a book called *The Incredible Journey*. Students complete the sentences by using the correct tense. Ask them to compare answers with a partner before feedback.

Answers
2 had happened   3 had been forgotten   4 had been treated   5 had been travelling   6 had had   7 had faced   8 had been told   9 had been looking

OPTIONAL ACTIVITIES

Weaker classes: If students have difficulty understanding the concept of the past perfect tenses, you may like to do the following activity. Read the following passage aloud two or three words at a time, pausing while students write down what you say. Make sure you give students time to write each group of words before repeating them.

Yesterday, I was very hungry. I bought a hamburger and went to the park. When I had eaten my hamburger I was thirsty, so I went to buy some water. When I got to the shop, I realised I had lost all my money – £10!! I went home and when I opened the door, I screamed because my dog had eaten my shoes. I sat down to watch TV. I had been watching TV for twenty minutes when my friend called. He was very happy. He told me that he had found £10 while he was walking in the park and he asked me if I wanted to go for a coffee.

Let students compare their texts. Help students with any words they have missed. Ask them to work in pairs and underline the examples of the past perfect tenses. Ask students to draw a vertical line in their books and place the actions in the text on that line in the correct order. Check their answers in open class, using the text to clarify the different uses of the tenses.

Stronger classes: Tell students that the past perfect tenses are commonly used in newspaper stories. Stories often start with a sentence in the past before going on to describe the actions leading up to that event using the past perfect tenses. Write the following sentences on the board:

Arnold Schwarzenegger was arrested this morning.

Police say they have discovered a wolf-boy in Northern England.

Explorer Joey Deacon said he was happy to be alive when he was rescued this morning.

Ask students to write down the events leading up to them. Encourage them to use examples of the past perfect continuous and past perfect passive in their stories. In pairs, students tell each other their stories. Listen to some of their ideas in open class.

Grammar notebook
Remind students to note down the rules for the past perfect continuous, past perfect simple and past perfect passive and to write a few examples of their own.

3 Listen

If you set the background information as a homework research task, ask the students to tell the class what they found out.

BACKGROUND INFORMATION

Silkworm: is the larva or caterpillar of a moth that is very important economically as the producer of silk. Its Latin name *Bombyx mori* means "silkworm of the mulberry tree" and a silkworm's diet consists solely of mulberry leaves. It is entirely dependent on humans for its reproduction and no longer occurs in the wild. It is native to northern China where silk culture has been practised for at least 5000 years.

a) Ask students to look at the pictures and discuss what they know about each of the creatures. Listen to some of their ideas in open class. Ask students to match the words with the pictures. Check answers.

Answers
1 butterfly   2 chameleon   3 silkworm   4 shark   5 cricket

b) Read through statements a–g with students. Check understanding of difficult vocabulary: *antennae, membrane, presence*. Students match the animals to the statements. Students compare answers with a partner before feedback.

Answers
2 e   3 f   4 g   5 b

c) 🔊 Students listen to the recording to check their answers. Emphasise that they should not worry about unknown vocabulary, but should listen for the main points. If necessary, play the recording again, pausing for students to check answers.

TAPESCRIPT

Host   Good evening ladies and gentlemen, and welcome to *Animal Antics*, the show that brings the amazing world of animals right into your living room. My name's Ron Harris, and I'm your host on today's show. As always, we start with our weekly animal quiz. Let's have a big hand for our contestants: Gillian Knowles, who is our defending champion, and tonight's challenger, Scott Boyd.

Scott/Gillian   Hello.

Host   Welcome to you both.

OK, the rules are the same as ever. First person to buzz gets the chance to answer. One point if the answer's correct. If it's wrong, of course, the other player gets a chance to answer and get the point. So, fingers on the buzzers for the first question. Butterflies have highly developed chemoreceptors. What exactly are chemoreceptors?

And it's Scott who's first off the buzzer.

Scott Chemoreceptors are taste receptors, Ron. They allow us to taste things. We've got ours in our tongues, but butterflies have them in their feet.

Host That's correct, Scott. Butterflies, bees and houseflies all have chemo or taste receptors on their feet. Before a female butterfly lays her eggs on a leaf, she walks across it to make sure that it's OK for her babies to feed on. Now, not many people know that! And so, on to question two. Name an animal that can look in two different directions at the same time. And it's Scott again.

Scott An eagle?

Host No, I'm afraid you're wrong this time, Scott. Gillian, do you have an answer?

Gillian I hope so, Ron. Is it a chameleon?

Host Yes, indeed it is. Chameleons can not only change their colour to camouflage themselves, blend in with the background and become invisible, but they can also move their eyes independently, meaning they can look in different directions at the same time. Imagine that! If my mother could do that, I'd have been in real trouble when I was a boy!

Now, question three, how does a male silkworm find a partner? And it's Scott this time …

Scott I think it's by spinning a trail of silk that the female follows all the way to his cocoon.

Host Sorry, no … Gillian?

Gillian Is it by producing low-level vibrations that only female silkworms can pick up?

Host No, I'm afraid you're both wrong. It's through smell. The female gives off a special smell, and the male silkworm can smell a potential mate from as far away as eleven kilometres! But the male can't smell anything apart from female silkworms, and he's as blind as a bat, too. And now we move on to sharks … Always popular! Question four. In what way do sharks detect movement? Scott?

Scott Well, they detect the electrical charges that are sent when another animal, or fish of course, moves a muscle. So they know exactly when there's prey close by.

Host That's correct, Scott. And it's no good staying still because your heart is a muscle too, and sharks can even detect that. Now, doesn't that make you want to go into the water?! And now it's time for the last question. How do crickets hear? And it's Scott again.

Scott That's an easy one, Ron! They use their antennae. On top of their heads.

Host Well, Scott, the question isn't that easy. I'm afraid you're wrong. Gillian, can you tell us the answer?

Gillian Err, I think they pick up sound vibrations through a membrane on their legs …

Host That's absolutely right, Gillian. Well done to you both, but this week's winner and still champion is …

(d) 🔊 Play the recording again. Students listen to find out who won the quiz.

Answer
Gillian

┌─ OPTIONAL ACTIVITY ─────────

Divide the class into two teams and ask each team to write ten questions based on their knowledge of nature and the animal world. Students ask their questions to the other team. Allow the team to confer before answering and to use dictionaries if they do not know the answer in English, but only allow one attempt! You may like to use the following questions to get them started:

Which animal lays the biggest egg? (ostrich)
How many stomachs does a cow have? (four)
Which animal's babies are called foals? (horse)
What was the first animal to be sent into space? (dog)
What African animal kills the most people? (crocodile)

4 Vocabulary
Animal sounds

(a) 🔊 Look at the pictures with students. Students may be interested to know that different languages give different sounds to animals. What sounds do the animals make in their country? You may like to ask students to imitate the sounds made by the animals before listening to the recording! Before listening ask students to repeat the names of the sounds after you. Listen to the recording and ask students to match the sound to the animal. The words are onomatopoeic (they sound like what they refer to) so it may help students remember the words if they repeat them in an exaggerated fashion to sound like the animal in question.

Answers
1 f   2 e   3 g   4 a   5 b   6 d   7 c

(b) In pairs, ask students to complete the sentences. It may help to imagine which animal sound would be most likely in each situation. Check answers.

Answers
2 roared   3 grunted   4 hissed   5 croak
6 crowed   7 bleats

Vocabulary notebook
Encourage students to start a new section *Animals and animal sounds* in their notebook and add these words. They may find it useful to note down translations of the words too.

Write the following idioms on the board. Ask students to complete the sentences using the animals from Exercise 4a. In pairs, students compare answers and discuss the meaning of each idiom before feedback.

1 *John's in the* _____ *house.* (dog: someone is annoyed with him)
2 *Philip is the black* _____ *of the family.* (sheep: the rest of the family think he's a bad person)
3 *He was sweating like a* _____ . (pig: he was sweating a lot)
4 *He felt as if he had a* _____ *in his throat.* (frog: he can't speak clearly, perhaps because of a sore throat or a cold)
5 *He took the* _____ *'s share of the work.* (lion: he did most of the work)
6 *He is a real* _____ *in the grass.* (snake: he pretends to be your friend while secretly doing things to harm you)

5 Read and speak

(a) Pre-teach *toddler* and *playpen*. Tell students they are going to read a report involving animals. Then, in groups of three, they retell the story they have read in their own words.

(b) Open the discussion by asking students what makes a person a hero (somebody who has committed a very brave act, often used if somebody has saved another person from danger). Ask what makes the animals in the stories heroes. Let students discuss in pairs and listen to some ideas in open class.

(c) In small groups, students discuss any similar stories they may know. To encourage conversation, give an example of your own. Circulate and monitor, helping with vocabulary where required. Listen to a few examples in open class.

Weaker classes: Students can write their answers before speaking. Encourage them to look at their notes as little as possible.

If students enjoy this activity, you could ask them to write up their stories from Exercise 5. Point out that each report in Exercise 5a begins with an introduction in the present simple before explaining the events using past tenses and giving details. Two of the reports use quotes from witnesses. Encourage students to follow a similar structure. In a subsequent lesson, divide the class into groups of four and ask them to create a news programme with each student reading their report. Students practise reading their reports before reading them to the whole class. If you have access to a tape recorder, these can be recorded and played back to students. Use this opportunity to focus on pronunciation and intonation.

Literature in mind

6 Read

If you set the background information as a homework research task, ask the students to tell the class what they found out.

BACKGROUND INFORMATION

The Call of the Wild: is a novel by American writer Jack London, published in 1903. A modern classic, it is sometimes classified as a children's book because the protagonist is a dog, but it is dark in tone and contains scenes of cruelty and violence.

Jack London: was born in San Francisco on 12 January 1876. His family were poor and Jack sold newspapers to make money to support his family. He left school at ten and educated himself at the public library. As a teenager, London led a rough life, spending time as a pirate and as a tramp. In 1897, he went to seek his fortune in the Klondike gold rush. This gave him plenty of material for his career as a writer and, for a while, he was one of the most widely read authors in the world, publishing over fifty books. London died on 22 November 1916, aged 40.

Klondike Gold Rush: In 1897, gold was discovered in the Klondike region of Canada. Within six months, 30,000 people had rushed to the area to make their fortune.

Warm up

Books closed. Write *The Call of the Wild* on the board and tell students it is the title of a book. Ask students to guess what the story is about.

(a) Ask students if they have heard of Jack London. Tell students they are going to read an extract from *The Call of the Wild*. Pre-teach *sledge*. Students look at the cover of the book and read the summary of the story to decide if they'd like to read the book. Discuss students' ideas and help with vocabulary.

(b) Ask students to read through the extract to find the answers to the questions. Tell them not to worry about difficult vocabulary, but just to concentrate on the task. Check answers.

Answers
1 They became more acute: he heard the faintest sound; an ability to scent the wind.
2 To hunt and kill, to fight like a wolf, to howl at the stars.

(c) Students read the texts more closely to find words with the same meanings as expressions 1–8. Allow students to use dictionaries to help them with difficult words and to compare answers with a partner before feedback. During feedback encourage students to express the idea behind the words rather than expecting them to produce an exact synonym.

Possible answers

2 without worrying how difficult it is
3 protect himself
4 most distant parts
5 most solid muscles
6 left him
7 chased and caught it
8 inherited characteristics of that type of dog

(d) Students read the text more closely to find words with the same meanings as expressions 1–8. Allow students to compare answers in pairs before feedback.

Answers

2 fang   3 loathsome   4 acuteness   5 peril
6 snug   7 packs   8 trait

OPTIONAL ACTIVITY

If you would like your students to do more close comprehension work on the text, you can use the following *true / false / don't know* exercise. Ask students to explain the reason for their answers during feedback.

1 *Buck stole because he was hungry* (**true**)
2 *Buck's sense of smell improved* (**true**)
3 *Buck was an old dog* (**don't know**)
4 *Buck used to live with a pack of wolves* (**false**)
5 *Buck howled when the sun was very hot* (**false**)

7 Write

The planning for this exercise can be done in class and the writing can be set for homework.

(a) Pre-teach *Golden Retriever* and *puppies*. Tell students they are going to read a magazine article about a dog. Students read the story and answer the questions. Allow them to compare answers with a partner before feedback.

Answers

1 He felt sorry for her and he thought she was beautiful
2 She was very unhappy and felt like she was in a strange place – she didn't eat very much
3 Because she realised it was her home

(b) Ask students to work in pairs and discuss the questions. Circulate and help with ideas. Discuss answers in open class.

Weaker classes: If students have difficulty answering the questions, read through the text in open class and point out the techniques used by the author.

Possible answers

- A sense of mystery – the author uses "she" and doesn't immediately explain what he is describing
- By including direct speech, asking the reader questions, building up tension by referring to what might happen later
- The author doesn't clearly explain what happened, but leaves it to the reader's imagination. He also ends with the moral to the story

(c) Ask students to read the story and find examples of each of the techniques. Allow some time for students to analyse the story individually, then to discuss their ideas in pairs. Circulate and help as necessary. Listen to some of their ideas in open-class feedback.

Possible answers

1 *She was so unsettled; … such an air of sadness …; as loyal and loving as an animal could be; It was such a shock*
2 Paragraph 1 includes several examples of direct speech
3 *maybe if I had known what was going to happen …*
4 *No way could I have sent her away. No way – not me anyway; my heart melted; I do miss Goldie*

(d) Students look at the questions and plan their story. Make sure they spend a lot of time on this, to emphasise the importance of planning before writing the first draft. Students could be asked to create a story following a similar pattern to the example in the book, with less creative input. This might be written in the class or set as homework.

OPTIONAL ACTIVITY

A more interactive activity is known as process writing. After a planning session, students write their first draft. This is written quickly with more emphasis on fluency than accuracy. This first draft is then read by another student who gives the writer ideas on how to improve it. At this first reading, they should concentrate on content and clarity and on how to make the story more interesting, rather than correcting grammar. The writer then rewrites the story to include the new ideas, with more emphasis on accuracy. This is then read again, possibly by the first partner, possibly by another. This time, the reader focuses on accuracy. The teacher may read the story at this stage to give further corrections. The story is then rewritten a third time to include these corrections. After so much work it is a good idea to put the stories on the wall, where the whole class can circulate and read them.

2 Snap decisions

Unit overview

TOPIC: Making decisions

TEXTS
Reading and listening: an article about a musician in an orchestra
Listening and speaking: a conversation about thin-slicing
Listening: a book review programme
Reading: three scenarios about making decisions
Writing: a letter of complaint

SPEAKING AND FUNCTIONS
Being interviewed
Discussing the consequences of decisions

LANGUAGE
Grammar: future in the past
Vocabulary: making decisions
Pronunciation: sounding polite or angry

1 Read and listen

If you set the background information as a homework research task, ask the students to tell the class what they found out.

BACKGROUND INFORMATION

The Munich Philharmonic Orchestra: was founded in Munich in 1893 by Franz Kaim, son of a piano manufacturer, as the Kaim Orchestra. In 1895 it took up residence in the city's Tonhalle (concert hall). By 1910 it had become known as the Munich Konzertverein Orchestra but during the Second World War, the Tonhalle was destroyed and the orchestra was shut down. After the war, fortunes recovered and the orchestra was raised to the highest world-class standards. It is now housed in the Gasteig Culture Centre.

Abbie Conant: was born in the United States and started playing the trombone at school. She was recognised as especially talented at an early age and received a scholarship to the Interlochen Arts Academy in Michigan, where she received a diploma in 1973. In 1976 she studied at Yale University, and in 1979 she received her Master's degree. Between 1979 and 1980 she was solo trombonist of the Royal Opera of Turin and was solo trombonist of the Munich Philharmonic until 1993.

Warm up

To introduce the topic of music, ask students to make a list of three male musicians and three female musicians. Listen to some of their examples and make a list of some of the most well-known musicians on the board. Discuss whether men or women make better musicians and ask students to give reasons for their opinion.

a 🔊 Students listen to the extracts and decide whether a man or woman is playing the instruments. Allow them to compare their ideas with a partner and encourage them to give reasons for their choices. You may also like to ask them which instrument is being played in each case.

Answers
The instruments are an electric guitar, a violin, drums and a trombone: they could be being played by either a man or a woman in each case.

b Students read the text to answer the questions. Tell them it is not important to understand every word at this stage. If students have any questions about difficult words which appear in the later vocabulary exercise, tell them to try to guess the meaning and that you will refer to it later. Check answers.

Answers
1 Abbie Conant was playing
2 The selection committee
3 Letting what you see affect what you hear

c 🔊 Read through the questions with students to check understanding. Play the recording while students read. You could pause as necessary to check understanding and clarify any difficulties. Students answer the questions and compare answers with a partner before feedback in open class.

TAPESCRIPT
See the reading text on page 12 of the Student's Book.

Answers
1 She had to play behind a screen while the selection committee listened.
2 She thought she'd failed because she missed a note but the committee thought she was best.
3 They had expected a man.
4 Because the fact that she was a woman made them question their own prejudices.
5 She first went to court when she was demoted to second trombone – after some years she was reinstated to first trombone. She went to court again when she was paid less than male colleagues – she was given equal pay.
6 The fact that they couldn't see her got her the job.

(d) Read through the definitions and ask students to find words and expressions with the same meaning in the text. The words are in the order of the text. To make the exercise more challenging, you could write them on the board in a different order. Check answers.

Answers
1 prejudices   2 openings   3 an audition
4 a screen   5 astounded   6 passed with flying colours   7 demoted   8 reinstated   9 unbiased

─── OPTIONAL ACTIVITY ───

Tell the class they are going to imagine a conversation between the main characters from the text. Divide the class into three groups and give each group one of the following characters: Abbie Conant; the head of the selection committee; the conductor of the orchestra. Students discuss some of the things their character might say. When students have some ideas, re-assemble the class into groups of three containing one student from each of the three groups. Students act out a conversation between the three people. This may be more effective if girls take the role of Abbie Conant and boys are the head of the selection committee. The conductor of the orchestra is a neutral character.

2 Listen and speak

(a) Write the expression *in seconds flat* on the board and ask students to find it in the text. Ask them how they would define the expression. Listen to some of their ideas.

(b) 🔊 Tell students they are going to listen to a conversation about making snap decisions. Students listen and make notes. Ask students to write a definition in their own words and listen to some of their ideas as feedback.

TAPESCRIPT

SPEAKER 1:   In the book *Blink*, the author Malcolm Gladwell uses the term 'thin-slicing' to describe how we react when we have to make sense of something very quickly, or when we are in a situation that is new to us. When we don't have a lot of time we can't evaluate a situation fully, we can't look at all the details. We have to focus on the details of a part of the situation, a thin slice, for a second or two, and make a snap decision based on what we see in those few seconds.

SPEAKER 2:   There are several examples in the book of how people who are excellent in certain fields thin-slice. In basketball, for example, there are players who can assess and understand everything happening around them extremely quickly and make the right decisions. These players are said to have 'court sense'. Basically, they are good at making snap decisions.

SPEAKER 1:   There are, of course, situations when people thin-slice, and their decisions are completely wrong. This often happens when people are prejudiced, and they only see what they want or expect to see. An example that Gladwell gives is about a time in his life when he decided to grow long hair. He claims that all of a sudden, he started to get fines for speeding, although he wasn't driving any faster than before. So whilst the traffic policemen were using thin-slicing, they were actually biased against his long hair, and so they got it all wrong. An example of when making snap decisions based on someone's appearance can create problems.

(c) Play the recording again and ask students to find positive and negative examples of making snap decisions. Students discuss answers with a partner before feedback.

Answers
positive – basketball players making quick decisions and having court sense
negative – traffic police bias against a man with long hair

(d) In pairs, students discuss situations when they made a snap decision. You may like to give them an example of your own to get them started. Encourage students to go into as much detail as possible. Listen to some of the best examples in open class feedback.

> **Discussion box**
> **Weaker classes:** Check understanding of *equal rights*; *qualities*; *stereotype*. Students can choose one question to discuss.
> **Stronger classes:** In pairs or small groups, students go through the questions in the box and discuss them. Monitor and help as necessary, encouraging students to express themselves in English and to use any vocabulary they have learned from the text. Ask pairs or groups to feedback to the class and discuss any interesting points further.

3 Grammar
Future in the past

(a) **Weaker classes:** Ask students to think of examples of future tenses and write the following simple examples on the board:

I am going to visit my friend this evening.
I think it will rain tomorrow.
Draw this timeline on the board:

```
                              I think it will
                              rain tomorrow.
_____ Thursday _____↑____→
        (time of speaking)    ↓
                         I am going to
                         visit my friend
                         this evening.
```

Tell students that we can use *was going to* and *would* when we are talking about a point in the past and want to say that something was still in the future at that time.

I was going to visit my friend that evening.
I thought it would rain the next day.

Draw this timeline on the board:

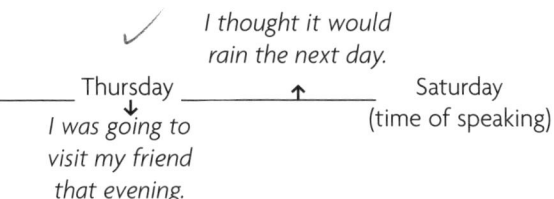

Point out that *was going to* and *would* follow the same basic rules as *is going to* (used for plans / decisions / intentions / future events with present evidence) and *will* (predictions).

If students are unclear, write the following questions on the board and elicit answers from the class.

I was so surprised I forgot what I _____ say. (**was going to**)

They decided that they _____ go on holiday in June. (**would**)

We _____ buy a new car, but we didn't have enough money. (**were going to**)

Continue with the procedure for stronger classes.

Stronger classes: Write the three example sentences on the board. Elicit the names of the tenses used and draw attention to the forms (past of *to be* + *–ing*; *would* + infinitive). Ask students which action each verb refers to and which happened first: *They were waiting* or *they were going to meet*, *she found out* or *she was going to be demoted*, *she knew* or *she would*. With weaker classes use the timelines to clarify the examples.

Rule
Read through the rule with students and ask them to complete it in open class. Refer back to the examples in the previous exercise to clarify.

Answers
were/was going to; would

(**b**) Read the sentences with students and check understanding of difficult vocabulary: *shame* and *risk*. Go through the first sentence as an example. Students complete sentences with phrases in the box.

Answers
2 wasn't going to be   3 would be   4 was going to be released   5 were going to buy   6 would be

Language note
Remind students that the future in the past follows the same rules as other future tenses and cannot be used in clauses beginning with time expressions such as: *when, before, after, by the time, while, as soon as, if* etc. Instead of using future in the past, you must use the past simple.

I told him that as soon as we would get there, we would buy a drink. ✗

I told him that as soon as we got there, we would buy a drink. ✓

You may also like to point out that the future in the past is commonly used when reporting speech:

He told me he was going to buy a new car.

He said he would call at seven o'clock.

(**c**) In pairs, students discuss things that they were going to do but didn't. Give some examples of your own to get them started. Listen to some of their ideas in open class.

Grammar notebook
Remind students to note down the rules for the future in the past and to write a few examples of their own.

4 Listen

If you set the background information as a homework research task, ask the students to tell the class what they found out.

BACKGROUND INFORMATION
Blink: The Power of Thinking Without Thinking: is a book by Malcolm Gladwell in which he explores the power of the trained mind to make split-second decisions or in other words to use instinct. It was first published in 2005.

Thin-slicing: is a phenomenon described by Malcolm Gladwell in his book *Blink*. It means making very quick decisions based on small amounts of information. Gladwell says that spontaneous decisions are often as good as, or even better than, carefully planned and considered ones. Gladwell draws on examples from science, advertising, sales, medicine and popular music to reinforce his ideas. Gladwell says that thin-slicing allows us to 'read' other people's actions. This is commonly called intuition, but is really the result of unconscious rapid cognition, fast information processing that goes on subliminally.

ECG: an abbreviation for electrocardiogram, which is the drawing made of the electrical activity of the heart.

CEO: a business acronym, which means Chief Executive Officer, or chairman of the board.

Warm up
Books closed. Ask students if they have read any good books lately. Ask how they decide which books to read or music to listen to. Elicit some answers and write *review programme* on the board. Discuss what types of review programmes they have seen and whether they always agree with the opinions of the people on the programmes.

a 🔊 Books open. Tell students they are going to listen to a book review programme in which reviewers discuss *Blink*. Play the recording while students listen and answer the questions. Encourage students to concentrate on the task and not to worry if they don't understand every word. Check answers.

TAPESCRIPT

Host And now it's time for our weekly book review. Please welcome our panel of reviewers back into the studio. Hello everyone, and what have you been reading this week?

Anne Well, this week we read *Blink*, Malcolm Gladwell's latest bestseller.

Host Malcolm Gladwell? He wrote *The Tipping Point*, didn't he?

Anne Yes, he did, and it was extremely well received.

Host And Anne, what exactly is *Blink* about?

Anne It's a book about rapid cognition. That is, those moments when you have to make split-second decisions. It's about the type of thinking that takes place in the blink of an eye.

Host What exactly do you mean, Anne? Can you give us an example?

Anne OK. Imagine you're meeting someone for the first time, or you're viewing the house you're thinking of buying. The first few seconds you see this person or property are crucial. Your mind jumps to lots of conclusions and you make your mind up about lots of things. *Blink* is a book about those first two seconds of quick conclusions.

Host A whole book about two seconds of decision making? That seems excessive.

Brian It's actually very interesting. Gladwell tries to analyse what goes on in our heads when we make snap decisions rather than dithering over things for hours or days. He also talks about how we can improve our decision-making skills.

Host Thanks, Brian. Well, I guess I should read it, or should I? I'm hopeless at making decisions! What did you think of the book, Claire?

Claire At first I was a bit dubious, but I must admit that I really got into it. There's some fascinating stuff. Before I read the book, I thought that it was much better to mull things over; that well thought-out decisions were the only ones that really worked. Look before you leap, haste makes waste, you know that kind of stuff. But after reading *Blink* I'm not so sure any more. Gladwell gives us lots of examples where that philosophy just doesn't work.

Host Can you share one with us, Claire?

Claire Well, one of the stories that particularly struck me was the one about the Emergency Room doctors at Cook County Hospital in Chicago. A few years ago they changed the way they diagnosed heart attacks. The doctors were told to gather *less* information on their patients.

Host Less information? And how did that work?

Claire I know, it sounds weird, doesn't it? Instead of gathering lots of information they focussed on a few key issues.

Host Such as?

Claire Well if the patient is suffering from chest pain, they simply check their blood pressure and do an ECG, ignoring everything else, like the patient's age and weight and medical history. And guess what? Cook County is now one of the best places in the United States for diagnosis of chest pain.

Host Wow! That's impressive! But what about the times when we jump to the wrong conclusion. Surely we don't always come to the right decision in the first two seconds. Brian?

Brian Well, that's a big part of the book too. For example, there's an interesting section on what it means to be tall. Gladwell discovered that almost all the CEOs of the top companies in the US are tall. Now there is no correlation between height and intelligence, or height and judgment, or height and the ability to motivate and lead people. But for some reason companies overwhelmingly choose tall people over shorter people for leadership roles. He claims it is an example of bad rapid cognition when something goes on in the first few seconds of meeting a tall person which makes us think of that person as an effective leader, and this stops us from making an informed decision.

Host So what's the general verdict? Did you like it? Or is the jury still out on that decision? You go first, Anne.

Anne Well I found parts of it interesting but all in all it didn't grab me.

Brian I don't agree, I really enjoyed it. It certainly made for interesting reading. I liked it because it's quite scientific yet it's very accessible to the general public.

Host Would you go along with that, Claire?

Claire Yes, I found I really got into it. I couldn't put it down once I started it.

Host So, listeners. Our panel recommends *Blink*, by Malcolm Gladwell. Now, the next book we're looking at this week is a new novel by the very successful ...

Answer
Claire and Brian enjoyed it. Anne only found parts of it interesting.

b 🔊 Read through the sentences with students and check difficult vocabulary: *blinking, diagnose, correlation, predisposed, cognition*. Play the recording while students listen and answer the questions. Students check answers with a partner before feedback. Play the recording again, pausing if necessary.

Answers
1 a   2 b   3 a   4 b

Stronger classes: A method of answering multiple choice questions is to decide which of the possible answers are obviously wrong. Ask students to justify their answers to the questions by demonstrating that all the other answers are wrong. Write these phrases on the board to help students express themselves:

X can't be right because ...
The recording doesn't say/mention ...
There is nothing in the recording about ...
X doesn't make sense!
X is obviously not the right answer.

(c) 🔊 Students listen again to answer the questions. Encourage them to take notes on what each speaker says and during feedback ask them to give reasons for their answers. Students check answers with a partner before open class feedback.

Answers
1 the host 2 Claire 3 Brian 4 Anne

┌─ OPTIONAL ACTIVITY ─────────────
If students are interested in this topic, you may like to set up the following speaking activity. Write the following occupations on the board and ask students to work in pairs and discuss how thin-slicing could be positive or negative for each of them. Listen to some of their ideas in open class.
1 teacher 2 soldier 3 policeman 4 taxi driver

5 Vocabulary
Making decisions

Warm up

Books closed. Draw a picture of a brain on the board and ask students what they do with their brain. Write some of their ideas on the board. Examples might be *think, have ideas, remember, dream, invent, fantasise, analyse* and so on. Elicit *decide* by asking students what they do if they want to buy two things but only have enough money for one. Discuss the process of making a decision, in L1 if necessary. Try and elicit some of the phrases used in the exercise.

(a) Tell students they are going to do an exercise based on expressions used to describe the process of making decisions. Students match the sentence halves and check their answers with a partner before whole class feedback.

Answers
2 e 3 a 4 g 5 b 6 h 7 d 8 f

┌─ OPTIONAL ACTIVITY ─────────────
To check understanding of the expressions in Exercise 5a, ask students to divide them into three groups:
thinking (dither over; think things over)
deciding quickly (jump to the wrong conclusion; snap judgement; split-second decision)
deciding after thinking (come to a decision; make an informed decision; make your mind up)

(b) Books open. Tell students they are going to read a newspaper advertisement offering to help people make confident decisions. Students complete the text using the expressions from the box. Let them check their answers with a partner before feedback.

Answers
2 dither
3 making your mind up
4 mull things over
5 an informed decision
6 snap
7 jumping to the wrong conclusion

┌─ OPTIONAL ACTIVITY ─────────────
In pairs, students write a short dialogue which contains one or more of the expressions in Exercise 5b. You could ask pairs to act out the dialogue to the class and vote on the most interesting. In weaker classes, students can write their sentences before speaking. Encourage them to look at their notes as little as possible.

Vocabulary notebook
Encourage students to start a new section *Making decisions* in their notebook and add these words. They may find it useful to note down translations of the words too.

6 Read and speak
Warm up

Ask students if they think they are good at making decisions. Do they tend to make decisions quickly or do they take a long time to decide? Do they like it when other people make decisions for them? Listen to some of their ideas in open class.

(a) Books open. Tell students they are going to read three scenarios based around a decision. Pre-teach *pier, paddle, tide, cut off, coastguard.* Ask students to read the texts and decide what they would do in each situation. Give students a time limit of three minutes to make their decisions.

(b) Divide the class into groups of four or five and ask them to discuss their answers. Encourage students to use vocabulary from Exercise 5. Where students have chosen different options, ask them to justify their choices. They should try to come to agreement as to the best thing to do in each situation. Circulate and help with vocabulary as required. As feedback, hold an open class discussion and vote on the best action to take in each of the scenarios.

┌─ OPTIONAL ACTIVITY ─────────────
Tell students that they are going to write some new scenarios. In small groups, students choose a situation to write questions about. Ask groups to think of three options for each scenario. Students read out their questions to students from other groups and record

their answers. They then re-assemble in their original group and compare results. Encourage them to draw some general conclusions, e.g. *Most students we spoke to are brave because ...* and to present them to the class.

7 Speak and listen

a) In pairs, students look at the photographs to answer the questions and discuss the differences between them and what is happening in each situation.

Answers
Students' own answers

b) Tell students they are going to listen to three interviews. Play the recording. Students listen and decide which of the situations in Exercise 7a each interview is from.

TAPESCRIPT

1

Kate So, tell us a bit about yourself, Martin.

Martin Erm – well, I'm Martin Richards, I'm 19, I live in Coventry – erm, as you know, I'm at Queen Elizabeth the First High School. And – sorry, I'm a bit nervous, I don't really know what to tell you.

Kate That's OK – don't worry. Why not tell us something about your interests?

Martin You mean, outside school?

Kate That's right.

Martin Hmm, let me think a moment. Well, I like reading, of course, and I'm very keen on cinema, films, I go to the cinema a lot and I watch a lot of DVDs too ... erm ...

Kate Any favourite films, directors?

Martin Yes, I'm a big fan of Inarritu, actually ...

Kate The Mexican director?

Martin Yes, I think he's done some wonderful films.

Kate Great. OK. Let's move on a bit, shall we, Martin? Perhaps you could tell us why you'd like to come and study here ...

2

Phillipa ... and I think it was probably down to the way I was brought up, really.

Sue Right. And where were you brought up?

Phillipa Well, it's a bit of a long story really. Erm – the thing is, my parents moved around quite a lot because my father was in the diplomatic service, so we lived in lots of different places over the years ... erm ...

Sue For example?

Phillipa Well, let me think – this isn't in chronological order, OK? – erm, we spent some time in Ghana in West Africa, then there was a short stint in South America, in Paraguay, and another place we went to was, erm, Vienna, we were in Vienna for a while, that's where I learned to speak German of course ...

Sue Oh that's right, you speak German, don't you?

Phillipa I do, yes – it's a little rusty now, but I can get by.

Sue I've heard that you can do more than just get by! But anyway, let's talk a bit, if we may, about how you really started your career in music, because it was a bit by chance, wasn't it, ...

3

Jill Hi! Would you mind if I asked you a few questions?

Bobby Hmm, I don't have much time.

Jill It won't take a minute.

Bobby All right, but I'm in a bit of a hurry – what's it about?

Jill I'm doing a marketing survey, it's to do with how you use your mobile phone, is that all right?

Bobby OK, what do you want to know?

Jill Right – well, first of all, can I ask you if you live here?

Bobby I do, yeah.

Jill OK. And have you got a mobile phone?

Bobby Course I have – who doesn't?

Jill Right, yeah, of course. OK, next question – do you use the phone primarily for a) social contacts, b) work purposes or c) both?

Bobby Hmm, I really don't know, just give me a moment, OK?

Jill Sure, no problem.

Bobby Erm, I think I'd have to say that it's mainly for work.

Jill Work?

Bobby Yeah.

Jill So that's b. OK, thanks. Can we go on to the next one?

Bobby Yeah, sure, fire away ...

Jill OK. Question number 3. Are you the only person in your household who's got a mobile phone?

Answers
1 c an interview for university
2 a a TV chat show
3 b an interview in the street

c) Read through the phrases with students and check understanding. You may like to draw students' attention to the pronunciation of the phrases to help recognition in the listening exercise.

Play the recording while students listen to answer the questions. After the first listening, let students compare their answers with a partner. Check answers. If necessary, play the recording again, pausing to clarify any problems.

Answers
1 I   2 Ie   3 Ie   4 Ie   5 Ie   6 I   7 I   8 I
9 Ie   10 Ie

d) To introduce this exercise, you may like to briefly mention different levels of formality and how the language we use changes in different situations depending on who we are talking to. Students read the phrases and decide if they are formal, informal or neutral. Allow them to check answers with a partner before open class feedback.

Answers
1 formal   2 neutral   3 informal   4 formal
5 neutral   6 informal   7 informal   8 formal
9 informal   10 informal

(e) Tell students they are going to carry out some interviews. In pairs, students read the situations, decide if they are formal or informal and write six questions for each situation. Circulate and ensure students are using the right formality of language. Students interview each other, changing roles for the second activity. As feedback ask some individuals to explain how successful their partners were at the interviews.

Weaker classes: Elicit ideas for questions in open class and write the best examples on the board for students to refer to during the interviews.

8 Pronunciation
Sounding polite or angry

(a) 🔊 Students turn to page 122 and read through the sentences. Play the recording. Students listen and decide what the speaker will say next.

Answers
1 b   2 a   3 b   4 b

(b) 🔊 Play the recording again, pausing for students to repeat each sentence. Encourage students to mimic the recording.

(c) 🔊 With the whole class, say the sentences politely or angrily. In pairs, students practise saying the sentences in the two different ways. Their partner tells them how they are feeling.

9 Write

The planning for this exercise can be done in class and the writing can be set for homework.

Warm up

Ask students what sort of things people complain about in shops. Ask them if they have ever complained in a shop. If they haven't, ask them to think about the type of situations in which they would complain in a shop. Listen to some of their examples in open class. Ask students to imagine that a shop assistant has been rude to them in a shop and they want to complain to the manager. What sort of things would they include in the letter? Discuss in open class.

(a) Tell students they are going to read a letter of complaint. Students read the letter quickly and answer the question. Remind students not to worry about understanding every word, but to focus on the task.

Answer
They were disrespectful, unhelpful and rude.

(b) Students read the letter again and match the titles A–C with the paragraphs. Check answers.

Answers
1 C   2 A   3 B

(c) Students read the letter again to find techniques used by the writer to make the letter more convincing. Let students discuss their findings with a partner before feedback.

Answers
The general tone of the letter is polite and formal. The writer clearly describes the events with attention to detail (Virtual Focus digital camera, Jeremy Baldwin etc.) and the use of quotation marks. She also clearly states the action she will take if she does not receive an apology.

(d) Students read the text again and underline words and expressions the writer used to convey her feelings to the reader.

Answers
She uses adjectives and intensifying adverbs to express her feelings (*deeply disappointed, appalled, totally unacceptable*). She addresses the reader directly, inviting him to share her feelings (*I think you can understand perfectly why I left your shop*). She also mentions the fact that she was a loyal customer.

(e) Read through the sentences 1–8 with students and ask them to replace the underlined words with an expression from the box. Encourage them to look back at the letter to see the expressions in context. Stronger students may be able to do the exercise without looking back at the text. Students compare answers with a partner before feedback in open class.

Answers
1   express my annoyance
2   am not prepared to
3   wish
4   dismayed
5   it is my opinion
6   would like to point out
7   have no objection to
8   discovered

(f) Tell students they are going to write a letter of complaint to a shop manager. Ask them to take some time to think of an incident (real or fictional), then make notes of the main points of the story and to plan the order in which to tell them. Encourage them to keep to the structure of the example letter and to use as many of the techniques and expressions as possible. In a subsequent lesson, ask students to read each other's letters and decide which of the complaints would be successful.

③ Advertising

Unit overview

TOPIC: Advertising

TEXTS
Reading and listening: how we use emotions and logic when buying things
Listening: an expert talking about advertising on the Internet and in magazines
Reading: an article about 'Buy Nothing Day'
Writing: a covering letter of application

SPEAKING AND FUNCTIONS
Designing a marketing campaign
Discussing ways of reducing consumption

LANGUAGE
Grammar: position of adverbs, adjective order
Vocabulary: advertising

1 Read and listen

Warm up

Books closed. Brainstorm a list of typical things that teenagers spend their money on and write ideas on the board. Then make a separate list of things that influence our choices when buying things (advertising, recommendations, necessity, appearance, price, availability etc.).

(a) Ask students to look at the three adverts and decide what is being advertised. Picture a is an advert for a knife, picture b is an advert for a car and picture c is an advert for a chewing gum. Ask students how effective they think the adverts are. Students discuss with a partner whether the adverts make them want to buy the products or not. Ask for a few comments in open class.

(b) Explain the meaning of *logic* and *justification*. Read through the instructions with students and ask them to read the text to find the answers. Encourage students not to look up every new word but just to read and focus on finding the examples.

Answers
1 petrol, rice, airline seats
2 shoes that light up, mobile phone wallpaper, streamers, a faster car, a bigger lawn mower

(c) 🔊 Read through the questions with the students and help with any difficulties. Play the recording while students read and listen to answer the questions. After the first listening, let students compare their answers with a partner. Check answers. If necessary, play the recording again, pausing to clarify any problems.

TAPESCRIPT
See the reading text on pages 18 and 19 of the Student's Book.

Answers
1 B   2 C   3 B   4 D   5 B   6 C   7 D   8 A

(d) Read through the sentences to check understanding. In pairs, students choose the correct preposition to complete each definition and check their answers in the text. For further practice of this vocabulary, you could ask students to write their own sentences including the phrasal verbs and listen to some of their ideas in open class.

Answers
2 on   3 in   4 out   5 up   6 on

┌─ **OPTIONAL ACTIVITY** ────────────
As an extension of Exercise 1b, cut out some adverts from magazines and remove any slogans or brand names. Show adverts to the class for them to guess what is being advertised. Write slogans on the board for students to match with the adverts. Stronger classes can be encouraged to invent their own slogans.

2 Grammar
Position of adverbs

Students covered the position of adverbs in SB4, Unit 6.

(a) **Weaker classes:** If students need reminding about adverbs, write the following words on the board and ask students what type of words they are:

quickly
slowly
badly

Explain that they are adverbs and that they can be used to describe verbs and adjectives. Then write the following:

He played badly.
He left suddenly.
He walked in a strange way.
It was really cold.

Ask students to find the adverbs in the sentences. They should find the first two (*badly*, *suddenly*) easy. Point out that *in a strange way* is an adverbial phrase and describes the verb in the same way as an adverb. Explain that in the fourth sentence, the adverb *really* adds meaning to the adjective and that this is called qualifying an adjective. Continue with the procedure for stronger classes.

Stronger classes: Read through the sentences with students. Check students understand *qualifying*, *adverbial phrases*. Ask students to try to think of example sentences for each rule. Listen to some of their ideas in open class, but do not comment at this stage.

(b) Ask students to match sentences 1—6 with the rules in Exercise 2a. Let students compare their answers in pairs before getting feedback. Pay particular attention to the position of the adverbs in the sentences.

Answers
b rule 4 c rule 6 d rule 1 e rule 5 f rule 3

Discussion box

Weaker classes: Students can choose one question to discuss.

Stronger classes: In pairs or small groups, students go through the questions in the box and discuss them.

Monitor and help as necessary, encouraging students to express themselves in English and to use any vocabulary they have learned from the text. Ask pairs or groups to feedback to the class and discuss any interesting points further.

(c) Ask students to complete the sentences with the adverbs in brackets. Refer students back to the rules in Exercise 2a and encourage them to use these as a guide.

Answers
1 It was a really fascinating film. (rule 1)
2 I didn't really enjoy the meal. (rule 2)
3 Buying something is clearly a personal decision. (rule 2)
4 We thought about it carefully before deciding. (rule 3)
5 I bought the wrong thing unfortunately. (rule 5)
6 I honestly don't know the right answer. (rule 2)
7 Proudly, he showed us the medal he'd won. (rule 4)
8 She showed me how to do it in an interesting way. (rule 6)

Language note
We avoid putting an adverb between a verb and a following *-ing* form or *to* infinitive:

He started singing quietly
(not *He started quietly singing*)
He tried to leave quietly
(not *He tried quietly to leave*)

(d) Students check answers to Exercise 2c in pairs and discuss any other possible options before open class feedback. Ask students to match each sentence to a rule from Exercise 2a (see answers above) and during feedback, use the sentences to clarify the rules.

Answers
Other possible answers are:
1 It really was a fascinating film.
2 I really didn't enjoy the meal. / I didn't enjoy the meal really.
3 Clearly, buying something is a personal decision.
4 We carefully thought about it before deciding. / We thought carefully about it before deciding.
5 Unfortunately, I bought the wrong thing. / I unfortunately bought the wrong thing.

6 I don't honestly know the right answer. / Honestly, I don't know the right answer.
7 He proudly showed us the medal he'd won.
8 No other possibilities

Language note
Students may make mistakes with word order when using adverbial phrases at the end of a sentence, making sentences like: *He plays football on Tuesdays in the park. *He played in the game very well last week.* Tell students that if we want to say how, where and when something happened, we use the words and expressions in that order (how, where, when): *He plays football in the park on Tuesdays. He played very well in the game last week.*

Grammar notebook
Remind students to note down the rules for the position of adverbs and to write a few examples of their own.

┌ OPTIONAL ACTIVITY ══════════
Tell students that some words can be used as both adjectives and adverbs. Write the following sentences on the board for students to decide whether the underlined words are adjectives or adverbs. Let them compare answers with a partner before checking answers in open class.

1 *It was getting late.* **(adjective)**
2 *The Guardian is a daily newspaper.* **(adjective)**
3 *He speaks French well.* **(adverb)**
4 *Why are you driving so fast?* **(adverb)**
5 *She is hard to live with.* **(adjective)**
6 *She works very hard.* **(adverb)**
7 *I'm not very well.* **(adjective)**
8 *We arrived late, so we couldn't get in.* **(adverb)**
9 *We speak daily.* **(adverb)**
10 *He is a very fast runner.* **(adjective)**

Tell students that *early* and *loud* can also be used as both adjectives and adverbs and ask students to write their own sentences, e.g. *He arrived early. We caught the early train. He has a loud voice. He talks very loud.*

3 Vocabulary
Advertising

(a) Ask students to match the words with the pictures. Check answers. As a follow-up ask students to work in pairs and think of as many examples of logos, jingles and slogans (in English) as they can.

Answers
1 d 2 c 3 e 4 a 5 f 6 b

(b) In pairs, students discuss the questions. Monitor and encourage students to answer in full sentences and expand on their answers. Ask a few pairs to tell the class about their partner's answers.

Vocabulary notebook

Encourage students to start a new section *Advertising* in their notebook and add these words. They may find it useful to note down translations of the words too.

4 Listen

(a) Ask students how often they use the Internet and where they see advertising there. Students discuss the differences between adverts on the Internet and adverts in magazines. Ask them which they think is the most effective and why. Which type of advertising do they pay most attention to? Discuss answers in open class, but do not comment at this stage.

(b) Students discuss the question in pairs. Ask them how they feel about the use of pop-ups and if they can remember any particularly interesting ones. Listen to some of their ideas in open class.

(c) Tell students they are going to listen to an advertising expert. Play the recording. Encourage students to listen only for the answer to the question and not to worry about every word. Students check their answers with a partner before feedback.

TAPESCRIPT

Principal   Our next guest is Steve Wilson: one of the leading web advertising experts in the country. Steve's worked as an online marketing consultant with some of the top companies for several years now and today he's here to answer any questions you may have about his job or about a career in advertising in general. So let's have a nice loud round of applause for Steve Wilson.

Steve Wilson   Thank you.

Principal   OK let's have our first question from Jenny.

Jenny   Yes, I'd like to ask Mr Wilson if he always knew that he wanted to work in advertising.

Steve Wilson   No I didn't actually. When I left school I didn't really have any idea what I wanted to do so I took a year off to decide what I wanted to study at University. I got a temporary job walking around town with a sandwich board, you know, one of those signs that people wear advertising a restaurant or something like that. So there I was wearing my sandwich board and handing out flyers, which if you think about it, was actually my first experience in advertising I suppose. I started looking at the hoardings and billboards in the streets and I realised that some of them were clever and interesting. And I thought "I'd like to do that." So the next year I went to University to study media and communications. That was back in 1988 and I've been working in advertising ever since.

Principal   Paul, yes. What's your question?

Paul   Have you always worked in online advertising?

Steve Wilson   No. I spent about two years writing radio adverts. Thinking up all those annoying jingles and things like that. But I wanted to do more and the Internet was getting bigger and bigger so I thought it would be a good idea to get involved in that. And I've never looked back.

Principal   Helen?

Helen   Yes. Mr Wilson. You mentioned that you wrote jingles for radio adverts. What do you think is the most important thing for an online ad?

Steve Wilson   That's a very good question. I think I'd have to say that it's the headline. You know, the title, if you like. That's the first thing that people see and if that doesn't grab their attention then they're not going to stop and read the rest of the ad. It's a bit like a slogan in a magazine advert. It's designed to get people to want to know more about what you're selling. The headline is extremely important. Sometimes I'll spend three or four days just deciding on those four or five words.

Principal   OK, let's have a question from Ahmed.

Ahmed   Um, I'd like to know what's the most difficult thing about writing ads on the Internet and how is it different from writing TV commercials, for example?

Steve Wilson   I think one of the biggest challenges of Internet ads is trying to change people's conception of them. I mean most people have fairly negative ideas about advertising on the Internet and find it too intrusive. They associate it with annoying, multi-coloured pop-ups that cover up what you're trying to read. There's also very little tradition unlike on TV or in magazines where many people actually enjoy watching or reading a good bit of publicity.

Now the reason that pop-ups are used so much is that people can't ignore them, they have to close them down before they can carry on whatever it was they were doing. However, our research suggests that although they certainly do get people's attention, very few people actually read them. Furthermore, those who do read them, don't believe them. Pop-ups are the online version of the junk mail we get through our letter box, and what happens to that? It goes straight in the bin.

Now, of course, not all Internet advertising is done through pop-ups and the good news for people like me is that the Internet allows us to be very creative. We can use a range of different formats to get our messages across, from text, to video, to animation, to audio, to visual. I'm also lucky that I work for some famous Japanese companies and when people see their familiar logos on their computer screen, they're more willing to stop and read the ad.

Principal   OK, time for one more question. Yes, James.

James   Yes, my question is about advertising in general. Is there any golden rule when it comes to writing a good advert?

Steve Wilson Well, you can't go far wrong with the classic A.I.D.A approach. Attention, Interest, Desire and Action. First you get the attention of your potential customer. Then you work on getting that customer interested. Next, create a desire in the reader to buy your product or service and finally you direct this customer to take action immediately! The attention span of most readers is quite limited so you have to interest them quickly by making them an offer that they can't resist. Now one of the advantages to online advertising is that we can get our readers to act quickly by asking them to click on links – it's a very interactive medium. We can make it very easy for them to take their interest further.

Principal OK, well, I hope that's created an interest in some of you in the world of advertising! If you want to ask Steve any more questions, he will be outside in the careers fair. So, for now, thank you, Steve, and thanks everyone for your questions.

Answers
Internet adverts use pop-ups, video, animation, audio and visual

(d) 🔊 Students read through the notes and try to complete the gaps (in pencil, so that they can change answers later). Let students compare answers with a partner before listening to the recording again to check, pausing if necessary.

Answers
1 communications 2 headline 3 attention
4 negative 5 annoying 6 avoid 7 screen
8 read 9 believe 10 text 11 video
12 animation (audio, visual) 13 interest 14 action

5 Grammar

Adjective order

Warm up

Write the following instructions on the board:

Choose an object in the classroom: How big is it?
What colour is it? What is it made of?
Which country is it from?

Ask students to write one sentence which answers all the questions and describes the object. Point out that they will need to pay attention to the order of the adjectives. Listen to some of their answers and ask the rest of the group to say if the adjective order is correct. There will probably be some mistakes, but do not give correct answers at this stage.

(a) Read through the examples with students, paying attention to the adjectives in bold. Ask them which of the adjectives gives an opinion (*annoying, nice*) and which describes a fact (*multi-coloured, loud*). Students complete the rule.

Rule
opinion

(b) 🔊 Tell students they are going to listen to a short dialogue. In open class, fill in the four category titles. Play the recording while students listen and complete the table. Check the answers. You may want to play the recording again, pausing as necessary.

TAPESCRIPT

Female 1 She's got a gorgeous dark brown Italian leather jacket.

Male 2 Could I have one of those round chocolate cakes, please?

Female 3 You should visit the semicircular Italian garden while you're there.

Male 4 He bought her an expensive drop-shaped pearl necklace for her birthday.

Male 5 I've just finished *The Stolen White Elephant* by Mark Twain. It's a farce about a white Siamese elephant that disappears in New York. You should read it.

Female 6 I bought a cheap round blue frame at the market, but it suits the picture well.

Answers

Quality	Shape	Colour	Origin	Material	Noun
gorgeous		dark brown	Italian	leather	jacket
	round			chocolate	cakes
	semi-circular		Italian		garden
expensive	drop-shaped			pearl	necklace
most innovative modern					building
		white	Siamese		elephant
cheap	round	blue			frame

Language note
Tell the students that if we use two adjectives from the same category, we put a comma between the two adjectives and tend to put the shorter adjective first, e.g. *She had bright, cheerful eyes. It was a soft, comfortable sofa.*

If adjectives come after the noun (predicative adjectives), the order is less fixed. We tend to use **and** before the last adjective, e.g. *We were all hot, tired and thirsty.* An adjective expressing opinion often comes last: *The city is old and beautiful.*

(c) Students complete the phrases by putting the adjectives in the correct order. Ask them to compare answers with a partner before feedback.

Answers
2 a useful reference book
3 the old plastic cup
4 beautiful blue eyes
5 an expensive German sports car
6 comfortable Chinese running shoes
7 my best white cotton shirt
8 an enormous American advertising company

(d) In pairs, students think of adjectives to describe the nouns. If students find it difficult to think of adjectives, you might like to have an open class brainstorm and add more adjectives to each of the categories in Exercise 5b. Circulate and ensure students are using adjectives in the correct order.

Answers
Students' own answers

OPTIONAL ACTIVITY

Write the following paragraph on the board or dictate it to students:

My mother lives in a house. She has a car. She went to buy a hat. She has a dog. The dog saw a cake on the table.

Ask students to add adjectives to the paragraph and make any other changes necessary to make it more interesting. They should also finish the story in their own words. Encourage students to read each other's stories and check for errors. Listen to some of the best endings in open class.

Grammar notebook
Remind students to note down the rules for adjective order and to write a few examples of their own.

6 Speak
Planning a marketing campaign

(a) Tell students they are going to design a marketing campaign for a product of their choice. Explain that they have an unlimited budget and that they can use any type of advertising they choose. Read through the questions with students and quickly elicit some ideas for each one. You may like to point out that subtle advertising is sometimes very effective. Students work in small groups to decide the approach they will take, using the questions to help them form their ideas. Encourage students to use ideas from previous exercises. Circulate and monitor, helping with vocabulary as required.

(b) Draw students' attention to the four areas and give them some time to organise their ideas accordingly and to elect individuals to carry out each of the instructions. Let students practise their presentations before listening to each of them as whole class feedback. After the presentations, give students the opportunity to work in groups and discuss which of the marketing campaigns they think would be most successful. Students may like to vote on which they think is the best.

Weaker classes: Students can write their presentations before speaking. Encourage them to look at their notes as little as possible.

Culture in mind
7 Read and speak

If you set the background information as a homework research task, ask the students to tell the class what they found out.

BACKGROUND INFORMATION

Buy Nothing Day: started in 1993 and is now an international event celebrated in over 55 countries. The idea is to make people stop and think about how much what they buy affects the environment and developing countries. It is a day where you challenge yourself, your family and friends to try simple living for a day, spend time with family and friends, rather than spend money on them. A day without spending!

(a) Students look at the picture and answer the question. Listen to some of their ideas in open class.

(b) Ask students what they think Buy Nothing Day might be and why people might celebrate it. Ask students to read through the text quickly to check their answers. Tell them not to worry about difficult words, but just to concentrate on the task. Students write a sentence defining Buy Nothing Day in their own words. Listen to some of their ideas as feedback.

(c) If students have found the text difficult, you may like to explain some vocabulary at this stage. Check understanding of *detox, zombie, shopaholics, consumer binge, over-consumption*. Read the paragraph titles with students. Students read the text again and then match the topics to the paragraphs. Allow students to compare their answers with a partner before feedback.

Answers
A 3   B 5   C 2   D 4   E 1

(d) Read through the questions with students. Give students time to read the text more closely and to check their answers with a partner.

Answers
1   Paragraph 2
2   Paragraph 5
3   Paragraph 4
4   Paragraph 3

(e) Students work in pairs to write questions corresponding to the quotations 1–4 in Exercise 7d. Circulate and help with vocabulary as necessary. If students are interested in this topic, ask them to imagine they are going to interview a Buy Nothing Day activist. Students work in pairs to write questions and then act out an interview.

Possible answers

1 Was it good at the Buy Nothing Day event?
2 How has Buy Nothing Day affected you?
3 What will happen if we keep consuming at the same rate?
4 Why do you take part in Buy Nothing Day?

OPTIONAL ACTIVITY

Write the following definitions on the board and ask students to find words and expressions with the same meaning in the text.

1 *protesters* (activists)
2 *event* (phenomenon)
3 *shopping centres* (malls)
4 *frenzied* (frantic)
5 *difficult situation* (dilemma)
6 *extensive* (wide-ranging)
7 *fall* (plunge)
8 *responsibility* (onus)

Discussion box

Weaker classes: Students can choose one question to discuss.

Stronger classes: In pairs or small groups, students go through the questions in the box and discuss them.

Monitor and help as necessary, encouraging students to express themselves in English and to use any vocabulary they have learned from the text. Ask pairs or groups to feedback to the class and discuss any interesting points further.

8 Write

The planning for this exercise can be done in class and the writing can be set for homework.

Warm up

Write *Public Relations* on the board. Ask students to discuss what the term means (the practice or profession of establishing, maintaining or improving a favourable relationship between an institution or person and the public).

(a) Tell students that they are going to read a job advertisement for a PR assistant. Pre-teach *faint-hearted*. Students read the advert quickly and write a list of personal qualities the candidate needs.

Answers

The candidate should not be faint-hearted. They should be open, dynamic and willing to learn.

(b) Ask students to imagine they are going to apply for the post. What should they include in the covering letter? Students complete the list of points and compare answers with a partner. Tell students there may be more than three points to add to the list.

Answers

Other points to include are:

- Your recent work experience
- Your qualifications
- Your reason for changing jobs
- What you can offer the company
- What you are good at

(c) Students read through the model answer and underline examples of the points in the list in Exercise 8b. Check answers.

(d) Draw students' attention to the construction of the letter in Exercise 8c. Point out the introduction and the closing sentences. Emphasise the importance of planning a letter before writing. Tell students they are going to write a covering letter of application. Read through the two job adverts and check understanding of *dealing with people* and *keep your cool under pressure*. In pairs, students discuss the personal qualities required for each of the jobs and choose one to apply for. After planning, they could complete the writing at home. In a subsequent lesson, encourage students to read each other's letters and decide which would secure an interview.

OPTIONAL ACTIVITY

Write the following on the board. Ask students to write the words in their notebook in the correct order. They should also decide if the sentences are formal or informal.

1 writing apply to for I job as advertised Evening Standard teacher the in yesterday's am
2 I ask job want about teacher the to as.
3 enclosed CV please copy my also a find of.
4 my CV with this I've letter put.
5 I have you hope that post suitable I am a the I candidate convinced for.

Answers

1 *I am writing to apply for the job as teacher advertised in yesterday's Evening Standard.* (formal)
2 *I want to ask about the job as teacher.* (informal)
3 *Please also find enclosed a copy of my CV.* (formal)
4 *I've put my CV with this letter.* (informal)
5 *I hope I have convinced you that I am a suitable candidate for the post.* (formal)

4 Fight or flight?

Unit overview

TOPIC: Dealing with stressful situations

TEXTS
Reading and listening: an article about possible reactions to stressful situations
Speaking and listening: song: *Stand My Ground*
Writing: a report and proposal for the principal of your college

SPEAKING AND FUNCTIONS
Discussing how to deal with stressful situations

LANGUAGE
Grammar: talking about tendencies
Vocabulary: feeling stressed; coping with stress

1 Listen

Warm up

Write the words *I am afraid of ...* on the board. Ask students to create a list of people or things that they are afraid of. You may like to give a couple of examples of your own to get them started. They could discuss their answers in pairs or in small groups. Listen to a few examples in open class.

(a) Ask students to describe the pictures and say which of the cavemen they identify with. Students discuss in pairs. Use the pictures to explain the meaning of: *Fight or flight?*

(b) 🔊 Tell the students that they are going to listen to the beginning of a magazine article that describes one of the pictures. Play the recording while students listen to decide which of the pictures is described.

TAPESCRIPT

Imagine you're a caveman. As always you are out in the forest looking for berries to take home for your family. The forest can be a dangerous place but you're young and strong and tend to sense when danger is close. This morning you're lost in your own thoughts when suddenly you find yourself face to face with a sabre-tooth tiger. The sight of you makes his mouth water. Luckily for you, millions of years of evolution have given you a set of automatic weapons that take over in the event of an emergency. As soon as you see the tiger, a gland in your brain, the hypothalamus, sends a message to your adrenal glands and within seconds, you can run faster, hit harder, see better, hear better, think faster and jump higher than you could only seconds before. You don't have time to think of what your family back at the

camp would be doing, your only instinct is to survive. Your heart is pumping quickly and the blood is running through your body two to three times faster than normal. Your eyes get smaller so you can see better. All the functions of your body that are not needed for the fight that is about to start are temporarily shut down. You look at the tiger, it looks back at you, back arched and ready to pounce. You quickly look at the area around you, bend down slowly and pick up a sharp stone.

Answer
Picture 1

(c) 🔊 Play the recording again while students take notes. Tell students not to worry about the meaning of every word, but to concentrate on the task. Students compare answers with a partner before checking in class.

Answers
His brain sends a message to his adrenal gland and he can run faster, hit harder, see better, hear better, think faster and jump higher. His heart pumps quickly and blood runs through his body two to three times faster than normal. His eyes get smaller so he can see better.

OPTIONAL ACTIVITY

Students may like to learn some of the terms used to describe fears and phobias. Write the following words on the board:

1 *bibliophobia* 2 *pyrophobia* 3 *zoophobia*
4 *tropophobia* 5 *lachanophobia* 6 *obesophobia*
7 *xenophobia* 8 *panphobia*

In pairs, students discuss the meaning of the words. With weaker classes, you may like to write the answers on the board in random order for students to match to the words.

Answers
1 fear of books 2 fear of fire 3 fear of animals
4 fear of change 5 fear of vegetables 6 fear of putting on weight 7 fear of foreign people
8 fear of everything

2 Read and listen

(a) Students write a definition of a 'sabre-tooth tiger' situation using their own words. Circulate and help with vocabulary as necessary. Listen to some of their definitions in open class.

(b) In pairs, students discuss 'sabre-tooth tiger' situations in modern life. Encourage them to think not only of their own experiences, but of the world as a whole. Discuss any interesting answers in class.

c Tell students they are going to read a text and listen to a recording about 'sabre-tooth tiger' situations in modern life. Check understanding of *hunting*, *ancestor*, *threatened*, *trigger*, *counterproductive*. Tell students not to worry about the meaning of every word, but just to check how many of their examples from Exercise 2b are mentioned. Check answers.

Answers
A teacher asking to see a student in his classroom; mothers lifting cars off their trapped children; firemen heroically running into blazing houses

d Read through the sentences with students and check understanding. Play the recording while students listen and decide which one of the points is not raised. Play the recording again, pausing as necessary to clarify vocabulary and help with comprehension. Let students compare their answers before getting feedback.

TAPESCRIPT
See the reading text on page 24 of the Student's Book.

Answer
Point 5 is not raised

3 Vocabulary
Feeling stressed

a Ask students to match the underlined words and expressions with the meanings a–g. Encourage students to look back at the text. During feedback, explain the meaning of each of the phrases, say the full expressions and ask students to repeat them.

Answers
1 b 2 f 3 c 4 g 5 a 6 d 7 e

b In pairs, students write a sentence for each of the expressions in Exercise 3a, describing a situation in which they experience each of the physical symptoms. Circulate and check students are using the expressions correctly. Invite some of the students to read a sentence to the class.

c Read through the examples with students. Ask them to work together with a partner to make a list of non-stressful situations when they would experience the symptoms in Exercise 3a. Listen to some of the best ideas as feedback. You may like to ask students to write sentences which include each of the phrases.

Discussion box
Weaker classes: Students can choose one question to discuss.

Stronger classes: In pairs or small groups, students go through the questions in the box and discuss them.

Monitor and help as necessary, encouraging students to express themselves in English and to use any vocabulary they have learned from the text. Ask pairs or groups to feedback to the class and discuss any interesting points further.

Vocabulary notebook
Encourage students to start a new section *Feeling stressed* in their notebook and add these words. They may find it useful to note down translations too.

┌─ OPTIONAL ACTIVITY ──────────────
This activity works as a review of any new vocabulary. Students work with a partner. Ask one student in each pair to turn their back to the board. Write three items of vocabulary that students have recently studied on the board: *clammy, pounding, racing*. Give students a time limit of a minute. Students must try and describe the word or phrase without using any of the words, e.g. for *pounding* students might say 'what your heart starts doing when you are nervous'. The student who can't see the board must try and guess the word. When students have finished, ask them to change positions and write three new words or phrases on the board.

4 Grammar
Talking about tendencies

a **Weaker classes:** Ask students to think of things that they do on a regular basis. Ask them which tense they use to describe regular or habitual actions (present simple) and remind them of the use of adverbs to describe frequency. Write the following questions on the board and ask students to discuss what they do in each situation.

What do you do when you are hungry? (**I tend to buy a banana.**)

What do you do when somebody is talking too much and you are bored? (**I will usually walk away.**)

Who makes you angry? Why? (**My brother. He's always telling bad jokes.**)

Listen to some answers and try to elicit *tend to* and *will* and *always*. Explain the use of each of the expressions and follow the procedure for stronger classes.

Stronger classes: Look at the three sentences in the book with students. You may like to write them on the board to make explanation easier. Students answer questions 1–3 as a whole class exercise.

Answers
1 no specific time
2 often true
3 no specific time at all

b Students complete the rules. Refer them back to the sentences in Exercise 4a to clarify the difference between the structures. Explain that *will* is used to talk about characteristic behaviour or habits and often doesn't add any extra meaning to the sentence.

Rule
present continuous; will; tend

c Students complete the text. Make sure they only use one word to fill each gap. Allow them to compare answers with a partner before feedback.

Answers

2 to   3 will   4 doing   5 not   6 will   7 tends

d Students discuss which of the characters they sympathise with. Encourage them to give reasons for their choice and allow open class discussion.

e Ask students to think of a situation when they were picked on. Give an example of your own to get them started and encourage students to use the structures from Exercise 4a when describing their situation. In pairs students give each other advice on what to do in such situations.

> **Language note**
>
> In speech we can put stress on *will* to criticise people's characteristic behaviour or habits. It often suggests that criticisms have been made before but ignored:
>
> *She just won't do the washing up when I ask her.*
> *He will keep his mouth open when he is eating.*
> We can also criticise a person directly using *will*:
> *Well, if you will stay up late, you can expect to be tired in the morning.*

Grammar notebook

Remind students to note down the rules for talking about tendencies and to write a few examples of their own.

5 Listen

Warm up

Books closed. To introduce the topic and remind students of expressions used to give advice, tell students that a friend of yours is not happy because he has lost his job. Ask students to give your friend advice and elicit expressions such as: *He should ...,* *He ought to ..., If I were him, I would ...* etc.

a Books open. Draw students' attention to the photograph and ask them to work in pairs and answer the questions. For question 3, students should create a dialogue. Listen to some of the dialogues in open class. In weaker classes, students can write their sentences before speaking. Encourage them to look at their notes as little as possible.

b ◁)) Tell students they are going to listen to a man talking about his stressful experiences. Read through the symptoms to check understanding. Students listen and tick the symptoms which are mentioned. Encourage students to concentrate on the task and not to worry if they don't understand every word. Check answers.

TAPESCRIPT

Presenter   Hello and welcome to another edition of *Health Line*, the show where we look at health problems affecting many young people today and hopefully suggest ways to lead a healthier life. Today, we're looking at stress.

Now, stress is a natural part of being human. It's your body responding to changes in the world around you. It changes how your body works and puts your mind into different moods. During revision and exam periods, anxiety and stress are very common problems for students – even for those who appear confident and calm. A small amount of anxiety can actually be beneficial – it can make you alert and focused and stimulate you to work even harder – but too much anxiety means you will have trouble thinking clearly and this means you aren't likely to do as well as you could.

So how do you know when you're getting too stressed? Keith McMahon is a chemistry student. He's currently doing well in his third year at Edinburgh University but things weren't always so easy. When Keith first arrived at university, he found that life suddenly became much harder.

Keith   I'd always done pretty well at school so I wasn't particularly worried going to university. At school I didn't really study very hard and I would often work long hours a few days before an exam or sit up all night to get an essay in. Suddenly things were very different. Just before my first exam I realised that the way I had tended to study before just wasn't going to work. There was no way I was going to learn everything in time! I failed that exam and no matter what I did I just couldn't catch up. I started getting bad headaches and I noticed that I was constantly feeling tired and also getting more colds and feeling fluey. I also started to feel extreme anxiety for no obvious reason and there were days when I just couldn't leave the house. I didn't associate my symptoms with stress at first. I thought it was because I wasn't eating properly and going out more than I used to when I was living at home. Then I talked to another guy in my chemistry class and he said that he'd been getting rashes and finding it difficult to get to sleep so he'd gone to the doctor and she had said that it might be stress related. So I decided to go to the doctor and she diagnosed me as being overly stressed.

Presenter   Luckily the doctor had some very useful advice for Keith.

Keith   She told me to take a short break and to try to get back into a routine of sleeping and eating well. She also told me to take plenty of exercise and also to set myself realistic goals. It took a while but now I feel as if I'm back on top of things again. Next year my younger sister hopes to come to Edinburgh and I'm forever telling her how to avoid getting into my situation and how to beat stress before it beats her.

Answers

tiredness; insomnia; skin problems; colds and flu; headaches

c Read through the questions with students. Play the recording while students listen and answer the questions. Students check answers with a partner before feedback. Play the recording again, pausing if necessary.

Answers

1 It can make you alert and focused and stimulate you to work even harder.
2 He would often work long hours a few days before an exam or sit up all night to get an essay in.
3 Because he wasn't eating properly and he was going out more than he used to.
4 She told him to take a short break and try to get back into a routine of eating and sleeping well. She told him to take plenty of exercise and try to set realistic goals.

OPTIONAL ACTIVITY

This exercise gives you the opportunity to practise the language of advice. Write the following on the board:

If I were you, I would …
It's a good idea to …
You should …
You had better …

Ask students to look at the symptoms in Exercise 5b that were not mentioned in the listening. Elicit endings to the sentences on the board. Ask students to create a dialogue in which a patient is suffering these symptoms. The doctor should use the language of advice in his/her responses. Listen to some of the dialogues in open class.

---

6 Vocabulary

Coping with stress

a To introduce the topic ask students if they can think of any good ways of dealing with stress and if they know any expressions that might be used to help someone relax if they are stressed. Ask students to match the words in the two columns to make expressions connected with stress. Check answers. Read the expressions aloud using suitable caring intonation patterns and ask students to repeat them.

Answers

2 a 3 f 4 e 5 h 6 g 7 c 8 d

b Pre-teach *stress-buster, the block, self-esteem, stand up straight, straight away*. Tell students they are going to read some advice about reducing stress. Ask students to fill the gaps with one of the expressions from Exercise 6a. Tell them there may be more than one possible answer for some of the gaps. Students compare answers with a partner before feedback.

Answers

1 Take a break   2 put your feet up   3 Don't overdo it   4 Take some exercise   5 Don't be too hard on yourself   6 Don't let things get on top of you   7 chill out   8 take a deep breath

---

Language note

You may like to point out the usage of the expressions in this exercise. *Chill out, put your feet up, don't be too hard on yourself, don't let things get on top of you* are used informally. It is also important to note that, as imperatives, these expressions should be expressed with sympathetic intonation so as not to be misunderstood by the listener. They can be softened with phrases like *Have you thought about …, You should try to …* etc.

---

c In pairs, students discuss their answers to Exercise 6b. Do they think it is good advice? Ask them to talk about which of the suggestions they do themselves. Do they do anything else to reduce stress? Listen to some of their ideas in open class and encourage comments from other students.

Vocabulary notebook

Encourage students to start a new section *Coping with stress* in their notebook and add these words. They may find it useful to note down translations too.

7 Speak

Divide the class into pairs and give each student a letter A or B. Tell student A to look at the picture on page 27 and student B to look at the picture on page 123. Give students a short time to imagine their situation and the physical effects it might have on them. Students take it in turns to describe their situation to their partner, who gives advice. Circulate and help with difficult vocabulary as required. Ensure students are using vocabulary from Exercises 5 and 6. Listen to some of the dialogues in open class.

8 Speak and listen

If you set the background information as a homework research task, ask the students to tell the class what they found out.

BACKGROUND INFORMATION

Within Temptation: a Goth-metal band formed in 1996 by guitarist Robert Westerholt and vocalist Sharon den Adel. Even though they were all still in college, the band released their debut album *Enter* the following April. It attracted a great deal of critical and commercial acclaim but in 1999 the band took a break to finish their studies, returning with a second album, *Mother Earth,* in December 2000. Their third and most successful record to date, *The Silent Force,* was released in 2004 and from this came the massive international radio hit *Stand My Ground.*

---

a Tell students they are going to listen to a song called *Stand My Ground*. Read through the sentences and check understanding of *set eyes on, stare, face*. In pairs, students decide what the *it* refers to in each case. Listen to some of their ideas in open class.

Answers
Students' own answers

b (( )) Play the recording while students listen and fill the gaps with the phrases in Exercise 8a. Students compare answers with a partner. Play the recording again. Check answers.

TAPESCRIPT
See the song on page 28 of the Student's Book.

Answers
1 Does it feel right?
2 once it's set its eyes on you.
3 have to stare it in the eye.
4 I've got to face it.
5 If I don't make it, someone else will
6 It's all around
7 it's time for me to face it,
8 can I take it
9 I've got to face it.
10 If I don't make it, someone else will

c Ask students to read through the lyrics and decide what *it* refers to in each case. Tell them there is no right answer and encourage them to use their imagination. Students discuss their ideas in small groups before open class feedback.

Did you know ...?

Read the information in the box with the class and find out if students know any other songs by Within Temptation. Ask if they know any other groups that contain a boyfriend and girlfriend.

Language note
You may like to draw students' attention to some common expressions using *it*. Write the following on the board and elicit suitable sentence endings from students (possible endings in brackets)

It's no secret that ... (the manager is going to reduce spending next year)
It's no surprise that ... (Brazil lost the game)
It's no use ... (planting potatoes in July)
It's no coincidence that ... (John and Mary go to the same karate club)

Tell students that *it* is also used with certain verbs, e.g. *amaze, annoy, concern, frighten, shock, surprise, upset, worry*, in the pattern *it* + verb + object + *to* infinitive clause

It shocks me to hear that ... (people are starving in Africa)
It amazes me to think that ... (so many people watch TV on Saturday evenings)

It frightened me to be told that ... (the desert is growing so quickly)

Ask students to work in pairs and think of endings to each of the sentences. Circulate and help with vocabulary as required, before listening to some examples.

9 Write

The planning for this exercise can be done in class and the writing can be set for homework.

Warm up

Books closed. Ask students whether they get stressed at school and ask them what they find most stressful. Exams? Homework? Their teachers? Their colleagues? Encourage them to discuss as a group.

a Books open. Tell students that they are going to write a report and a proposal on the subject of stress at school. Students read through the task and work through the questions. Let them compare their answers with a partner before feedback of questions 1–5.

Answers
1 A report and a proposal
2 The aim of the report is to show the principal of your college the activities that tend to cause the most anxiety and the signs of pressure that students most commonly show. The aim of the proposal is to suggest things that the college can do to help students who suffer from stress.
3 Possible questions: *When do you feel stressed? Do you find exams stressful? How do you know that you are stressed?*
4 In the report, statistics are useful. In the proposal, there should be recommendations and suggestions.
5 Language should be formal and factual.

b Read through the phrases with the class and ask them to decide whether they are normally used in a report or a proposal. Students compare answers with a partner before feedback.

Answers
1 proposal
2 report
3 report
4 proposal
5 report
6 proposal
7 report
8 proposal
9 proposal

c Students read the report and proposal and check their answers to Exercise 9b. Ask students to underline the phrases in the text and pay close attention to the words that follow them. Go through the answers with students and deal with any questions.

d Tell students they are going to write a report and a proposal. Read through the tasks and check understanding. Let them choose one of the two tasks and encourage them to use the example in Exercise 9c as a guide and to include the phrases in Exercise 9b. If there is time in class and you feel students would benefit from further guidance in writing reports and proposals, give students time to plan their answers and make some notes on what they will include. Let them compare these with a partner and in open class, before going on to write the final version. If you set this activity as homework, encourage students to read each other's answers in a subsequent lesson and decide which is the best report and proposal.

Module 1 Check your progress

1 Grammar

a 2 had been waiting
3 had been saving
4 had been stolen
5 had been killed
6 had not been listening
7 had been working
8 had been built

b 2 a 3 a 4 b 5 c 6 c 7 a 8 b

c 2 It's an old plastic toy.
3 It's a new Japanese invention.
4 It's a cheap white cotton shirt.
5 They've got a large round dining table.
6 They live in a huge five-bedroomed house.
7 He drives a red Italian sports car.
8 She's wearing beautiful black high-heeled shoes.

d 2 This is a really good idea.
3 It was a very nice day for an excursion.
4 Give that book back to me immediately.
5 We enjoyed the trip to Canterbury enormously.
6 Unfortunately I did not get the job.
7 She looked at me in a curious way.

e 2 My parents are always complaining about the music I play.
3 Some people will go to the doctor with the smallest problem.
4 He's always telling me what to do.
5 Teenagers tend not to eat healthy food.
6 My father will tell the same old jokes!

2 Vocabulary

a 2 barks
3 hiss
4 baaing
5 grunted
6 roaring
7 crow

b 2 false
3 true
4 true
5 true
6 false

c 2 slogan
3 logo
4 hoarding
5 sandwich board
6 jingle

d 2 pound
3 hard
4 race
5 overdoing
6 feet
7 soared
8 take
9 Chill
10 top of

How did you do?
Students work out their scores. Check how they have done and follow up any problem areas with revision work for students.

Module 2
Fiction and reality

YOU WILL LEARN ABOUT ...

Ask students to look at the pictures on the page. Ask them to read through the topics in the box and check that they understand each item. You can ask them the following questions, in L1 if appropriate:

1   What is the man carrying?
2   What are the two boys pretending to be? Why?
3   When do you think this picture was taken?
4   What is happening? Is this a real place?
5   What do you think this building is?
6   What job does the man in this picture do?

In pairs or small groups, students discuss which topic area they think each picture matches. Check the answers.

Answers
1   Metaphors we use and what they mean
2   War and peace
3   Women spies in World War II
4   Virtual worlds on the Internet
5   Inspiring buildings
6   Frank Abagnale, fake pilot and fraudster

YOU WILL LEARN HOW TO ...

Use grammar
Students read through the grammar points and the examples. Go through the first item with students as an example. In pairs, students now match the grammar items in their book. Check answers.

Answers
Reporting verb patterns: She apologised for having misled me.
Deduction and probability: The exhibition will be opened by the Queen.
Causative *have*: *have something done*: Have you ever had a suit made for you?
Modal passives: It sounds awful. You must have been terrified.
Cleft sentences: What most inhabitants do first is find themselves a profession.

Use vocabulary
Write the headings on the board. Go through the items in the Student's Book and check understanding. Now ask students if they can think of one more item for the *War and peace* heading. Elicit some responses and add them to the list on the board. Students now do the same for the other headings. Some possibilities are:

War and peace: *heavy casualties, sign a treaty*

Expressions with *story*: *cut a long story short, her side of the story*

Metaphors to describe emotions: *cut up, down in the dumps*

Money: *economical, take out a loan*

(5) Double lives

Unit overview

TOPIC: People who lead double lives

TEXTS
Reading and listening: an article about Frank Abagnale, the conman
Reading: an article about spies in World War Two
Listening: a radio programme about two women spies in World War Two
Reading: an extract from *Charlotte Gray* by Sebastian Faulks
Writing: a biography of Kofi Annan

SPEAKING AND FUNCTIONS
A discussion about peace

LANGUAGE
Grammar: reporting verb patterns
Vocabulary: crime; war and peace

1 Read and listen

If you set the background information as a homework research task, ask the students to tell the class what they found out.

BACKGROUND INFORMATION

Catch Me If You Can: is a 2002 film set in the 1960s. It was directed by Steven Spielberg and adapted loosely from the book by Frank Abagnale Jr. and Stan Redding.

Leonardo Wilhelm DiCaprio: was born on 11 November 1974 in Los Angeles, California. He has an Italian-born father and a German-born mother. Leonardo has appeared in over 20 films and TV series including *Titanic* (1997), *The Departed* (2006) and *Blink* (2007).

Warm up

As an introduction to the topic of fraud, ask students to imagine that they were going to pretend to be a policeman for a week. What would they have to do to convince people that they were a real policeman? What would be the difficulties? Do they think it would be possible to do without being discovered? Give students a short time to discuss in pairs before open class discussion.

In pairs, students make a list of different kinds of crime, then order them according to how serious they think they are. Allow a fair amount of time for this as it should lead to an interesting discussion.

Circulate and help with vocabulary as required. When students have a fair list, listen to some of their ideas as feedback and try to draw up a list of crimes on the board and come to some agreement as to which is the most serious.

(**a**) Students read the text quickly to find the answer. Encourage students not to look up every new word but just to read and get the general idea of the text.

Answers
He changed the 'four' on his driving licence to a 'three'; misled people into depositing money into his account; forged a law diploma; passed himself off as a doctor; forged a university degree; passed himself off as a stockbroker and FBI agent; pretended to be a Pan Am pilot; defrauded people; forged and cashed paychecks to the value of $2.5 million using four different false identities.

(**b**) (🔊) Read through the questions with the students. Check any problems. Play the recording while students read and listen to answer the questions. After the first listening, let students compare their answers with a partner. Check answers. If necessary, play the recording again, pausing to clarify any problems. Take note that several words from the text are explained in Exercise 2, so if students have any questions about these words, tell them to try to understand the word from the context and wait until the next exercise for an explanation.

TAPESCRIPT
See the reading text on page 34 of the Student's Book.

Answers
1 Because his parents separated and he didn't want to live with either of them.
2 To make himself ten years older.
3 attorney; doctor; sociology teacher; stockbroker; FBI agent; Pan Am pilot
4 So that he could fly all over the world.
5 No, he managed to give them the slip for years.
6 So that he could work for them and help them understand how a conman operates.

OPTIONAL ACTIVITY

If you would like your students to do some further work on the vocabulary in the text, you can use the following exercise. Write the following definitions on the board and ask students to find words and expressions with the same meaning in the text.

1 ... how a young man *acted more cleverly than* the authorities ... (para. 1)
2 He made a lot of money through a *plan to give people wrong information* ... (para. 2)
3 He started a life of *hiding the truth* ... (para. 3)

4 He got a job by *pretending to be someone else* ... (para. 3)

5 It wasn't difficult to get a *false identity card*. (para. 4)

6 He *illegally took money from* people all over the USA ... (para. 4)

7 ... he was able to *avoid being found and caught* for many more months. (para. 4)

8 ... he *said it was true* that he had *produced false documents* and paychecks ... (para. 5)

9 ... he *says* that he *never meant to hurt other people*. (para. 6)

Answers

1 outsmarted   2 scam   3 deception   4 passing himself off   5 fake ID   6 defrauded   7 give them the slip   8 confessed   9 denies having ever intentionally caused harm to any individual

---

Discussion box

Weaker classes: Students can choose one question to discuss.

Stronger classes: In pairs or small groups, students go through the questions in the box and discuss them.

Monitor and help as necessary, encouraging students to express themselves in English and to use any vocabulary they have learned from the text. Ask pairs or groups to feedback to the class and discuss any interesting points further.

---

2 Vocabulary

Crime

(a) Students match the words in the box with the definitions 1–9. Students should find the words in the text and check the meanings in context. Allow them to compare answers with a partner before feedback.

Answers

2 mislead   3 deception   4 fake   5 give someone the slip   6 confess   7 deny   8 defraud   9 forge

---

Language note

Point out to students that four of the words in Exercise 2a (*confess, defraud, mislead, outsmart*) have a slightly unusual stress pattern, in that they are stressed on the final syllable.

(b) Read through the sentences with students and check any difficult vocabulary: *on the lookout, signature, non-existent*. Students match the two parts of the sentences. Students check answers in pairs before feedback in open class.

Answers

2 j   3 b   4 i   5 h   6 a   7 c   8 d   9 f   10 e

Vocabulary notebook

Encourage students to start a new section *Crime* in their notebook and add these words. They may find it useful to note down translations of the words too.

3 Grammar

Reporting verb patterns

Students covered reporting verb patterns in SB4, Unit 4.

(a) **Weaker classes:** To reintroduce reported speech, ask students to make a list of verbs which can be used to report speech. Listen to some of their ideas in open class and write them on the board.

Write the following sentences on the board:

Did you steal my bicycle? He asked ...

I didn't steal the bicycle. Bill stole it. You should ask him. He said ...

Yes, John. I stole your bicycle. Sorry. I'll buy you a new one. He told John ...

In pairs, students work out answers. Write answers on the board as feedback.

He asked him if he had stolen his bicycle.
He said he hadn't stolen the bicycle and said that Bill had stolen it and that he should ask Bill.
He told John that he had stolen the bicycle and said he was sorry and that he would buy him a new one.

Point out the use of *if* after *ask* and the use of an object with *tell* and *ask*. Ask students if they know any other verbs which could be used to report the sentences. Write the following verbs on the board: *confess to, admit, deny, claim, apologise, offer* and *advise*. Work through the example sentences to clarify meaning. In pairs students decide how to report the sentences using the new verbs. During feedback, point out the words which follow each verb when reporting.

Answers

He denied stealing the bicycle.
He claimed that Bill had stolen it.
He advised him to ask Bill.
He confessed to stealing the bicycle.
He admitted stealing the bicycle.
He apologised for stealing the bicycle.
He offered to buy him a new bicycle.

Continue as for stronger classes.

Stronger classes: Students complete the sentences using the reporting verbs in brackets. Tell students that when using the verbs in brackets, it is not necessary to report every word of the original sentence. Students check answers with a partner before open class feedback.

Answers

2 He confessed to having forged / forging paychecks to the value of $2.5 million.

3 The Government offered to release him from prison early if he helped them understand how conmen worked.

4 Abagnale admitted that what he had done
was wrong.

5 He apologised for having caused / causing
so much trouble to the authorities.

6 He denied having intended / intending to
cause harm to any individual.

7 Frank claimed that identity theft was the
crime of the future.

8 He advised people to take the threat
very seriously.

(b) Read through the questions with students. In pairs,
students discuss the questions. Check answers. With
weaker classes, you might want to go through the
whole exercise with the class before students write
their answers.

Answers
1 + *that* + clause (–*ing* also possible for *admit*)
2 + –*ing* form
3 the use of *having* + past participle
(the perfect participle)

Language note
When reporting speech it is possible to report a
past action using either the gerund or the perfect
participle, e.g. *He denied causing trouble to the
authorities. / He denied having caused trouble to the
authorities.* Using the perfect participle makes it clear
that the action took place in the past. Using the
present participle does not make it clear whether the
action took place in the past or is still occurring.

The perfect participle is mostly used to report
speech in written English. When speaking, it is
quite normal for the present participle to be used
to report the past and for the time to be inferred
from the context.

(c) Students match the sentences with reporting verbs.
Students compare their answers with a partner before
feedback.

Answers
2 c 3 b 4 f 5 d 6 a

(d) Students rewrite the sentences using the reporting
verbs. Remind them that we can change the format of
the original sentence to make the reported speech
more natural and that we use the perfect participle to
emphasise that an action took place in the past.

Answers
2 The policeman admitted having been outsmarted
by the thief.

3 He asked if I had forged the document.

4 He claimed that it was very easy to deceive
people.

5 She confessed to having defrauded the company.

6 He denied having passed himself off as a lawyer.

Grammar notebook
Remind students to note down the rules for reporting
verb patterns and to write a few examples of their own.

OPTIONAL ACTIVITY
Students work in pairs to create a dialogue that includes
an admission, a denial, a confession, an apology and a
claim. Circulate and help with vocabulary. Students
act out their dialogue to another pair, who retell the
story in reported speech using the verbs *admit*, *deny*,
confess, *apologise* and *claim*. Listen to some examples
in open class. Encourage the rest of the class to correct
any mistakes.

4 Read

Warm up

Write *Second World War* and *spy* on the board and
ask students what they know about them. Have they
seen any films about them? Students discuss in pairs
and make notes. Listen to some of the pairs' ideas and
write them on the board.

(a) Students read the text quickly and choose the best
title. Encourage students not to look up every new
word but just to concentrate on the title. Students
compare their answer with a partner before feedback
in open class.

(b) Read through the questions with students and pre-
teach difficult vocabulary from the text: *invade,
resistance, espionage, marksmanship, coded messages,
wilderness, casualties.* Students read the text again
and answer the questions, then compare with a
partner. Check answers.

Answers
1 Because Germany had invaded several European
countries

2 Local resistance movements

3 In places occupied by the enemy

4 People from a wide range of backgrounds

5 The ability to speak a European language like
a native

6 Marksmanship, using explosives, the transmission
of coded messages, survival in the wilderness, how
to resist interrogation

(c) In pairs, students discuss spies. Monitor and help
as necessary, encouraging students to express
themselves in English and to use any vocabulary they
have learned from the text. Ask pairs or groups to
feedback to the class and discuss any interesting
points further.

5 Vocabulary

War and peace

Read through the words in the box and check
understanding. If students are unclear of meaning,
ask them to find the words in Exercise 4a and elicit
the meaning from the context. Tell students they
are going to read about two imaginary countries,
Freedonia and *Sylvania*. Students read and complete
the gaps with the words in the box. Check answers.

Answers

2 declared war 3 recruited 4 battles
5 fought 6 casualties 7 surrendered
8 peace negotiations 9 signed

Vocabulary notebook

Encourage students to start a new section *War and peace* in their notebook and add these words. They may find it useful to note down translations too.

6 Listen

a 🔊 Tell students they are going to listen to a radio programme about two women who worked for the SOE in France in World War II. Play the recording while students listen and tick the correct boxes in the table. Encourage students to concentrate on the task and not to worry if they don't understand every word. Check answers.

TAPESCRIPT

PRESENTER Good evening, and welcome to *Women in War*. This week we listen to the stories of two brave women who were members of the Special Operations Executive – Lilian Rolfe and Odette Hallowes. First of all, here is the story of Lilian Rolfe.

SPEAKER 1 When war broke out in Europe in 1939, Lilian Rolfe was living in Rio de Janeiro in Brazil. As she watched events unfold thousands of miles away in Europe, she became increasingly frustrated. She badly wanted to be part of the war effort and so, armed with nothing more than her courage, her love of France and her ability to speak fluent French, she embarked on the long voyage to London with one aim in mind: to join the Women's Air Force.

This she did in 1943, but it was not long before Lilian's linguistic talents led her to the Special Operations Executive, where she was trained for the dangerous life of a wireless operator, working in the midst of the German occupying forces in France. Lilian had been born to British parents in Paris in 1914, and it was to the town of Montargis just 60 miles from her birthplace that Lilian, or 'Nadine' as she was now called, arrived by parachute in May 1944 with a tiny radio transmitter strapped to her body.

She spent two dangerous months in the heart of occupied France, moving from one hiding place to the next, sending and receiving coded messages between the resistance forces and London, risking torture if captured. Her job was to maintain the vital radio links that informed her French colleagues when arms and supplies were being delivered – and this allowed the resistance to continue their fight against the invaders.

On 3 July 1944 she was captured and held in a series of prisons in France and Germany. Despite eight months of continuous interrogation, Lilian refused to reveal any information that might have helped the enemy or put her colleagues and friends in danger.

Her story ended on 5 February 1945 when she was shot. After her death, Lilian Rolfe was awarded the highest French medal, the *Croix de Guerre*, in January 1946, and today in Montargis there is a street that's named after her, in honour of the sacrifices she made to save its people.

SPEAKER 2 Odette Hallowes' life as a spy began because of a simple mistake. She replied to an official advertisement asking for photographs of the British coast, to be used for security purposes, and at the same time Odette sent a letter offering her assistance – but she accidentally sent her letter to the wrong government department. It was not long before she found herself being interviewed for the job of a secret agent, and then working undercover in France.

Born near Paris in 1912, Odette Hallowes became a British citizen when she married an Englishman in 1931. Although she had three young daughters at school in England, Odette felt compelled to go and fight for France.

In October 1942 she arrived on the French Mediterranean coast, travelling by boat from Gibraltar and using the name 'Lise'. Within a few days, the Germans invaded the southern half of France, so instead of travelling north, Odette stayed in Cannes, working as a courier along the French Riviera, carrying messages to SOE agents in Marseilles and finding houses where her commanding officer could operate his radio transmitter safely.

She worked with great courage until April 1943, when the unthinkable happened: she was betrayed by a man she trusted, and both she and her commanding officer were captured by the enemy. On the long journey to prison in Paris, the two of them put a plan together. They agreed to pretend to be married, and despite much evidence to the contrary, their captors were eventually persuaded that Odette's 'husband' had only come to France on her insistence, and had no involvement in the French Resistance. She was interrogated 14 times, but she stuck to her story the whole time, drawing attention away from the commanding officer – and onto herself.

The Germans were sure that Odette was in possession of a great deal of valuable information. She alone knew where the wireless operators and the English officers she had worked with were. For the next two years, she was tortured to try to extract a confession, but without success. When she was moved to a concentration camp, she was denied food for a week and then locked in a cell where the only sounds she could hear were the screams of other prisoners – one of them being Lilian Rolfe. Odette revealed nothing. Her silence not only saved the lives of many people, it allowed them to continue their vital work in the French Resistance, and in 1945, a few months after the Allies invaded France, Odette Hallowes escaped from the camp. She hijacked a German car and held a German officer at gunpoint until he delivered her safely to the Americans.

Unlike many of her colleagues in the SOE, Odette Hallowes survived to see the end of the war and her beloved France made free again. She was awarded an MBE and the George Cross in recognition of her bravery, endurance and self-sacrifice. She died in 1995 at the age of 83.

Answers
1 Lilian Rolfe; Odette Hallowes
2 Lilian Rolfe; Odette Hallowes
3 Lilian Rolfe
4 Lilian Rolfe
5 Odette Hallowes
6 Lilian Rolfe; Odette Hallowes
7 Lilian Rolfe
8 Odette Hallowes

(b) 🔊 Read the questions with students and check difficult vocabulary: *parachute, deliveries, interrogated.* Play the recording again while students answer the questions. Check answers. Play the recording again, pausing if necessary.

Answers
1 F She went to join the Women's Air Force
2 F She carried a tiny radio transmitter with her
3 T
4 F She was interrogated, but she didn't reveal any information
5 F She delivered messages, but found houses where her commanding officer could use his radio
6 F They put their plan together before arriving at the prison
7 F She could hear Lilian Rolfe's screams from her cell, but they were not in the same cell
8 F She forced a German officer to take her to the Americans

(c) Tell students they are going to write a page from the diary of one of the women in Exercise 6a. Give them some time to work in pairs and discuss the type of things they are going to include. Advise them to include as much detail and descriptive language as possible to make the diary more realistic. If time allows, students write their page and then students read each other's work and vote on which is most realistic. You may like to set this activity for homework and read the pages in a subsequent lesson.

7 Speak

(a) Draw students' attention to the four photos. In open class, students discuss which one they would choose to define peace. Encourage them to explain the reasons for their choices.

(b) In pairs, students choose a picture and prepare to talk about it. Circulate and ensure students are using descriptive language and explaining their reasons for their choices. This activity is more effective if students practise their talks in pairs and then present their talk to a larger group or to the class as a whole. Listen to some examples in open class as feedback.

Weaker classes: Students can write their sentences before speaking. Encourage them to look at their notes as little as possible.

Literature in mind

8 Read

If you set the background information as a homework research task, ask the students to tell the class what they found out.

BACKGROUND INFORMATION
Charlotte Gray: is a 1999 book by Sebastian Faulks. It is a haunting story of love and war set in London and occupied France in 1942–3. A young Scottish woman goes to Occupied France on a dual mission: to run an apparently simple errand for a British special operations group and to search for her lover, an English airman who has gone missing in action. The story is thought to be based on the exploits of Nancy Wake, code-named 'The White Mouse', a member of the resistance in wartime France.

Warm up
Ask students what training would be required for a spy who was going to be undercover behind enemy lines. Elicit ideas and write examples on the board.

(a) Show students the picture of the book cover and ask them to guess what the book might be about. Discuss whether or not students would be interested in reading the book and why or why not. Tell students they are going to read a letter about a pilot. Students read the text quickly to find the answer. Encourage students not to look up every new word but just to read and get the general idea of the text.

Answer
Flight Lieutenant Gregory is missing. He is an extremely able pilot and a patriotic officer with a proper sense of duty.

(b) Check students understand the questions. Ask them to read the text and answer the questions. Check understanding of *cover story* and *derailed.* Pre-teach *refuel, begging, groomed.* Students compare answers with a partner before feedback in open class.

Answers

1 b   2 c   3 c   4 a

(**c**) **Weaker classes:** If students have found the text difficult, write the answers on the board in a random order and ask students to look at the text to find the context and match the words and meanings. Follow the procedure for stronger classes.

Stronger classes: Students find words or expressions in the text and write a definition for each. Circulate and help with vocabulary as necessary. Students compare answers with a partner before checking in open class.

Answers

1 b   2 d   3 f   4 g   5 c   6 e   7 h   8 a

(**d**) Refer students back to the phrase *She had confided in Daisy* in the text and discuss its meaning. Brainstorm ideas for what Charlotte might have said. Ask them to think about how Daisy might have reacted to Charlotte's plans. In pairs, students create dialogues between Charlotte and Daisy. Circulate and monitor, helping with vocabulary if necessary. Encourage students to use expressions from Exercise 8c where possible. Listen to some of the dialogues in open class as feedback.

Weaker classes: Students can write their dialogues before speaking. Encourage them to look at their notes as little as possible.

9 Write

If you set the background information as a homework research task, ask the students to tell the class what they found out.

BACKGROUND INFORMATION

The United Nations (UN): is an international organisation that promotes cooperation and peace between countries. It was founded in 1945 after the end of World War II by the victorious world powers in the hope that it would act to prevent conflicts between nations and make future wars impossible, by fostering an ideal of collective security. There are now 191 member countries and the UN plays a major role in peacekeeping around the world.

The World Health Organisation (WHO): is a specialised agency of the United Nations (UN) that acts as a coordinating authority on international public health.

Students can do the preparation for this in class and the writing can be set for homework.

(**a**) Tell students they are going to read a biography of the author of *Charlotte Gray*. Read through the instructions. Students read and underline the important information. If they underline different types of information in different colours, it will stand out more. During feedback, deal with difficult vocabulary in the text: *male-dominated*, *columnist*, *harrowing*, *acclaimed*.

(**b**) Read through the notes about Kofi Annan with students and check understanding of difficult vocabulary: *elite* and *tribal chiefs*. Tell students they are going to write a biography, using the biography of Sebastian Faulks as an example. Students could do the writing for homework. In a subsequent lesson, give them the opportunity to read each other's biographies.

--- OPTIONAL ACTIVITY ---

If your students have access to the Internet, ask them to research and write a biography on a famous person of their choice. If they cannot think of anybody, you may like to offer them one of the following: King Juan Carlos of Spain, Pelé (Brazilian footballer), Jimmy Page (musician), Audrey Hepburn (actress), Oprah Winfrey (chat-show host). Encourage students to follow a similar pattern to the Sebastian Faulks biography and to plan their biography carefully, writing a draft in note form before completing the final draft. In a subsequent lesson, give students the opportunity to read each other's biographies, or use the biographies as the basis of a spoken presentation on the famous person.

6 Legend or truth?

Unit overview

TOPIC: Urban legends and other stories

TEXTS
Reading and listening: an article about urban legends
Listening: a radio show about urban legends
Listening and speaking: a girl telling a dramatic story
Writing: a newspaper article about an urban legend

SPEAKING AND FUNCTIONS
A discussion about urban legends
Telling urban legends

LANGUAGE
Grammar: deduction and probability
Vocabulary: expressions with *story*
Pronunciation: stress in phrases

1 Read and listen

Warm up

Books closed. Tell students the following story:

A friend of mine went to New York on holiday last year and one day when she was walking in the street, she heard people screaming. She turned round and saw a crocodile coming out of a hole in the road! She ran away of course! That evening on the TV, she saw a report saying that the crocodile had been caught. It had been living underground in the sewers (the water system). It had been born in the New York zoo two years before, but they had too many baby crocodiles, so they had put it down the toilet! It had been living underground ever since. The reporter said this had happened several times before.

Ask students if they think the story is true. If not, ask them why not. Could it be possible?

a) Books open. Ask students to look at the three pictures and discuss what they think is happening in each one. Help with any difficult vocabulary and listen to some of their ideas in open class.

b) Tell students they are going to read an article in which the pictures are explained, in order to check their ideas in Exercise 1a. Encourage students not to look up every new word but just to read and get the general idea of the text. You could give them a time limit to encourage them to read the text quickly.

c) ◁)) Play the recording while students read, listen and fill the spaces in the text with one of the phrases. Allow students to compare answers with a partner before feedback.

TAPESCRIPT
See the reading text on pages 40 and 41 of the Student's Book.

Answers
A 4   B 7   C 1   D 6   E 2   F 5
Clause 3 is not used

d) Read through the questions with students to check understanding. Give students time to read the text closely and to check their answers with a partner before feedback.

Answers
1 Crime and horror, schools and universities, food contaminations and the Internet
2 Most urban legends are untrue
3 The story of a person who wakes up in a bath of ice with a kidney removed, which caused panic and police warnings
4 Spread urban legends easily, find websites dedicated to investigating the truth behind them
5 Mankind's compulsion for storytelling; the cautionary nature of many urban legends; why we get so much pleasure from passing on urban legends; a comparison between urban legends and traditional fairy tales
6 The fact that they change our behaviour

e) Check students understand the definitions. Ask them to find phrases or expressions in the text which have the same meaning. Let them compare answers with a partner before feedback in open class.

Answers
2 by word of mouth
3 crop up
4 led to
5 a wide range of issues
6 climate of fear
7 largely irrelevant
8 not one single case

Discussion box
Weaker classes: Students can choose one question to discuss.

Stronger classes: In pairs or small groups, students go through the questions in the box and discuss them.

Monitor and help as necessary, encouraging students to express themselves in English and to use any vocabulary they have learned from the text. Ask pairs or groups to feedback to the class and discuss any interesting points further.

2 Grammar
Deduction and probability

Students covered deduction and probability in SB3, Units 11 and 12.

(a) **Weaker classes:** Tell students an urban legend, either one of your own or the following story:

I have a friend called John who I have known for ten years. Last week, he went to the supermarket to buy some bread. He took it home and started to make a sandwich. When he cut into the bread he found a piece of paper with an address written on it. It was in his town, so he was curious and went to the address. He knocked on the door and a woman answered. He told her about the piece of paper and she was very surprised. She said that the same thing had happened to her and showed him the piece of paper she had found. On it was written John's address. They got married six months later.

Write the following on the board:

John is my friend.
John went to the supermarket.
They both found a piece of paper in a loaf of bread.
The pieces of paper had their addresses on them.
John married a girl who lived near him.

Ask students if they think the sentences are possible or if they really happened. Write *must, might, may* and *can't* on the board. Elicit the meaning and use of each verb from students. In pairs, students think of sentences using the modal auxiliaries.

Possible answers in brackets:

John is my friend. **(It must be true)**
John went to the supermarket. **(It might be true)**
They both found a piece of paper in a loaf of bread.
(It might be true)
The pieces of paper had their addresses on them.
(It can't be true)
John married a woman who lived near him.
(It might be true)

Ask students to focus on whether the action in the sentences took place in the past or the present and ask what happens when we use the modal auxiliaries in the past (modal + *have* + past participle). In pairs, students write sentences explaining why they think the sentences are true or not. During feedback, write correct answers on the board and focus on the use of the perfect participle.

Possible answers

John must be your friend.
John may have gone to the supermarket.
They might have found a piece of paper in the bread.
The pieces of paper can't have had their addresses on them.
John might have married a woman who lives near him.

Continue with the procedure for stronger classes.

Stronger classes: Ask students to look at the sentences in the book. Students work together to decide on the best answer. Check answers, focusing on the different levels of probability expressed by each of the modal auxiliaries.

Answers
1 a   2 b   3 c   4 a   5 b   6 a

(b) In pairs, students discuss the difference in meaning between the sentences. Encourage them to think about the context in which each sentence was said and the types of evidence that the speakers have based their assumptions on. Discuss in open class.

Answers
1 In sentence a, the speaker is almost certain that it is James at the door. In sentence b, it is possible that James is at the door.
2 In sentence a, the speaker is certain that Monica knows where her brother is, because she always knows where he is. In sentence b, the speaker is almost certain that Monica will know where her brother is, perhaps based on recent evidence.
3 In sentence a, the speaker is sure that her sister has reached New York. In sentence b, the speaker thinks it is very probable that her sister has reached New York.

(c) Check understanding of *pretty* (quite) and *hung up*. Ask students to complete the sentences using a suitable modal verb. Explain that there may be more than one answer.

Answers
2 can't be   3 will know / must know / might know
4 must have made / might have made
5 must have said   6 must have watched

(d) Before feedback on Exercise 2c, ask students to decide which sentences have more than one possible answer and explain the differences in meaning between the answers.

> **Language note**
> Students often make the following mistake:
> - **That mustn't be John at the door. He's in Spain.* (substituting *mustn't* for *can't*)
>
> Tell students that when using modal auxiliary verbs for deduction and probability, *can't* is the opposite of *mustn't*.
>
> - *May* and *might* often have a similar meaning when we talk about possibility. However, point out to students that *may* is more commonly used in formal written language and *might* is preferred in speech. *Might not* has a short form *mightn't*. *May not* cannot be shortened to **mayn't*.
> - We can add *well* to both verbs to express a strong possibility:

The picture may well be very valuable. (it is very possible)

- *Could* can also be used to express possibility.

In spoken English, expressions such as *maybe*, *perhaps* and *I think* are used instead of *may* and *might*.

Grammar notebook
Remind students to note down the rules for deduction and probability and to write a few examples of their own.

3 Listen

(a) Look at the pictures on page 42. In pairs, students describe what is happening in each story. Monitor and help with vocabulary if required. Listen to some of their ideas in open class, but do not tell them the correct order of the pictures at this stage.

(b) 🔊 Tell students they are going to listen to a radio show in which the stories in Exercise 3a are told. Students listen and number the pictures in the order that they hear the information. Encourage students to concentrate on the task and not to worry if they don't understand every word. Check answers.

TAPESCRIPT
Narrator: Story 1
Presenter: OK, it's just after twenty past ten and time for *A Likely Story*. And on the line we've got Kate from Huddersfield. How are you, Kate?
Kate: Hiya. I'm fine.
Presenter: And how's Huddersfield this morning?
Kate: A bit wet and cold!
Presenter: Well, let's see if we can bring a bit of sunshine into your morning. Are you ready to play?
Kate: Yes, I am.
Presenter: You know the rules. I'm going to tell you an urban legend and you've got to tell me if you think it's true or not. Get it right, and we'll send you a goody bag packed with nice things. Get it wrong and you get nothing.
Kate: OK.
Presenter: So, here we go. This story was sent to us by Jenny Goodwill who swears it's true because it happened to her friend's son. The only problem is that it's not the first time we've heard it. In fact our secretary swears it also happened to a friend of a friend of hers. So we're already a bit suspicious. But Kate, it's up to you. The story goes that Jenny's friend's son was making a cup of tea when he decided to heat the water up in the microwave oven. Anyway, after a minute or so, he took the mug out and looked into it. He thought it was a bit strange as the water wasn't actually boiling as it normally did. A second later the water exploded in his face, burning it quite badly and caused him to partially lose the sight in his

left eye. When he went to hospital, the doctor said that it wasn't the first time he'd had to treat similar burns from exploding water. So, Kate, there you have it. Exploding water in the microwave. True or completely made up?
Kate: Well, I've boiled water hundreds of times in the microwave and it's never happened to me.
Presenter: So you're saying it's false?
Kate: Yep. I am. I'm sure I would have heard if it was.
[*Buzzer sounds*]
Kate: No way! It's true?! I don't believe it!
Presenter: It is, Kate. I'm sorry. Apparently it's an extremely rare phenomenon, which some scientists refer to as superheated water. Now the conditions for this to happen are extremely difficult to achieve. First the cup must be extremely clean. If any foreign object such as sugar or milk is added before boiling the water, then this won't happen. Now if superheating has occurred, any sudden movement with the cup, such as picking up the mug or adding a spoonful of instant coffee can cause the water to erupt out of the mug – a bit like a volcano erupting in a way.
Kate: You're kidding me?
Presenter: No, I kid you not. In fact, the Food and Drug Agency warn people not to use microwaves to heat water but if you do have to, they advise that you heat it for the minimum time required in order to avoid superheating.
Kate: I think I'm going to use the kettle from now on.
Presenter: That sounds like a good idea, Kate. Thanks for playing. Sorry you got it wrong.
Kate: Well, I'm used to it – it's the story of my life! But no problem! Thanks. Bye!
Narrator: Story 2
Presenter: Our next listener is Phil from Manchester. Hi Phil, are you ready to play?
Phil: Yes, let's do it.
Presenter: Now this is a story that's doing the rounds on the Internet at the moment and I'll warn you – it's terrifying. Doctors have finally discovered what's behind a series of unusual deaths over the last few weeks in the south of England, and it'll make you think twice before you visit any public toilets for a while. The mystery started about a month ago when three women turned up at different hospitals in and around London. They were all suffering from the same symptoms: a high fever, skin rashes and vomiting. After a few days, they all died. Tests showed that all the women had died from blood poisoning. Doctors were puzzled, especially as they couldn't find any connection between the women. But they then found out that all three women had eaten at the same restaurant at Heathrow airport a few days before they died. So health workers rushed to the restaurant and immediately closed it down.

They did tests on the food, water and air-conditioning system but found nothing. So the restaurant opened again. Then a day later another woman was admitted to hospital with the same symptoms. Now, she'd been to the restaurant, but she hadn't eaten or drunk anything. The only thing she'd done was use the toilets. So one of the experts working on the case visited the restaurant and went to the toilet. He lifted up the toilet seat and there, hidden from view, he found a tiny red spider. The spider turned out to be an American Blush spider. They're normally found in South America, and they like dark damp places near water. They are also extremely poisonous, although it can take up to ten days for the poison to take effect. However, once it does start working the victim has less than two hours to get help. Upon this discovery, the doctors thought everything was under control. But then another man died yesterday from the same symptoms. He'd arrived on a plane from Bolivia and gone straight home. Just like all the other victims, he had a small puncture mark at the top of his leg. An immediate search was done on the plane he had flown on and another American Blush spider was found. Since then every plane coming from South America has been searched and a further six spiders have been found. Doctors now believe these spiders could be anywhere in the country, and they're telling people to lift the seat and check any public toilet before using it. Told you it was scary, didn't I, Phil?

Phil: Yeah, you did.

Presenter: So Phil, what do you think? Is there any truth in the story or do you think they're pulling our leg?

Phil: Well, it does sound kind of ridiculous. I mean, if it were true, it would have been on the news, wouldn't it?

Presenter: Maybe the government don't want us to know?

Phil: No. It isn't true. I'm sure of that.

[*Trumpet fanfare*]

Phil: Yeees!!

Presenter: Well done Phil. There's no fooling you. A bag of goodies will be making its way to you shortly.

Phil: Thank you very much.

Presenter: And if any listeners get an email with this story, delete it immediately. We did a bit of research and found out that this is a classic scare story that has been doing the rounds since 1999 although details have changed over the years. And that's it for today's likely story.

Answers
Story 1: a c b The story is true
Story 2: f e d The story is false

---

c In pairs, students use the pictures to retell each of the stories. If students need help in making their stories effective, spend some time eliciting vocabulary from the listening text and writing it on the board. Useful vocabulary in story 1: *heat the water up, boiling, exploded, jumped out, lose sight, burns.* In story 2: *symptoms, blood poisoning, test, toilet lid, dark damp places.* As feedback, listen to some of the stories in open class.

4 Vocabulary
Expressions with *story*

a Students match the expressions to the definitions. If they are unsure about any of the vocabulary, ask them to guess the meaning. Encourage students to think of these expressions as single pieces of vocabulary even though they are made up of various words. Let them check their answers with a partner before feedback. If students are still unclear about the meaning of any of the expressions, give them a context in which it would be used.

Answers
2 d 3 e 4 b 5 a 6 h 7 c 8 g

b Pre-teach *fault* and *broke*. Students read the dialogues and circle the correct words. Check answers.

Answers
1 end of story   2 to cut a long story short
3 her side of the story   4 It's the same old story
5 make up a story   6 a likely story   7 It's the story of my life!   8 told me a sob story

c Give students the opportunity to practise saying the dialogues in pairs. Make sure they pronounce the expressions correctly. Ask for some examples from a few pairs.

TAPESCRIPT / ANSWERS
See dialogues in Exercise 4b in the Student's Book.

Vocabulary notebook
Encourage students to start a new section *Expressions with story* in their notebook and add these words. They may find it useful to note down translations of the words too.

5 Speak

Tell students they are going to do an activity called *A likely story* in which they read some information, then tell a story to their partner who has to decide whether it is true or not.

Divide students into pairs and give each student a letter A or B. Ask students A to look at the instructions on page 43, while students B turn to page 123 and read their questions. Allow students to ask any questions about vocabulary to ensure they understand meaning.

Give students time to add details to their stories in order to make them sound convincing. Monitor and help with vocabulary as necessary. In pairs, students tell each other their stories. Listen to a few of the stories in open class.

At the end of the exercise, tell the class that student A's story is true and student B's story is not true.

Weaker classes: Students may benefit from working together with a partner when they are adding details to their stories. Allow students to write their stories before speaking. Encourage them to look at their notes as little as possible.

6 Listen and speak

Warm up

Books closed. Write the following words on the board: *airport*, *ticket*, *car park*, *holiday*, *barrier*. Tell students that these words appear in a story and ask them to discuss in pairs what they think the story might be about. Ask some pairs to give feedback.

(a) Students open their books to look at the pictures and tell you what they can see. You may like to ask students to try to order the pictures to tell the story.

(b) ◁))) Play the recording while students listen and write 1—6 in the boxes in Exercise 6a. Check answers.

Answers
f e a d c b

TAPESCRIPT
Boy 1   ... and it was really funny, the car was such a mess, we just had to laugh.
Girl   Well, you know, that reminds me of a couple of years ago when we all went on holiday to San Francisco in California, and erm, well, we'd just arrived in the USA. We did the usual at San Francisco airport, you know, got our luggage and everything ... well, my father had booked a hire car so we had to get in a little bus, one of those little buses the car hire places use.
Boy 2   A courtesy bus?
Girl   Yeah, that's it, and anyway, it took us to the place to pick up the car, and then we had to take all our luggage to the garage where the car was. In we all got and thought, 'Yeah, California here we come!'. They'd given us this fancy car, so off we went – well, I say 'off we went', but we only got as far as the exit where you have to put the ticket in ... Dad put the ticket in and the machine kind of ate the ticket – but would you believe it, the barrier didn't go up.
Boy 1   Where had he got the ticket from anyway?
Girl   Oh, they give you one at the car hire place.
Boy 1   Oh, right.
Girl   Anyway, so he waited a minute or two but the barrier still didn't go up, right, so he started pressing all the buttons and he pressed them again and again and again, but nothing happened

– until, finally, the machine made a strange noise and the ticket came flying out again but it fell on the floor. So Dad opened the car door and got out to pick it up, and lying on the ground there were about a hundred old parking tickets!!
Boy 2   Oh no!
Girl   Yeah, and by this time, of course, there were about another five cars behind us waiting to go out too ...
Boy 1   All hooting their horns I expect ...
Girl   Well, no – that was the amazing thing, they just sat and waited patiently, no one blew their horn at all ...
Boy 1   So what happened in the end?
Girl   Well, Dad was going crazy – you know how easily he loses his cool! – but he picked up a few tickets and started shoving them into the machine, and then, all of a sudden, up went the barrier! No one knew why it had gone up but Dad just leapt into the car, put his foot down and roared off! I think we were going at about a hundred miles an hour when we drove out of the garage, it was hilarious, and then Dad just started laughing like mad and we headed off towards San Francisco, all of us laughing till we nearly cried. I mean, I know it's not <u>that</u> funny, but at the time, you know ...
Boy 2   Traveller's tales.
Girl   Kind of, yeah ... we often talk about that one when we're ...

(c) ◁))) Read through the phrases with the class and check that students understand *pressed*. Play the recording again. Students listen to number the boxes in the order they hear the phrases. Students compare answers with a partner before feedback. You may want to play the recording again, pausing as necessary.

Answers
7, 1, 5, 2, 4, 3, 6

Language note
There are two examples of inversion in the text:
1 *Off we went* This pattern is often found in narrative to mark a change in events:
   Along came Joe, In came the policeman, etc.
2 *Lying on the ground were ...* This pattern is known as fronting. Information in a sentence is reordered to give emphasis to a particular place. This will often focus attention on another element later in the sentence.

(d) In pairs, students discuss how the phrases are used to make the story more dramatic. Listen to some of their ideas and draw attention to the fact that the intonation used when saying the phrases is very important. You may like to play the recording, pausing where necessary and asking students to repeat the intonation patterns.

(e) Tell students that they are going to tell a story that they have experienced or heard. Read through the instructions to check understanding. Ask students to make brief notes about their story before telling it to their group. You may like to give an example of your own to get them started. Monitor and check that they are including some of the phrases from Exercise 6c. When students have voted on the best story in their groups, listen to the best stories in open class.

7 Pronunciation
Stress in phrases

(a) Students turn to page 122 and read through the phrases. Ask them to underline the stressed words and syllables.

(b) 🔊 Play the recording for students to check answers, then play the recording again, pausing for students to repeat each sentence. Encourage students to mimic the recording.

TAPESCRIPT / ANSWERS
2 <u>Off</u> we went.
3 Would you <u>believe</u> it?
4 <u>All</u> of a sudden …
5 That was the <u>amazing</u> thing.
6 What <u>happened</u> in the end?

(c) Read through the phrases with the class, paying attention to stress and intonation. In pairs, students practise saying the sentences to each other and decide where the stress should go for each phrase. Listen to some examples in open class and correct stress patterns where necessary.

OPTIONAL ACTIVITY
Ask students to write a story which includes all of the phrases in Exercise 7c and all of the following things (or others of your choice).

a banana   a thief   two dogs   a spaceship   a kiss

In pairs, students plan their story. Circulate to help with vocabulary and to ensure students are using the phrases correctly. Students tell their story to another pair. You could ask some pairs to tell their stories to the class and vote on the most interesting.

8 Write

The planning for this exercise can be done in class and the letter set as homework.

(a) Tell students they are going to read an urban legend from a newspaper. Pre-teach *prick, cowboy boots, stamped to death, fang, embedded, sole*. Students read the text quickly and answer the questions. Encourage students not to look up every new word or worry about the words in italics, but just to read and get the general idea of the text. Check answers.

Answer
It is probably from a tabloid newspaper as it is very sensational in tone.

(b) Explain to students that all of the words in italics are adverbs which are used to describe the sentence. In pairs, students circle the adverb which does not fit into the sentence.

Answers
1 miraculously
2 tragically
3 overwhelmingly
4 mysteriously
5 Finally
6 Astonishingly

Language note
The adverbs in the text are used in three different ways. Ask students to look back at the text and decide which of the adverbs are used to describe:
1 a whole sentence or clause (adverbs 1, 4, 6, 8)
2 a verb (adverbs 2, 7)
3 an adjective (adverbs 3, 5)
The adverbs describing a whole sentence or clause are known as comment adverbs. These adverbs make a comment on what we are saying. They can:

show how likely we think something is:
apparently, obviously, probably, undoubtedly
show our attitude or opinion:
astonishingly, sadly, surprisingly, luckily
show our judgement of someone's actions:
kindly, stupidly, carelessly

Comment adverbs are most frequently placed at the beginning of a sentence, but can go at the end. They are separated from the rest of a sentence by a comma, or a pause when speaking.

Surprisingly, the champion lost the race.
The champion lost the race, surprisingly.

(c) Read through the titles with students. Ask them to discuss their ideas with a partner before open class feedback.

Possible answers
1 horror; supernatural story
2 a cosy story with a happy ending
3 the boots are responsible for death
4 a story of survival

(d) Tell students they are going to write one of the stories in Exercise 3. Tell them to use the story in Exercise 8 as a model and to ensure that they use adverbs to make the story exciting and interesting. This can either be done in class or as homework. In a subsequent lesson, encourage students to read each other's stories and decide which is the best.

7 Inspiration and creation

Unit overview

TOPIC: Inspiration and creation

TEXTS

Reading and listening: an article in which three artists describe their inspirations
Listening: an interview with an expert on metaphors
Listening and speaking: part two of an interview with an expert on metaphors and a discussion about metaphors
Reading: an article about three inspiring buildings
Writing: a poem including metaphors

SPEAKING AND FUNCTIONS

Discussion about having things done

LANGUAGE

Grammar: *have something done* (review); modal passives (present and past)
Vocabulary: metaphors to describe emotions

1 Read and listen

If you set the background information as a homework research task, ask the students to tell the class what they found out.

BACKGROUND INFORMATION

Darcey Bussell: was born in London on 27 April 1969. She studied at The Royal Ballet School aged 13 and joined the company six years later. She became the youngest Principal of The Royal Ballet at the age of 20. Her classical repertory includes Odette/Odile in Swan Lake, Princess Aurora in The Sleeping Beauty and the Sugar Plum Fairy in The Nutcracker. In 2006 she announced her retirement as Principal of The Royal Ballet after two decades, but is continuing to make appearances as a guest artist. She was awarded the CBE by the Queen in December of the same year for her services to dance.

Dr. Benjamin Zephaniah: was born on 15 April 1958 in Birmingham, but spent his early years in Jamaica, where he absorbed much of the music and poetry that influences his work. Benjamin had a difficult school life, and at 14 spent two years in prison. It was there that he decided to educate himself and become a poet. He moved to London in 1979 and published his first poetry collection, *Pen Rhythm*, in 1980. His other poetry collections include *Talking Turkey* (1994) and *Funky Chickens* (1996). He has also written

novels for teenagers as well as several stage and television plays. His most recent book is *We Are Britain!* (2002), a collection of poems celebrating cultural diversity in Britain.

Joan Armatrading: is credited with being the first black female singer/songwriter to gain prominence on the British music scene. She offered a unique take on folk and reggae that was highly influential to artists like Tracy Chapman. Born on the Caribbean island of St Kitts in 1950, she moved to Birmingham with her family when she was eight, where she taught herself to play piano and guitar. Her first commercial success was with her self-titled release in 1976, and she followed that with 1977's *Show Some Emotion* and 1978's *To the Limit*.

✓ Warm up ✓

(1) - what inspired you (film - music - person)?
(2) - Ask ss to give you eg's of things or people had big influence on them.

Books closed. Tell students some of the things that inspire or have inspired you. Refer to people, books, music, films, whatever has had a big influence on you. Ask students to give you examples of people or things that inspire them. Let students discuss their inspirations with a partner before listening to some examples in open class.

(a) Open books. In pairs, students make a list of ten things that could inspire writers, singers or dancers. Write some of their ideas on the board during feedback.

(b) Look at the photos and ask students to imagine what type of people they are and where they get their inspiration from. Students read the text quickly to check their answers. Encourage students not to look up every difficult word, but just to read and get the general idea of the text.

Answers

Darcey Bussell is inspired by bright colours and beautiful views.
Benjamin Zephaniah is inspired by the image of a starving child in the Biafran war.
Joan Armatrading is inspired by everyday conversations.

(c) Read through the questions with students. Pre-teach *swollen belly* and *association*. Ask students to read the text again and listen to the recording to answer the questions. Allow students to compare their answers in pairs before feedback.

TAPESCRIPT

See the reading text on page 46 of the Student's Book.

(3) Let them discuss their inspirations with a partner first.

(4) ss make a list of 10 things that could inspire writers, musicians etc.

(5) ss look at the photos and decide what type of people they think they are.

(6) ss gist read to find whether they were right or not.

Answers _bring back_ (handwritten)
1 They (revive her) enthusiasm for life.
2 They are (appalled.) _filled with horror or dismay_ (handwritten)
3 Because he saw a baby with thin arms and a swollen belly and discovered it was because of fighting between black people.
4 He felt suicidal.
5 By playing with associations between words.

(d) 🔊 Play the recording again while students read the text and answer the questions. Students check answers with a partner. Repeat the recording if necessary, pausing after the answers to the questions. Check answers in open class and invite students to comment on the information.

Answers
1 Benjamin Zephaniah   2 Darcey Bussell
3 Joan Armatrading   4 Benjamin Zephaniah

(e) Check students understand the definitions. Ask them to find the words in the text and choose the correct definition. Let them compare answers with a partner before feedback in open class.

Answers
1 make someone feel strong feelings of disapproval
2 very brightly coloured
3 done on purpose
4 the crime of intentionally starting a fire
5 show the connection between two or more things
6 make an activity happen faster

Discussion box
Weaker classes: Students can choose one question to discuss.

Stronger classes: In pairs or small groups, students go through the questions in the box and discuss them.

Monitor and help as necessary, encouraging students to express themselves in English and to use any vocabulary they have learned from the text. Ask pairs or groups to feedback to the class and discuss any interesting points further.

2 Grammar

have something done (review)

Students covered _have something done_ in SB3 Unit 7.

(a) Weaker classes: To remind students of this structure, write the following words on the board:

cut hair, repair car

Ask students these questions:

Do you do these things yourselves?
Who does them for you? Do you pay that person?

Elicit the following sentences from students and write them on the board:

I have my hair cut by the hairdresser.
I have my car repaired by a mechanic.

Clarify that we use this structure to describe services done for us by someone else. This is often, but not always paid for. Follow the procedure for stronger classes.

Stronger classes: Ask students to look at the sentence and answer the question. Tell students that the action was done by someone else.

Answer
We don't know

(b) Read through the rule with the class and ask students to complete it.

Rule
to have + object + the past participle of the main verb

Explain to students that the structure is often called the causative _have_ and that it is used to describe things that we want to happen.

Stronger classes: You could mention that this structure can also be used to describe bad things that have happened to us that we didn't intend to happen. For example: _I had my car stolen last week._

(c) Read through the sentences with students and check understanding of _hired_ and _look after_. Students complete the sentences and compare answers with a partner before feedback in open class.

Answers
2 had her house painted
3 had a suit made
4 had my letter published in my favourite magazine
5 had their cat looked after by their neighbours
6 have my blood pressure checked

Language note
We can use _get_ instead of _have_ in causative sentences:
When are you getting your hair cut?
This can be used to suggest that we have managed to do something:
It was difficult, but we got our car repaired in the end.
We can also use _get_ informally when we are talking about a job we do ourselves:
I must get the washing up done.
(= _I must do the washing up._)

Grammar notebook
Remind students to note down the rules for _have something done_ and to write a few examples.

OPTIONAL ACTIVITY
If you would like to give your students some practice in the use of the causative to describe things that we didn't intend to happen, write these sentences on the board:
1 _Someone has stolen my bicycle._
2 _Someone broke into our house yesterday._
3 _The wind blew my hat off._
4 _Someone broke John's nose in a fight._
5 _The police took his passport._

Go through the first sentence with the class, discussing how to make a causative structure. Students do the others in pairs, and then check in open class.

Answers
1 I have had my bicycle stolen.
2 We had our house broken into yesterday.
3 I had my hat blown off (in the wind).
4 John had his nose broken in a fight.
5 He had his passport taken.

3 Listen

a Write the word *metaphor* on the board and ask students what they understand by the term (the application of a word or phrase to somebody or something that is not meant literally but to make a comparison, for example saying that somebody is a snake). Can they think of any examples? Listen to some of their ideas. Ask students to look at the pictures and work out which metaphor is shown.

Answers
a He's got the whole world on his shoulders.
b He's got butterflies in his stomach.
c She could eat a horse.
d He's over the moon.

b 🔊 Tell students they are going to listen to an interview in which a professor of linguistics talks about metaphors. Play the recording while students listen to check their answers from Exercise 3a and find out what the metaphors mean. Tell students that the listening is quite long and remind them not to worry about every word, but to make a note of important information. Students compare answers with a partner before feedback.

TAPESCRIPT

Host How often do you complain that your feet are killing you when you're tired or say that you could eat a horse when you are hungry? Expressions such as these are a lifetime passion for our next guest, Jane Davis. A professor of linguistics, Jane's here to explain her love of the metaphor and tell us how metaphor analysis can help us understand ourselves. Jane, welcome to the programme.

Jane Davis Thank you for having me.

Host So, first question. How do you explain your passion for metaphors?

Jane Davis Well, it's quite easy really. I believe that metaphors are what bring languages alive. They allow us to take the language and make it our own. Let me put it another way: when we speak any language, we can't go around inventing new words or messing about with the grammar. If we do, we might be accused of not speaking the language properly. Metaphors allow us a certain amount of freedom within this set of rules. We can take those words and grammatical structures and use them to create our own images and

symbols. A good metaphor is a great example of how our language should be used.

Host OK, before we go any further, I think you'd better define exactly what a metaphor is.

Jane Davis OK. The first thing about metaphors is that they involve a comparison between two or more things. You might tell your girlfriend, for example, that *Her lips are fresh red roses*, or as my dad used to say when we never did what we were told, *I feel like I'm banging my head against a brick wall.*

Now the second thing we must remember is that these comparisons are figurative. That is, we don't actually mean what we're saying. Your girlfriend's lips quite clearly are not flowers and similarly my dad was not actually physically hurting himself. A metaphor gives our words a new, more imaginative meaning.

Host So how do they work exactly?

Jane Davis They only work if a connection can be made between the things that are being compared. We can picture a red rose and a pair of red lips and so the connection becomes obvious.

Host So we need to think carefully about our comparisons.

Jane Davis Absolutely. I mean if I told you that 'your lips were like cardboard boxes', you'd probably wonder what on earth I was talking about!

Host Unless we shared the same strange imagination.

Jane Davis That's possible I suppose. Now another thing that I should mention about metaphors is how frequent they are. One study that I read about said that the average person will use four metaphors in every minute of speech. Four metaphors a minute! Even if that's a bit of an exaggeration, it's still an incredible statistic.

Host So why are they so common in our everyday speech?

Jane Davis Well, metaphors often get used to talk about our emotions and feelings – the most important things we have to talk about in life. Let's look at a few examples. When you're happy, you might say that you're feeling over the moon, when you're sad perhaps you're feeling blue. When you get angry your blood boils; when you're nervous, you have butterflies in your stomach. The list goes on and on. We use metaphors to express what we feel.

Host Now, the expressions you've mentioned are phrases that I would find if I looked them up in a dictionary, aren't they?

Jane Davis   Indeed they are. Many metaphors have become so common that they've become standard phrases. Expressions like *I'm carrying the weight of the world on my shoulders* to tell you how much pressure I feel I'm under and *I think I'm cracking up* to tell you I can't take this pressure any more, expressions like these are used and understood by all of us. However, we also make up a lot of metaphors and these, I think, are more interesting because they tell us a lot about how we see the world.

Host   That's interesting, tell us some more about that …

Jane Davis   Well, let me give you an example. The other day I asked some students to use metaphors to say how they'd feel if they were on holiday in a foreign country where they spoke very little of the language. The images they came up with told me a lot about them. For example, one student said that he would feel like a fireman confronted by a huge forest fire. He said that it would be an exciting but frightening experience and one that he would have to learn how to control soon if he was going to survive.

Host   Very dramatic.

Jane Davis   And another student said she would feel like a rat floating on a piece of wood in the middle of a huge ocean.

Host   Wow, she must have been really scared by the idea.

Jane Davis   Exactly. So as you can see, the metaphors that the students chose helped us deal with their feelings more carefully. So like I said earlier, we can use metaphors to understand ourselves and other people better.

Answers
a He's got the world on his shoulders – He is under a lot of pressure
b He's got butterflies in his stomach – He is very nervous
c She could eat a horse – She is very hungry
d He's over the moon – He is very happy

c 🔊 Read through the questions with students and check understanding. Play the recording again while students circle the correct answer. You may like to ask stronger students to answer the questions from memory first, then play the recording again for them to check their answers.

Answers
1 a   2 c   3 b   4 b   5 a

4 Vocabulary
Metaphors to describe emotions
Warm up

Books closed. Ask students to think of as many adjectives to describe emotions as they can. This can be done as a competition with students working in

pairs to create as long a list as possible in a two-minute period. Listen to some of the longest lists in open class as feedback. Alternatively, ask students to work in pairs to think of an adjective for each letter of the alphabet, then, as feedback, build up a central list on the board.

a Open books. Pre-teach *banging* and *down in the dumps*. Students complete sentences using the words in the box. Remind them that the expressions in italics are metaphors and should be learnt as individual items of vocabulary. In most cases, they cannot be directly translated to other languages without a change in meaning. Allow students to use dictionaries and to compare their answers with a partner before feedback.

Answers
1 frustrated   2 nervous   3 happy   4 depressed
5 angry   6 mad   7 embarrassed   8 shocked
9 disappointed   10 calm

b Students complete the sentences using expressions from Exercise 4a. Remind students that they should write answers in the correct tense and using the correct pronouns where necessary. Students compare answers with a partner before feedback.

Answers
2 butterflies in my stomach
3 know where to put myself
4 really cut up
5 a bit down in the dumps
6 makes my blood boil
7 I'm banging my head against a brick wall
8 Keep your hair on

c Read through the questions with students and check understanding. In pairs, students make up a story using the questions as prompts. Circulate and help with vocabulary as required. Students tell their stories to another pair. Ensure that they are using some of the metaphors from Exercise 4a to describe emotions in their stories. Listen to some examples in open class and have a vote on which is the most imaginative story.

Vocabulary notebook
Encourage students to start a new section *Metaphors to describe emotion* in their notebook and add these words. They may find it useful to note down translations of the words too.

5 Grammar
Modal passives (present and past)
Students covered modal verbs in SB4, Unit 7.

a **Weaker classes:** To remind students of the use of modal verbs in the past and present, write the following mixed-up sentence on the board.

Where's John? He be garden the in or gone shops might the have he might to.
(He might be in the garden or he might have gone to the shops.)

Elicit the correct sentence from students and ask which verbs refer to the present (*might be*) and which refers to the past (*might have gone*).

Point to an object in the class, perhaps a piece of clothing or furniture, and ask students what it is made of. Elicit the sentence *It might be made of ...* Ask students where they think it was made. Elicit the sentence *It might have been made in ...* Write example sentences on the board and draw attention to the passive forms of modal verbs in the past and present. Continue with the procedure for stronger classes.

Stronger classes: Read through the sentences from the text with the class. Ask students to complete the sentences with the words in the box, then look back at the text to check answers.

Answers
1 accused of   2 used   3 scared   4 made

(b) Students decide which sentence in Exercise 5a refers to a past situation.

Answer
Sentence 3

(c) Students look at the sentences in Exercise 5a and complete the rule.

Rule
be; have been

> **Language note**
> Apart from *can*, all modal verbs can be used to express the past. They do not change form (*might be* becomes *might have been* etc.). *Can* cannot be used in the past: **It can have been ...*

(d) Look at the example sentence with students. Point out that *someone* or *people* is not usually necessary when we use the passive. In pairs, students write sentences using the passive and compare answers with a partner before feedback.

Answers
2 Applications can be sent by email.
3 The prize must be won.
4 His name will not be forgotten.
5 These things should be put back.
6 Your purse might have been stolen.
7 This door must have been opened.
8 She should have been invited to the party.

(e) Students look at the words in the box and fill in the gaps in the text.

Answers
1 have   2 be   3 can't   4 will   5 been   6 would
7 passed

> **Language note**
> Students may think *be* and *have* and *do* are modal verbs. They are auxiliary verbs and are used to form tenses. Modal auxiliary verbs like *can, may, should* etc. indicate the speaker's attitude to the verb. They have no infinitive, no continuous form, no passive form, no third person singular. Questions are formed by inverting the modal and the subject (*Must I, Can we* etc.).

⌐ OPTIONAL ACTIVITY
A fun activity to practise the use of modal passives is to bring a variety of objects into the classroom, e.g. a spoon, a piece of string, a box, anything really! Divide the class into small groups and give each group an object. They have two minutes to think of as many uses for the object as they can. During feedback, groups have one minute to talk about their ideas. Each use must be explained using a modal passive, e.g. *It could be used as a hat.* Give points for correct sentences.

To practise modal passives in the past, give students an object and tell them to imagine they are objects which were used 20,000 years ago that have recently been discovered. Students make sentences using modal passives in the past, e.g. *It could have been used for...*

Grammar notebook
Remind students to note down the rules for modal passives (past and present) and to write a few examples of their own.

6 Listen and speak

Tell students they are going to listen to the second part of the interview with an expert in linguistics from Exercise 3. Students listen and make a note of the metaphors used by the radio presenter. Let students compare answers with a partner before feedback. Divide the class into pairs and give each student a letter, A or B. Read through the instructions with students. Students draw the metaphors. Tell students they should not worry about artistic ability! In open class, discuss how Jane Davis invites the host to think differently.

TAPESCRIPT
Host   ... Fascinating! Now, you said we use our metaphors to learn how to change the way we think. Can you tell our listeners how?

Jane Davis   Well, there are a number of ways but let me take you through one exercise that I always find particularly effective. For this, you'll need a piece of paper and a pen.

Host   OK.

Jane Davis   Now, I want you to think of a situation when you get nervous and you don't think you act as well as you could.

Host   OK. I've got one.

Jane Davis   Can you tell us about it?

Host Sure. It's a bit embarrassing though. I hate flying. I get really, really nervous just before the flight.

Jane Davis There's nothing embarrassing about that at all. It's a common fear. You're certainly not alone. Now what I want you to do is draw a metaphor for how you feel during those few minutes before you get on the plane.

Host OK.

Jane Davis Now the reason I'm asking you to draw all this is because visualising the metaphor literally helps us get a clearer picture of your perceptions of the difficult situation and hopefully a better understanding of your exact problem.

Host OK, I've finished.

Jane Davis Right, now I'd like you to take us through your picture.

Host OK, now this is me and as you can see, I'm all alone. There are lots of other people around but they don't see me. It's like I'm invisible. All alone in the departure lounge. And I sit there – and I can't move really.

Jane Davis Excellent. And this time I'd like you to draw a picture which is a metaphor of how you would like to feel in this situation.

Host OK.

Jane Davis The key thing is that you use your imagination but don't think too much.

Host OK, I think this will do. Let me explain. This is a big white horse parading around on the runway where all the planes are ...

Jane Davis Wow. That's quite a difference. Now the next stage, and this is something we'll do together, is to think how you can bring qualities from your second picture into your first one. I know this gets kind of crazy, but working with metaphors can be quite like dreams at times. So see it as fun, really.

Host OK, so I want the horse in the departure lounge. That would be much better than the invisible me who can't move. Wow! You know what?

Jane Davis What's that?

Host This is really fascinating. The feeling I get is that I should try walking around the departure lounge rather than sitting down feeling I can't move. When I ride a horse, you know, I feel so in control. And this is the feeling I'd like to get before I fly – that I'm in control.

Jane Davis Uh-huh.

Host And I think I can get a little more of that feeling of being in control by standing up and walking around the departure lounge. By making myself visible ... how crazy this is! But what you are saying makes sense somehow.

Jane Davis Well, it all came from you, really. By thinking in metaphors and drawing them, you've gained more insights into your own thoughts and feelings than if I had just asked you why you're scared of flying.

Host Well, one thing's for sure – the next time I fly, I'll walk around the lounge – like a horse, really.

Answer

Jane Davis invites the host to bring the qualities from the second picture into the first.

Students think of a situation that is difficult for them and follow the instructions. Students discuss point 3 with a partner. Circulate and help with vocabulary as necessary. Listen to some of their ideas in open class and invite comments from other students.

Culture in mind

7 Read

(a) Look at the pictures of buildings on page 50 of the Student's Book. Students decide on the purpose of each building. Listen to students' ideas and ask students if they know anything else about any of the buildings.

Answers
1 b   2 c   3 a

(b) Students read the texts quickly to check their answers. Set a time limit to encourage students to read quickly.

(c) Pre-teach *helipad* and *atrium lobby*. Read through the questions with students and deal with any difficulties. Encourage students to answer the questions from memory before reading again to check. Students compare answers with a partner before feedback. Ask students to give reasons for their answers.

Answers
1a Casa Batlló (it resembles a dragon)
1b The Burj al-Arab hotel (it resembles a dhow)
1c The City Hall (it resembles a motorcycle helmet)
2a The City Hall (it opened in July 2002)
2b The Burj al-Arab (it has the tallest atrium lobby in the world)
2c Casa Batlló (casa dels ossos)

(d) Students think of other interesting buildings and tell the class about them. Give students some planning time and encourage them to look back at the descriptions in Exercise 7a for inspiration. You may like to give students some buildings to choose from and give an example of your own to get them started. In small groups, students listen to each other's descriptions.

Students work in pairs to discuss ways of making their school building more creative and inventive. Encourage students to think about interiors and facilities as well as external factors. You may like to give them an imaginary amount of money to work with. Listen to some of their ideas in open class. This can lead to some interesting discussion about the positive and negative aspects of the school and the activity can be extended to produce a report to be presented to the director or headteacher of the school, who can be invited to the class to hear their ideas.

If you would like your students to do some further work on the vocabulary in the text, you can use the following exercise. Write the following definitions on the board and ask students to find words and expressions with the same meaning in the text. The words are in the order of the text. To make the exercise more challenging, you could write them on the board in a different order.

1 *wealthy* 2 *curving* 3 *imagery* 4 *repeated, frequent* 5 *look like* 6 *false* 7 *globular* 8 *distorted* 9 *customised*

Answers

1 prosperous 2 flowing 3 symbolism 4 recurring 5 resemble 6 artificial 7 bulbous 8 misshapen 9 modified

8 Write

Warm up

To introduce the topic of learning, write the question *How do we learn?* on the board. Ask students to discuss in pairs, then listen to some of their ideas in open class. Ask them to think about which things are easiest to learn and which are the most difficult. Do they find English easy to learn? Do they approach learning English differently from how they would learn to repair a car, for example? Why? Encourage open class discussion.

a Tell students they are going to read an extract from a book on learning. Students read the text quickly to find metaphors. Tell students not to worry about the meaning of every word, but to concentrate on the task. Check answers and ask students if they think the act of juggling is similar to the learning process.

Answers

Juggling is used as a metaphor for learning (*keeping a number of things up in the air*) and for gracefully coping with mistakes (*dropping the balls*).

b Explain to students the difference between similes and metaphors. A *simile* is a figure of speech in which the subject is compared to another subject. Tell students that many similes are formed with *like*, e.g. *Juggling is like learning*. Another common type of simile uses *as*, e.g. *As white as a sheet, As old as the hills*. Metaphors are different from similes as they do not compare two things, they say two things are the same, e.g. *All the world is a stage, Love is a bed of roses*.

Read through the sentence openings with students to check understanding. In pairs, students create similes or metaphors using the prompts. Encourage them to be as imaginative as possible.

Answers
Students' own answers

c Students work in small groups to produce a list of words to be used for creating similes or metaphors. Use the list in the book as a starting-point, and after a few minutes, listen to some further examples and draw up a class list on the board.

d Choose a word or phrase from the list created in Exercise 8c. Individually or in pairs, students create as many metaphors or similes as possible, writing each one on a separate piece of paper. These can be read out as feedback or alternatively, stuck around the room for students to read.

e Students discuss which they think are the strongest metaphors or similes. Ask them to write a poem using the metaphors and similes. The planning for this exercise can be done in class and the writing can be set as homework, or students can write the poems in class.

A good vocabulary expansion activity related to learning. Ask students to think of an activity they know a lot about, e.g. horse-riding, skate-boarding etc. Students write ten words connected to that activity on a piece of paper. Ask students to circulate holding the piece of paper in front of them so that the ten words are visible to the rest of the class. Students read each other's words and guess the activity they describe, then ask for explanations of the words they do not know. Students make a note of any interesting new words in their vocabulary notebook. If students enjoy talking about their hobbies, you may like to encourage them to give a presentation to the rest of the class.

8 Virtual worlds

Unit overview

TOPIC: Virtual worlds and virtual holidays
on computers

TEXTS
Reading and listening: an article about the Entropia
Universe – a virtual world
Listening: a radio programme about virtual holidays
Listening: song: *Virtual World*
Writing: a letter politely refusing an invitation

SPEAKING AND FUNCTIONS
Discussing the advantages and disadvantages of
virtual holidays

LANGUAGE
Grammar: cleft sentences with *what* and *it* (review)
Vocabulary: money and word building

1 Read and listen

If you set the background information as a homework
research task, ask the students to tell the class what
they found out.

BACKGROUND INFORMATION

Entropia Universe: is an online virtual universe
designed by Swedish software company MindArk.
Entropia Universe has its own currency (PED –
Project Entropia Dollars) and virtual items
acquired inside Entropia Universe have a real
cash value. A participant may, at any time,
withdraw their accumulated PEDs back into real
world currencies according to the fixed exchange
rate. The Entropia online community claims to
have over 600,000 registered participants from
over 220 countries, with the average number of
players online at any one time said to be around
600. The community has produced several real-
world marriages as well as creating a multitude
of cross-border friendships. The Entropia
Universe claims to have entered the Guinness
World Book of Records in 2004 for the most
expensive virtual item ever sold.

Warm up

Books closed. Write the following words and phrases
on the board:

*downloading chatrooms email doing homework
shopping finding specific information*

In pairs, students discuss which of the activities they
use the Internet for and how much they do of each
thing. Ask them to add any other activities which
are not on the list. Listen to their ideas in open
class and create a list on the board of the most
popular activities.

(a) Open books. Ask students what they know about
virtual worlds and discuss in open class.

(b) In pairs, students make a list of things they would
expect to find in a virtual world. Listen to some of
their ideas in open class.

(c) Ask students if they think people would pay to enter
a virtual world. Ask students how much they would
pay and whether they think people would pay for
things when they were in the virtual world. Students
read the text quickly to check their answers.

(d) Read through the questions with the class. Ask
students to read the text and write the numbers of
the questions in the correct place. Allow students
to compare answers with a partner before checking
answers in open class.

Answers
in this order 8 4 1 10 5 6 2 7 9

(e) 🔊 Read through the sentences with the students
and help with any difficulties. Play the recording
while students read and listen to answer the
questions. After the first listening, let students
compare their answers with a partner. Check answers.
If necessary, play the recording again, pausing to
clarify any problems.

TAPESCRIPT
See the reading text on page 52 of the Student's Book.

Answers
1 F They are not rich   2 N   3 T   4 T
5 F They say it is a good way to make money

─── **OPTIONAL ACTIVITY** ───────────
Ask students to imagine that they have an unlimited
budget to create a virtual world of their own. What
would they call their world and what would they
include in it? Elicit a few ideas in open class and write
some ideas on the board. In pairs, students decide
what to put in their world. Circulate and help with
vocabulary as necessary. Students describe their
worlds to another pair before listening to some of
the best ideas in open class.

2 Vocabulary

Money

Warm up

Books closed. Write the word *Money* on the board and elicit as many words as possible connected to money. Write a list of interesting words on the board and, where possible, use these to elicit some of the words used in the exercise.

(a) Books open. Students match the words and phrases 1–10 to the definitions a–j. Do not answer any questions about vocabulary at this stage and ask students to guess the answer if they are unsure. Check answers, paying particular attention to pronunciation.

Answers
2 d 3 f 4 a 5 i 6 b 7 c 8 e 9 g
10 h

(b) Read through the questions with students to check understanding. Students complete the sentences using a word from Exercise 2a. Ask them to compare answers with a partner before feedback.

Answers
2 purchase 3 economical 4 take out a loan
5 interest rate 6 economy

Discussion box
Weaker classes: Students can choose one question to discuss.

Stronger classes: In pairs or small groups, students go through the questions in the box and discuss them.

Monitor and help as necessary, encouraging students to express themselves in English and to use any vocabulary they have learned from the text. Ask pairs or groups to feedback to the class and discuss any interesting points further.

Vocabulary notebook
Encourage students to start a new section *Money* in their notebook and add these words. They may find it useful to note down translations of the words too.

3 Grammar

Cleft sentences with *what* and *it* (review)

Students covered *what* clauses in SB4, Unit 5 and dummy *it* in SB4, Unit 7.

(a) Look at the sentences and ask students to rewrite them without the *what* construction. Write the correct answers on the board.

Answers
The thing that is so impressive about the Entropia Universe is the number of participants.
The thing most inhabitants do first is find themselves a profession.

(b) As a whole class exercise, ask students to underline the main focus of each of the sentences. If students find this difficult, look at some easier examples, e.g. *What I like is* strawberry ice cream. *What I want is* a cup of tea. Point out the main focus of these sentences and its position in the sentence.

Answers
the number of participants
find themselves a profession

(c) Students complete the rule. Use the sentences in Exercise 3a to clarify the rule.

Rule
end

(d) Look at the example with the class and draw attention to the main focus of the sentence (*spend real money on purchasing virtual property*). Students rewrite the sentences as cleft sentences with *what*. With weaker classes, you might like to go through the sentences and point out the main focus of each before asking students to write their sentences. Let students compare their answers with a partner before open class feedback.

Answers
2 What I would never do is transfer money into a virtual account.
3 What some players don't care about is how much money they spend on virtual reality games.
4 What's good is that some new cars are very economical.
5 What I don't understand is why people spend money on these games.
6 What I don't want to do is make things difficult.

Language note
This pattern is only usually used with *what* clauses. Rather than place clauses with *how, when, where, who, why* at the beginning of the sentence, we tend to use a noun before the clause:

The reason why/that I am late is that my alarm clock is broken. (not *Why I am late is …*)
The place where/that they met was near London. (not *Where they met was …*)
A person who/that I admire is Nelson Mandela. (not *Who I admire is …*)

(e) Look at the sentences with the class. Students say the sentences without the *it* construction. Write the correct answers on the board.

Answers
Jacobs made the headlines in October 2005.
You really expand your options by spending cash.

(f) In open class, ask students which words should be underlined as the main focus of each of the sentences.

Answers
Jacobs
spending cash

(g) Students complete the rule. Use the sentences in Exercise 3f to clarify the rule.

Rule

beginning

Read the *Look* box with students. Draw attention to the use of *it* as subject in the sentences in Exercise 3e.

(h) Read through the sentences with students. Point out the use of the *it* cleft in the example. Students write sentences with an *it* cleft and the information in brackets. Compare answers with a partner before feedback in open class. During feedback, point out that the correct information is heavily stressed when saying these sentences. Say the sentences for students to repeat.

Answers

2 No, it was Swedish scientists that invented Entropia.

3 No, it is new players that have to wear an orange jumpsuit.

4 No, it was Yuri Gagarin that was the first man in space.

5 No, it was Santos Dumont that was the first person to fly.

6 No, it's the Hulk that turns green when he's angry.

Language note

In cleft sentences, the clause after the *it* clause is usually a *that* clause. However, we sometimes use *which*, *who*, *when* or *where* instead of *that*:

It was in London where they met.
It was Yuri Gagarin who was the first man in space.

Note that *how* and *why* can't replace *that*:

It was by studying that he managed to pass his exams (not ...**how he managed to pass his exams*)

It was because of the weather that he stayed at home (not ...**why he stayed at home*)

Grammar notebook

Remind students to note down the rules for cleft sentences and to write a few examples of their own.

4 Listen

Warm up

Books closed. To introduce the topic of holidays, ask students where they have been on holiday recently and which are the most popular types of holiday in their country. In small groups, students describe different types of holiday. Listen to some of their ideas in open class.

(a) Open books. Individually, students remember their best holidays. Ask them to write down an example of an image, smell and sound they can remember. Give an example of your own to get them started if necessary.

(b) In small groups, students discuss their holidays, concentrating on the images, smells and sounds. Encourage them to go into detail in their answers and to describe their feelings as clearly as possible. As feedback, have an open discussion about which of the three things students find easiest to recall.

(c) Tell students they are going to listen to a radio programme about virtual holidays. Allow them to read through the questions and ask for clarification if they don't understand. Play the recording while students listen for the answers to questions 1–5. Let students compare answers with a partner before playing the recording again, pausing if necessary. Check answers.

TAPESCRIPT

Presenter And now with the latest science news here's Heather Difford.

Reporter Thanks Jill. And I've got some good news for those of you who dream of seeing the world but don't have the time or money to do so. A company called Remote Media have developed a multi-sensory holiday simulator which allows people to savour the sights and smells of exotic locations without leaving the comfort of their nearest travel agent. The system, which was developed for the travel company Thomson, combines three-dimensional imagery with aroma technology to create an experience that's second only to actually being there.

So far the only country that's been given the virtual makeover is Egypt. Visitors to Thomson travel agents can put on specially constructed headsets and lose themselves for three and a half minutes in some of the country's most famous sights such as the Temples of Karnak, the Valley of the Kings and deep sea diving in the Red Sea.

A special camera was used to film the different locations and it allows viewers a totally three-dimensional experience. Furthermore viewers are offered a 180° field of vision which basically means you're surrounded by Egypt wherever you look. The aroma system, which accompanies the visual one, has been developed by a separate company, Dale Air, who were previously famous for supplying the smell of Kylie Minogue's breath for her statue at Madame Tussaud's, among others. The aromas offered on this Egyptian adventure include the damp smells inside the pharaoh's tomb, the spices and herbs from Cairo's famous markets, cool sea breezes and coconut suntan lotions.

The new technology has already been introduced in Thomson's Leeds branch where it's met with considerable approval. The company plans to have the system in most other branches by January in time for the busiest time for holiday bookings.

Now all this doesn't mean that you'll be replacing your yearly fortnight in Portugal for three and a half minutes in your local travel agents – well, not for now, anyway. The use of the system is purely promotional and will be used to market and sell real holidays around the world – a 'try before you buy' scheme was how it was labelled by a Thomson sales director. The company also have plans to work with a number of different tourist boards so that they can create and promote a growing number of other locations over the coming years. Jill, back to you.

Presenter   So we're not talking Arnold Schwarzenegger in *Total Recall* quite yet?

Reporter   No, not quite. I think the idea that we will be able to have virtual holidays implanted into our memories is still a few years off yet. For now we'll have to content ourselves with this.

Answers

1 b   2 b   3 b   4 c   5 c

(d) 🔊 Read through the sentences with students and check any difficult vocabulary: *stressed, full surround, promote, headset*. Play the recording and ask students to choose the correct answers. Let students compare their answers before checking in open class. If necessary, play the recording again with pauses during feedback.

Answers

1 d   2 f   3 c   4 a   5 b   6 e

5 Speak

(a) Students work together to discuss the questions. Circulate and help with vocabulary as necessary. In open class, ask some pairs for their ideas and write them on the board. Try to create a list of the places, smells and sounds to include which the whole class agrees upon.

(b) Students discuss the questions in pairs or small groups. If this issue is of particular interest to students, you might like to arrange a debate. Divide the class into two halves (one half saying virtual holidays are a good thing and the other half saying they are not). You might also ask one student to be neutral and leader of the debate. Students present their arguments. At the end, you can make a decision about which side won the debate and give reasons.

6 Vocabulary
Word building

(a) Students choose the best word to complete each sentence. Encourage students to work without your help at this stage, but allow them to use a dictionary. Let students compare answers with a partner before feedback.

Answers

2 dimensional; technology   3 special   4 breath
5 considerable   6 create; promote   7 memories

(b) Students work together to decide which part of speech each word is. You may like to ask stronger students to think of sample sentences to show the meaning and use of each word.

Answers

1 adjective; noun; adjective   2 noun; noun; adjective / noun; adjective   3 adjective; adverb; noun   4 noun; verb; verb   5 verb; adjective; verb   6 verb; adjective; noun / verb; noun; adjective   7 noun; noun; noun

Vocabulary notebook

Encourage students to start a new section *Word building* in their notebook and add these words. They may find it useful to note down translations of the words too.

(c) Students read the text and use the correct form of the words in the box to complete the sentences. They compare answers with a partner before feedback in open class.

Answers

2 reality   3 construction   4 imaginary
5 horribly   6 dead   7 recording   8 flight
9 freedom   10 constantly

7 Listen

If you set the background information as a homework research task, ask the students to tell the class what they found out.

BACKGROUND INFORMATION

Andru Donalds: is probably better known in recent years as one of the lead vocalists of the group Enigma. He was born in Jamaica and later spent some time in England, Holland and France trying to make it as a musician. The result was his very successful debut album *Andru Donalds,* released in 1995. The single *Mishale* reached number four in the US charts and as a solo artist, he has released five albums, the latest being *Andru Donalds V* in 2006.

Virtual World: is a song by Andru Donalds and comes from his fourth solo album *Let's Talk About It* (2001).

(a) 🔊 Ask students to look at the picture and the title of the song. In pairs, students discuss what they think the singer feels about virtual worlds. Listen to any interesting ideas in open class. Play the song while students check answers. Tell students not to worry if they don't understand every word, but just to focus on the task.

Answer

The singer has a negative view of virtual worlds

b 🔊 Ask students to quickly read through the lyrics of the song. Play the recording again while students listen to find six words which are different to those in the book. Allow students to compare answers with a partner before feedback.

TAPESCRIPT / ANSWERS
(Words different from text in book are shown in bold)

Nowadays so many things have changed
I can feel the cold
Don't be blind and **start** to realise
You're just a morphing soul
In a virtual world (homeless heart, left alone,
    looking for a home)
Children hypnotised in front of a TV
Playing lonely, just with best friend TFT
People **surfing**, chatting all around the world
Ignoring time and the ones they will need
When they sit in the cold
Think about if that's the way life should be
    (you need a touch)
You'll never get that thrill from talking to a **screen**
    (it means so much)
I just doubt, that is the way you want to get old
Without the feeling of love, you'll be lost
In a virtual world (homeless heart, left alone,
    looking for a hold)
But from the very start, it was a world **apart**
Looking for the digital horizons
I can trust in love and my soul
Instead of a virtual world
Night and day, I see these people on the streets
    (they need a touch)
Cyber junkies, losing sense of **reality** (it means
    so much)
Surrounded by **machines** without a bit of soul
Ignoring time and the ones who will help
When they sit in the cold
Think about if that's the way life should be
    (you need a touch)
You'll never get that thrill from talking to a **screen**
    (it means so much)
I just doubt, that is the way you want to get old
Without the feeling of love, you'll be lost
In a virtual world

c Ask students to read through the lyrics and answer the questions. Check answers.

Answers
1 verse 2   2 chorus   3 verse 1   4 chorus

Did you know ...?

Read through the information and invite students to say anything else they know about Andru Donalds. Ask students to discuss whether they would choose an academic career or a career in music and why. Listen to some of their ideas in open class and invite comments.

8 Write

The planning for this exercise can be done in class and the letter set as homework.

a Tell the students they are going to read an informal letter. Students read the letter quickly and answer the questions before feedback. Encourage students not to look up every new word but just to concentrate on the answers. You may like to set a time limit of two minutes for this exercise.

Answers
The purpose of the letter is to say thank you for a birthday present. The writer is the sister of the addressee.

b Ask students to read the text again to find informal and colloquial expressions that have the same meaning as 1–6. Allow students to compare answers with a partner before feedback.

Answers
2 kids   3 place   4 piece of cake   5 grab a bite
6 dash off   7 guess   8 funny   9 check me out

c Read through the questions with students to check understanding. Students work together to answer the questions. Encourage students to keep a record of letter beginnings and endings and informal expressions in their notebooks.

Answers
1 She doesn't refer to the actual date or write her actual address.
2 Students' own answers (example beginnings: *Hello Chris, All right Chris, Hey!, Yo!* etc. Possible endings: *see you later, yours, all the best*).
3 The letter has a conversational style and uses exclamation marks and brackets. Starting sentences with *Well, Anyway, Seriously, So.* Leaving out subjects and articles, e.g. *kidding, won't tell you, piece of cake*. Other phrases, e.g. *quite some time, I guess, a bit funny, very, very much, great fun, watch out for, must go now, P.P.S.*
4 The writer uses contracted forms.
5 The writer uses brackets to speak directly to the addressee.

d Read through the information with students. Ask them to write a reply to the invitation. After planning, they could complete the writing at home. In a subsequent lesson, encourage students to read each other's letters.

Module 2 Check your progress

1 Grammar

(a)
2 to stealing
3 getting
4 to know
5 to go
6 to pay
7 cheating
8 to trying

(b)
2 must have lost
3 can't have studied
4 must know
5 can't help
6 can't have
7 might have missed
8 I'll have left

(c)
2 My father is having his car repaired at the garage.
3 I have had these invitations designed for me.
4 She had her appendix taken out.
5 They are going to have their living room decorated.
6 He had his photograph taken.

(d)
2 be built
3 be sent
4 have been broken
5 have been told
6 be fixed
7 have been written

(e)
2 What I don't understand is why people want to play computer games.
3 It's people wasting their time and money that makes me really angry.
4 What's important is being careful with your money.
5 It was the end of the film that was the really interesting bit.
6 It's sitting in front of a computer for a long time that I don't like.
7 What was difficult for me was trying to understand the rules of the game.
8 What will be more and more common in the future are virtual worlds.

2 Vocabulary

(a)
1 invaded
2 treaty
3 recruited
4 casualties
5 battle
6 surrendered
7 negotiations
8 declare

(b)
2 sob
3 likely
4 cut
5 side
6 making
7 End
8 same

(c)
2 butterflies
3 boil
4 loose
5 hair
6 of the world
7 where to put
8 a brick wall

(d)
2 creativity
3 speciality
4 argumentative
5 considerable
6 memorable
7 systematically

How did you do?
Students work out their scores. Check how they have done and follow up any problem areas with revision work for students.

Module 3
Alone and together

YOU WILL LEARN ABOUT ...

Ask students to look at the pictures on the page. Ask them to read through the topics in the box and check that they understand each item. You can ask them the following questions, in L1 if appropriate:

1 What are the two girls doing?
2 Where do you think this famous landmark is?
3 What is the man in the picture famous for?
4 What is the girl doing?
5 How do you think the man feels?
6 Why do you think the woman is lying down in the boat?

In pairs or small groups, students discuss which topic area they think each picture matches. Check the answers.

Answers
1 Why we copy behaviour
2 Landmarks in Brasília
3 World-famous superheroes
4 Habits and gestures
5 What it's like to live alone in the wild
6 Winning and losing in sport

YOU WILL LEARN HOW TO ...

Use grammar

Students read through the grammar points and the examples. Go through the first item with students as an example. In pairs, students now match the grammar items in their book. Check answers.

Answers
Hedging: This seems to be an area that is worth investigating.
Boosting: This discovery has unquestionably been one of the most important steps forward in recent neuroscience.
could, be able to, manage to: He was hurt but he was able to play on.
Negative inversion: Under no circumstances can I recommend this film.
Mixed conditionals: If I had never come here, I wouldn't know how valuable solitude is.
Alternatives to *if*: I'd just have to phone someone, otherwise I'd go crazy!

Use vocabulary

Write the headings on the board. Go through the items in the Student's Book and check understanding. Now ask students if they can think of two more items for the *Habits and gestures* heading. Elicit some responses and add them to the list on the board. Students now do the same for the other headings. Some possibilities are:

Habits and gestures: *fiddle with your hair, bite your nails*

Success and failure: *overcome, blow it*

Physical abilities: *squint, X-ray vision*

Expressions with time: *kill time, have time on your hands*

9 Understanding others

TAPESCRIPT
See the reading text on pages 62 and 63 of the
Student's Book.

Unit overview

TOPIC: How humans communicate and understand
each other

TEXTS
Reading and listening: an article about mirror neurons
Listening: an expert talking about human
communication skills
Reading: an extract from *The Life of Pi* by Yann Martel
Writing: a discursive composition

SPEAKING AND FUNCTIONS
A discussion about mirror neurons and imitation
Talking about things that interest you
Talking about headlines using hedging and boosting
phrases

LANGUAGE
Grammar: hedging and boosting
Vocabulary: habits and gestures

1 Read and listen

Warm up

To introduce the topic of imitating actions, write the
following words and phrases on the board: *walk, talk,
smile, eat, write, read*. In pairs, students discuss the
order in which babies learn to do the things. Listen to
some of their ideas as feedback. Ask students to discuss
how babies learn each of the things – are they natural
or do they have to be taught? Discuss in open class.

a) Ask students to look at the photo and the title and
discuss what they think the article is about. Don't
comment on their ideas at this stage.

b) Students read the text quickly to check their answers.
With weaker classes, you may like to pre-teach *yawn,
electrode, raisin*. Tell students it is not important to
understand every word at this stage. Let students
compare answers with a partner before feedback.

Answer
The text explains how mirror neurons work and affect
our behaviour, causing us to understand people.

c) 🔊 Check that students understand the statements.
Pre-teach *empathy*. Play the recording while students
read. You could pause as necessary to check
understanding and clarify any difficulties. Students
match the statements with the paragraphs and
compare answers with a partner before feedback. If
students find this exercise difficult, you may like to do
this activity in open class and point students towards
important parts of the text.

TAPESCRIPT
See the reading text on pages 62 and 63 of the
Student's Book.

Answers

1 B   2 D   3 A   4 C   5 A   6 E

d) 🔊 Check students understand the questions. Ask
them to read the text as they listen to the recording
and answer the questions. Students compare answers
with a partner before feedback in open class. If
necessary, play the recording again, pausing to clarify
vocabulary and help with comprehension.

Answers

1 They found that when one of the monkeys
  observed a scientist picking up and eating a raisin,
  the neurons in the monkey's brain fired in the
  same way as when the monkey ate a raisin itself.
2 They have found that every time we see someone
  else do something, our brains imitate it.
3 We use them to understand other people and
  have empathy with them, or not.
4 If scientists gave subjects sentences to listen to,
  the same mirror neurons were triggered as when
  the action was actually performed.

e) Check students understand the definitions. Ask them
to find phrases or expressions in the text which have
the same meaning. Let them compare answers with a
partner before feedback in open class.

Answers

1 neurons
2 replicate
3 neuroscience
4 empathise
5 subtle
6 social disorders
7 to incorporate
8 a driving force

OPTIONAL ACTIVITY

Separate the class into groups of six for this memory
activity. Write the following words on separate cards:
stretch, yawn, laugh, blink, wink, cough. In groups,
students take one card each and decide on a sequence
of actions. They carry out the sequence without saying
the words. When they finish, the rest of the group
must remember the sequence of actions and say the
words in the same order. Continue around the group
and see who can remember the longest sequence!

Discussion box
Weaker classes: Students can choose one question
to discuss.

Stronger classes: In pairs or small groups, students go
through the questions in the box and discuss them.

Monitor and help as necessary, encouraging students to express themselves in English and to use any vocabulary they have learned from the text. Ask pairs or groups to feedback to the class and discuss any interesting points further.

2 Listen

As an introduction to the listening, ask students how they establish rapport with other people. Does it depend on the things you say, or the way you act? Students discuss in pairs before discussion in open class. Tell students they are going to listen to an expert talking about human communication skills. Read through the sentences with students to check they understand. Pre-teach *rapport* and *misuse*. Play the recording. Students listen and complete the sentences. Ask them to compare answers with a partner before listening again, pausing the recording if necessary. Check answers in open class.

Weaker classes: If students find listening exercises difficult, write the answers on the board in the wrong order and ask students to fill the gaps.

TAPESCRIPT

Presenter   Thanks very much Mark, for those insights. Now let's move on to our next item, which is about mirroring. Joan Myers is here to tell us all about it. Joan.

Speaker   One of the things that perhaps we all want to improve is our ability to establish rapport with other people. Rapport: you know, that feeling that you and another person understand each other, you're on the same wavelength, you can communicate to each other with little or no problem. But rapport is sometimes a little bit elusive, hard to achieve – just how do we get other people to like us and be on our wavelength?

Well, there are a number of things that we can do, things that are used by effective communicators and by people like therapists – and salespeople! Perhaps one of the best known is an approach called 'mirroring'. As the name suggests, mirroring is a technique in which you try to mirror, or reflect, the behaviour of the people you're with. To be more precise: you mirror micro-behaviour, the little things that people do. Some examples are: body posture, gestures – the things people do with their hands, the angle they hold their head at, how frequently they blink, the expression on their face – and so on and so on.

So what does mirroring involve? Roughly the following. You note something in the behaviour of the person that you're going to mirror, and then you do the same thing in a similar way. Let's take an example: if the other person moves their head slightly to one side, then you wait a few seconds and do more or less the same thing, moving your head to the same angle, not in exactly the same way as the other person, but approximately. If you can do this kind of thing smoothly and elegantly, the other person won't even notice. And this is a key point. You need to not just mimic the other person, but give the person a feeling that you're on the same wavelength as them, and somehow create that same feeling in yourself, too. It's something we do naturally anyway. Let me give you an example: when two people who have a good rapport are sitting opposite each other and they're having a conversation, and one of them leans forward, the chances are that the other person will soon lean forward too. When this happens, mirroring the other person's behaviour comes really naturally, almost as if you couldn't <u>not</u> do it, you know.

Presenter   OK, fine. But let me ask you a question here. Imagine I'm talking to somebody, and I want to try this technique of mirroring. Isn't it a strange feeling for the other person if whatever they do, I do too? Wouldn't they feel that I'm trying to take the mickey out of them?

Speaker   Well, that's a good question. Yes, they might feel you want to make fun of them, especially if you exaggerate this mirroring, you know, if you immediately start imitating exactly everything they do and doing it like you were some kind of robot or something. So here's the key point: do it gently and respectfully – and see it as a way that helps you to understand the other person better. And there're a couple of other things to remember, too. First of all, going back to the example I gave a little earlier: if the person tilts their head to the left, you should tilt yours to the right – so that for the other person it's a bit like looking in a mirror – hence the name. But don't over-do it, or you will look and feel silly! Secondly, don't forget that with mirroring, you can build up a strong sense of trust in the other person very quickly – so it's your responsibility not to misuse that trust. And thirdly – if you want to practise mirroring, a good way to start is by trying to mirror people you're watching on television, in things like interviews – that way, you won't upset anyone!

Presenter   Fine. Got that – that's a good idea.

Speaker   Right! OK, let's move on a bit. Now, the mirroring we've talked about so far is physical, but of course we can mirror verbally, too – mirroring the way that people speak and the words that they use. Let's look at an example – the way doctors talk when they're interviewing patients. So, what I'm going to do now is play a recording I made of a doctor talking to a patient – a doctor who, if you like, is talking 'normally', without any mirroring. Let's listen.

Doctor   Do you have any major medical problems?

Patient   No, I'm pretty healthy.

Doctor   OK. Have you ever had any operations?

Patient Never.

Doctor OK. Do you have any allergies to medicines?

Patient Not that I know of.

Doctor OK. Do you smoke?

Patient Oh, my goodness, no. Never.

Doctor OK. Do you drink?

Patient No.

Speaker And so on. Now, up to this point, the doctor might actually seem to be more interested in going through a standard list of questions than in understanding the patient's real concerns. Now let's listen to another version of the interview. This time the doctor's going to use some verbal mirroring – and you can assume that she's doing some physical mirroring too! Here we go.

Doctor Do you have any major medical problems?

Patient No, I'm pretty healthy.

Doctor You're pretty healthy. Have you ever had any operations?

Patient No . . . never.

Doctor Never? Do you have any allergies to medicines?

Patient None that I know of.

Doctor None. Do you smoke?

Patient Oh, my goodness, no. Never.

Doctor Never?

Patient Never. My father's just been diagnosed with lung cancer, and he's smoked all his life.

Speaker Did you hear the differences? When the patient says, 'Oh, my goodness, no. Never,' the doctor has no idea why the word 'never' was used. By mirroring it, saying the word 'never' and then pausing, it reminds the patient of the emotion that made him say 'never', and the patient then says more about it. It's a pretty good example of how mirroring can lead to better rapport and more effective communication with the patient. And it's also an example of how mirroring can bring us closer to other people, and create a better rapport with them. If you'd like more information about this idea, please visit our website – website address details will follow at the end of this programme.

Presenter Thank you Joan. Now, let's move on and ...

Answers
1 wavelength   2 body posture   3 mimic
4 responsibility   5 verbally   6 concern

3 Vocabulary
Habits and gestures

Warm up

Books closed. To introduce the topic of habits and gestures, carry out some actions and ask the class to describe what you are doing. Use some of the examples from Exercise 3a and try to elicit the words from students.

(a) Books open. Ask students to cover the box in Exercise 3a and look at the pictures. Ask them to name the actions. Listen to their answers but do not comment at this stage. Uncover the exercise. Students match the words and the pictures, writing the words under the pictures. They compare answers with a partner before checking answers in open class.

Answers
 1 rub your forehead
 2 yawn
 3 fiddle with your hair
 4 stroke your chin
 5 fold your hands behind your head
 6 cough
 7 bite your nails
 8 tilt your head
 9 blink
10 rub your hands together

(b) In pairs, students decide which of the actions people do in each of the situations. Tell students there are several possible answers for some of the situations. Check answers.

Answers
1 blink, fiddle with hair, bite nails
2 tilt head, yawn, cough
3 stroke chin, rub forehead
4 yawn, fold hands behind head
5 rub forehead

(c) Put students into pairs and ask them to discuss the questions. Ask one of them to give feedback and encourage class discussion on interesting points.

Answers
Students' own answers

Vocabulary notebook
Encourage students to start a new section *Habits and gestures* in their notebook and add these words. They may find it useful to note down translations too.

4 Speak

Divide the class into groups of three. Read through the instructions with students. Before starting the activity, give students some time to choose a subject from the box and plan what they are going to say. Make it clear that in the first stage of the activity, only student A is talking, while the others either just listen or listen and take notes. When each of the students has spoken and the group has discussed what they have learnt, listen to feedback from a member of each group. Allow comments from the rest of the class and encourage open class discussion.

5 Grammar

Hedging and boosting

(a) **Weaker classes:** To introduce the topic of hedging and boosting, ask students to draw a horizontal line in their notebooks with *timid* written at one end and *confident* at the other. Ask students to put a cross somewhere on the line to describe their personality, then compare in small groups.

Ask students what phrases might be used by a confident person and what phrases might be used if someone is unsure of what they are saying. Elicit *undoubtedly, unquestionably, appears to* and *seems to*. Continue with the procedure for stronger classes.

Stronger classes: Ask students to look at the sentences and decide which are assertive and which are cautious. During feedback ask students to say the sentences without hedging or boosting.

Answers
1 and 4 assertively
2 and 3 cautiously

(b) Read through the rules with the class and check that students understand the meaning of the verbs. If they need further practice, ask them to make sentences using some of the hedging and boosting structures.

Rule
1 avoid 2 direct 3 formal

(c) Read through the sentences with students to check understanding. Students rewrite the sentences and compare answers with a partner before feedback. Check the answers. For further practice, ask students to rewrite the sentences using other hedging and boosting devices.

Answers
2 This seems to be an area that is worth investigating. / This is an area that seems to be worth investigating.
3 Further research in this area would unquestionably be a waste of time.
4 Some great advances appear to have been made.
5 Understanding more about how the brain works can undoubtedly be useful.
6 Scientists are believed to have made enormous progress in this area.

┌─ OPTIONAL ACTIVITY ───────────
Students may have difficulty with the word order of sentences using hedging or boosting. Write the following jumbled sentences on the board and ask students to put the words in the correct order. If you have a competitive class, you may like to do this exercise as a race. Tell students that there may be more than one correct answer, especially to number 6!

1 *for to cancer discovered appear a cure have they*
2 *definitely crime been an in violent year in last has the increase there*
3 *to there believed are undiscovered of millions be planets*
4 *need definitely more will to if exam pass he he the wants to study*
5 *tigers are thought be 4,000 than India left in to there fewer*
6 *definitely boys more are than girls intelligent*

Answers
1 They appear to have discovered a cure for cancer.
2 There has definitely been an increase in violent crime in the last year.
3 There are believed to be millions of undiscovered planets.
4 He will definitely need to study more if he wants to pass the exam.
5 There are thought to be fewer than 4,000 tigers left in India.
6 Boys are definitely more intelligent than girls.

Read the *Look* box with students and draw attention to the position of adverbs in Exercise 5c.

┌─────────────────────────────────
Language note
Hedging phrases are most commonly used in written English. Journalists and other writers often use hedging when they do not have enough proof to make a direct statement, e.g. *X is believed to be making a new film. Y is thought to be living in Peru.*

In some social situations, many people do not like making direct statements and use hedging to avoid doing so, e.g. *You seem to have some tomato ketchup on your shirt.*
└─────────────────────────────────

Grammar notebook
Remind students to note down the rules for hedging and boosting and to write a few examples of their own.

6 Speak

Explain that hedging and boosting is often used in newspapers and in news broadcasts. Tell students that they are going to describe, and respond to, news stories. Read through the headlines and sample dialogue to check understanding. In pairs, students create dialogues following a similar pattern to the example. Circulate and monitor to ensure students are using the hedging and boosting expressions in an appropriate context and saying them with the correct stress and intonation.

Weaker classes: Students can write their answers before speaking. Encourage them to look at their notes as little as possible.

┌─ OPTIONAL ACTIVITY ───────────
Depending on the sensitivity of the class, you may like to have further practice of hedging and boosting by asking students to write dialogues based on imaginary research carried out by other members of the class. For example:

A: It appears Juan has invented a new way of writing.
B: Really. I don't believe it!
A: It is believed to be the only type of writing which is impossible to understand. What is most surprising is that he can read it!
B: That is incredible.

Students create dialogues in pairs. Listen to some dialogues in open class.

Literature in mind

7 Read

Warm up

Books closed. Write the following words on the board: *ship, zoo, wreck, tiger, boy, zebra*. Tell students that these words appear in the summary of a novel and ask them to work in pairs and discuss what the story might be about. Ask some pairs to give feedback. Students open their books and read the summary of the story. Were they right? Look at the photo and discuss whether or not students would be interested in reading the book, and why or why not.

(a) Check the meaning of *tanker* and *lifeboat*. Students read the text quickly to find the answers to the questions. Encourage students not to look up every new word but just to read and get the general idea of the text. You could give them a two-minute time limit to encourage them to read the text quickly. Check answers.

Answers
1 The tiger
2 The tanker does not hit the lifeboat.

(b) Read through the sentences with the class. Students read the text again to put the sentences in the order in which they appear in the extract. There is quite a lot of new vocabulary in this text, but encourage students to work without help from you or a dictionary at this stage. Ask students to underline specific words and phrases they don't understand. Let students compare answers with a partner and to discuss the possible meanings of new words together. After feedback, you may want to read through the text with the students, pausing to check their comprehension and their grasp of vocabulary.

Answers
The statements appear in the following order:
4 1 10 3 5 8 6 7 9 2

(c) Read through sentences 1–8 and explain the meaning of *trudged, bent, lowered, spot*. Give students time to read the text closely and to check their answers with a partner before feedback.

Answers
1 relentlessly   2 looming   3 crouched
4 languishing   5 with all his might   6 to no avail
7 speck   8 anguish

(d) In pairs, students answer the questions. Check answers.

Possible answers
1 The tiger thinks the boy is another tiger /
   he needs the boy to do the rowing.
2 The tanker didn't see them.
3 Because he has no one else.

8 Write

The planning for this exercise can be done in class and the composition set as homework.

(a) Tell students they are going to read a composition about animal testing. Write the title of the composition on the board. In pairs, students make a list of the arguments they expect to find in the text. Listen to some of their ideas in open class as feedback.

(b) Students read the composition quickly to check their answers. Tell them not to worry about understanding every word, but to focus on the main arguments in the text. Students compare answers with a partner. Check answers in open class and invite students to comment on the information in the composition and to say which of the statements they agree with.

(c) Pre-teach *dilemma*. In pairs, students discuss the questions. During feedback, draw special attention to the order of paragraphs in the composition.

Answers
1 Students' own answers. Possible attention-grabbing ways of introducing the topic might be to tell a story that happened to a friend of yours, or to give statistics showing the number of people whose lives have been saved by medicines tested on animals.
2 On the other hand; however; There is no doubt that this is a complex issue; It is probably one of the most controversial issues of our times; there are so many convincing arguments on both sides.
3 Paragraph 1: Introduction
   Paragraph 2: For animal testing
   Paragraph 3: Against animal testing
   Paragraph 4: Conclusion and opinion

(d) Read through the titles. Tell students to plan their composition using the same paragraph structure as in the sample composition. Encourage them to think about arguments for and against the statement. This task could be extended into a class presentation, with students putting their writing on walls, passing them round for cross-reading or giving oral presentations based on their texts. If you set the writing as a homework task, ask students to read each other's work in a subsequent lesson. Invite some students to read out their work to the class.

10 The sporting spirit

Unit overview

TOPIC: Winning and losing at sport

TEXTS
Reading and listening: three newspaper articles about sport
Listening: a conversation about cheating at sport
Reading and speaking: famous sporting quotations
Listening and speaking: a presentation about Brasília
Writing: a description of a sporting event

SPEAKING AND FUNCTIONS
Discussing cheating in sport
Giving a presentation

LANGUAGE
Grammar: *could / be able to / manage to*
Vocabulary: success and failure
Pronunciation: linking sounds

1 Read and listen

If you set the background information as a homework research task, ask the students to tell the class what they found out.

BACKGROUND INFORMATION

John Akhwari: was born in Mbulu, Tanganyika and represented Tanzania in the Olympic marathon in 1968 in Mexico City. During the race he fell, badly cutting his knee and dislocating the joint. Rather than giving up, he continued running. He finished last among the 74 competitors. When asked why he continued running, he said simply, "My country did not send me to Mexico City to start the race. They sent me to finish." There was an article written up in Delta's *Sky Magazine*. Akhwari has lent his name to the John Stephen Akhwari Athletic Foundation, an organisation which supports Tanzanian athletes training for the Olympic Games.

Sally Robbins: was born 15 July 1981 and is an Australian rower, who was a member of Australia's 2004 Summer Olympics Women's Eight Rowing crew. In the final the team were well placed for Bronze when, 500 metres from the finish, she appeared to collapse and lay back. Robbins was publicly humiliated in the Australian media as "Lay-down Sally" and called "un-Australian". Most Australians were outraged that, whilst given the nation's highest honour in representing the country, she gave up.

Zinedine Yazid Zidane: was born 23 June, 1972. He is a French former football midfielder who played for four European clubs, including Juventus FC and Real Madrid, and was a member and later captain of the French national team for which he participated in three World Cups and in three European Championship tournaments. Zidane was elected FIFA World Player of the Year a record-equalling three times (1998, 2000, 2003), and was named European Footballer of the Year in 1998. Zidane retired from football after the 2006 FIFA World Cup.

Warm up

Books closed. To focus on the topic, quickly brainstorm as many different sports as possible. Put students into small groups and ask them to make a list of the five most demanding sports and to discuss what makes them demanding. After five minutes, ask a representative of each group to read out their list and have an open class discussion to create a list which the whole group agrees on.

(a) Books closed. Write *The sporting spirit* on the board and ask students to say what they understand by the expression. Can they think of any examples of the sporting spirit that they have seen? Open books. Students look at the photos and answer the questions. Discuss their answers in open class.

Answers
1 a rowing   b a marathon   c football
2 and 3 Students' own answers

(b) Tell students they are going to read three texts about different sports. Read through the instructions to check understanding. Tell students not to worry about the meaning of every word, but to concentrate on the task. Let students compare answers with a partner before giving feedback.

Answers
1 texts 1 and 2   2 text 1   3 text 1   4 text 3
5 text 2   6 text 1   7 text 2   8 text 3

(c) Read phrases 1–8 with students. Explain the meaning of *community service* and *hit the wall*. Play the recording while students read and listen to the text then match the phrases to the gaps in the text. Pause where appropriate to check comprehension and help with difficult vocabulary. Check answers.

TAPESCRIPT
See the reading text on pages 68 and 69 of the Student's Book.

Answers

1 F   2 G   3 C   4 A   5 H   6 B   7 D   8 E

─── OPTIONAL ACTIVITY ───

If you would like your students to do some further work on the vocabulary in the text, you can use the following exercise. Write the following definitions on the board and ask students to find words and expressions with the same meaning in the text. The words are in the order of the text. To make the exercise more challenging, you could write them on the board in a different order.

1 *very surprised or shocked* (text 1) (stunned)
2 *achieve what he wanted to do* (text 1) (fulfil his ambitions)
3 *will only become clear in the future* (text 1) (remains to be seen)
4 *loud clapping while standing* (text 2) (a standing ovation)
5 *taken quickly* (text 2) (rushed)
6 *hit with the head* (text 3) (butted)
7 *when someone stops something happening for a period of time* (text 3) (suspension)
8 *not right for the situation* (text 3) (inappropriate)

Discussion box

Weaker classes: Students can choose one question to discuss.

Stronger classes: In pairs or small groups, students go through the questions in the box and discuss them.

Monitor and help as necessary, encouraging students to express themselves in English and to use any vocabulary they have learned from the text. Ask pairs or groups to feedback to the class and discuss any interesting points further.

2 Grammar

could / be able to / manage to

Warm up

Hand each student a small piece of paper and ask them to write down something they can do which they think others in the group can't do, e.g. *speak French, run very fast, cook a roast dinner*. Give students examples to get them started. Take in the pieces of paper and read out the abilities for the rest of the group to guess who has that ability. Ask students to describe their ability and when they first did it. Do not correct any grammatical errors at this stage.

(**a**) Books closed. Write *ability* on the board and elicit as much information as possible from students: the modal verbs used to talk about ability in the past, present and future; any other verbs which can be used and examples of each usage. Books open. Read through the rules with students in open class and ask them to help you complete them.

Rule

general; specific; non-ability; ability; modal verbs

(**b**) Read through the sentences with students. Check understanding of *shots*. Students fill the gaps using one of the words from the rule. Check the answers. Refer back to the examples in Exercise 2a and use these for further explanation if necessary.

Answers

2 managed to / were able to   3 couldn't
4 managed to   5 been able to   6 be able to
7 could   8 be able to

─── OPTIONAL ACTIVITY ───

Write the following questions on the board:

What abilities do you have now that you didn't have when you were younger (and vice versa)?

Think of a situation in the past where you (or someone you know) had a problem and resolved it.

Give students some thinking time before they start to discuss the questions with a partner. Students work in pairs and discuss the questions. Monitor and ensure students are using *could / be able to / manage to* correctly. During feedback, ask the rest of the class to correct any mistakes in usage and explain why a certain verb should be used.

Language note

Students may say **I will can do it if I try* or **I might can help you*. Point out that *can* is not an infinitive but is part of the verb *to be able to*. In structures requiring an infinitive we use *be able to* instead of *can*, e.g. *I will be able to do it if I try* or *I might be able to help you*.

Grammar notebook

Remind students to note down the rules for *could*, *be able to* and *manage to* and to write a few examples of their own.

─── OPTIONAL ACTIVITY ───

Write the following sentences on the board. Ask students to correct the errors. Check answers.

1 *After a long climb, I could reach the top of the mountain.*
2 *When I was young I wasn't able to swim.*
3 *I managed to ride a bike when I was seven. It was easy.*
4 *I looked everywhere, but managed to find it.*

Answers

1 After a long climb, I managed to reach the top of the mountain.
2 When I was young I couldn't swim.
3 I could ride a bike when I was seven. It was easy.
4 I looked everywhere, but couldn't find it.

3 Listen

a Students look at the photos. Ask them to say what they know about the people and to guess what they have in common (cheating and breaking the rules in sport). Ask students if they can think of any other examples of sportsmen/sportswomen cheating.

Answers
a a tennis player arguing with the umpire
b rugby players fighting

b Write the names Jenny and Paul on the board. Tell students they are going to listen to these two people talking about cheating in sport. Play the recording while students answer the questions. Tell them not to worry if they don't understand every word, but to concentrate on understanding the general topic. Check answers.

TAPESCRIPT

Girl So, did you see the match, Paul? Brilliant, wasn't it!?

Boy Yeah, great game. Better than last week!

Girl Last week? Oh yeah, I remember – they were winning until the last minute, that's right, then they blew it and lost. No, last night was a lot better.

Boy It was, yeah. Pity about the penalty, though.

Girl Pity? Why? We won the game because of that penalty!

Boy That's right – but it wasn't a penalty, was it, Jenny? I mean, it was clear as a bell – the defender never touched him.

Girl Look, it doesn't matter – it's a penalty if the referee says so.

Boy But our player dived – he was trying to get a penalty.

Girl I know – so what? All that matters is that our team won, right?

Boy Yes. No. I don't know. I just wish we'd won fairly, I suppose.

Girl Look – it happens all the time. Every team tries to win if they can, and sometimes that means ...

Boy Means what? Breaking the rules?

Girl Yeah, Paul – breaking the rules. That's how it is nowadays. It's like – like, you know, when a player fouls another player to stop him scoring a goal, or handles the ball or something like that. It's part of the game.

Boy Yeah – the worst part! So a player handles the ball and the ball goes in the net, but the referee doesn't see him handle the ball and gives the goal. Well, it's just cheating, isn't it!?

Girl Well, maybe the problem is the referee, not the player.

Boy Well, you've got a point – but even so, it's the player who cheats, not the referee.

Girl And what do you want the player to do? Is he going to stand up and say 'Oh, sorry ref, actually it wasn't a goal because I used my hand'? If the other players don't kill him, the fans will!

Boy No, I don't want players to do that – what I'd like them to do is not handle the ball intentionally in the first place. There are lots of sports where you don't get cheating like that, like you get in football.

Girl For example?

Boy Tennis. Golf. Erm – athletics. In fact – individual sports. You only really get players cheating, breaking the rules, when it's a team game.

Girl Well, I'm not so sure about that. I mean, tennis players get angry and shout at the referee sometimes, don't they? And disagree with the line calls, whether the ball was in or out, all that stuff. I've seen loads of tennis players arguing.

Boy Sure, but that's different. I mean, they're not cheating, are they? They're not trying to win points by doing things that aren't in the rules, or are against the rules. They're just disagreeing.

Girl So what's your definition of cheating, then, Paul?

Boy Well, not <u>my</u> definition, anyone's definition – it's doing something that you know isn't allowed, in order to gain an advantage. And I reckon it happens much more in football than any other sport.

Girl No, that's crazy. It's all over the place.

Boy I don't know, I mean, I love rugby too and you just don't see cheating like that. I mean, players make mistakes and sometimes they get into fights with each other, but it isn't actual cheating, not like you get in professional football.

Girl So you're against football?

Boy No! I'm against cheating. I mean, I know I'm wasting my breath ...

Girl Hey, I'm listening!

Boy No, I mean I'm wasting my breath saying that there shouldn't be cheating in sport. It's big money and there's cheating all over the place, I don't think it's ever going to be stopped, in fact I reckon it'll just get worse. And I think that's a real pity, because I really like sport.

Girl Yeah, I see what you mean – a bit. But I'm not as negative as you, I think sport's great even if there is a bit of cheating here and there.

Boy Hang on, Jenny, I'm not being negative! What did I say that was negative?

Girl Oh, that cheating will just get worse and so on and all that stuff ...

Answers
1 football, tennis, golf, athletics, rugby
2 c

c Read through the sentences with students and then play the recording again. Students listen to identify the speakers. Play the recording again to check answers, pausing where necessary for clarification.

Answers
1 J 2 J 3 P 4 J 5 P 6 J

(d) 🔊 Ask students to read through the sentences quickly. Play the recording while students complete the sentences with a word from the box. With stronger classes you may like to ask them to complete the sentences from memory, before playing the recording again to check.

Answers
1 dived   2 fairly   3 intentionally   4 shout
5 advantage

(e) In small groups, students discuss their opinions. Ask different groups to report back to the class and invite others to comment.

> **Discussion box**
> **Weaker classes:** Students can choose one question to discuss.
>
> **Stronger classes:** In pairs or small groups, students go through the questions in the box and discuss them.
>
> Monitor and help as necessary, encouraging students to express themselves in English and to use any vocabulary they have learned from the text. Ask pairs or groups to feedback to the class and discuss any interesting points further.

4 Vocabulary
Success and failure
Warm up

Books closed. To introduce the topic, write the words *success* and *failure* on the board. Ask students to think of examples of each from their own lives. Put students into small groups and ask them to discuss what can help people be successful and what can cause people to fail. Listen to some of their ideas in open class as feedback.

(a) Books open. Pre-teach *get the part*. Students read the sentences and complete the table with the underlined words. Allow them to compare answers with a partner before feedback.

Weaker classes: You may like to give students extra examples to help them understand the meanings of the words.

Answers
SUCCESS: overcome, pull something off, fulfil, make it
FAILURE: fall through, blow it, mess up, go wrong

(b) Ask students to read through the sentences and choose the correct option, referring back to the table as necessary. You could ask stronger students to complete the sentences without looking at the table in Exercise 4a. Students check answers in pairs before feedback in open class.

Answers
2 blow it   3 made it   4 fell through
5 pull it off   6 overcome   7 fulfils
8 messed up

(c) Students complete the sentences. To make this exercise a little more difficult, you may like to ask students to cover the previous exercises.

Answers
1 up; went   2 through   3 make   4 overcome

(d) In pairs or small groups, students discuss two of the questions in Exercise 4c. Encourage them to use the new vocabulary as they speak and to ask their partners to expand on their sentences and give further information. Ask a few pairs to tell the class about their partner's answers.

Vocabulary notebook
Encourage students to start a new section *Success and failure* in their notebook and add these words. They may find it useful to note down translations of the words too.

5 Read and speak
Warm up

Write the following sentences on the board. Check understanding and ask students which they agree with. Listen to some of the students' ideas in open class.

It's not the winning, it's the taking part.
It's the winning, not the taking part.

(a) Tell students they are going to read six famous quotations about sport and winning. Pre-teach *bunch* and *dime*. Students complete the sentences with the words in the box. Tell students that there may be more than one possible answer in some cases. Students compare answers with a partner before feedback. If students have alternative answers, ask them to explain the meaning.

Answers
1 play together   2 take the game-winning shot
3 come second   4 get it right   5 can't win
6 win or lose

(b) In pairs, students discuss their opinions. Encourage them to use some of the language from the quotes to help them express their opinions.

(c) Remind students of the use of metaphors and see if they can remember any of the metaphors used in Unit 7 Exercise 4. Students work in pairs and complete the sentences. Give them some examples of your own to get them started. Students write their answers and compare answers with another pair before feedback.

Possible answers

1 swimming without water
2 better than coming last
3 born
4 making friends

6 Listen and speak

If you set the background information as a homework research task, ask the students to tell the class what they found out.

BACKGROUND INFORMATION

Brasília: is the capital of Brazil. It was built during the 1950s when it was decided that the capital of Brazil should be in the centre of the country (the former capital Rio de Janeiro was on the coast). It was inaugurated in 1960 and now has about 2.3 million inhabitants.

a 🔊 Look at the pictures with the class. Tell students they are going to listen to a presentation given by a student about the city of Brasília. Play the recording while students listen and number the pictures in the order in which they are mentioned. Check answers in open class.

Stronger classes: You may like to ask stronger students to make notes as they listen and ask them to explain what Marco says about each of the pictures.

TAPESCRIPT

Teacher   OK, for the last few minutes of the lesson we're going to have another presentation and this time it's Marco who's going to tell us a bit about his home town – so Marco, over to you.

Marco   Thanks. Hi everyone. OK, I'm going to talk to you about the city of Brasília. It's my home, and it's the city which, as you might already know, is the capital of Brazil. Now the first thing I want to say about the city is that it is relatively new, it was built during the 1950s and inaugurated in 1960. There'd been plans for a new city for decades but it was a man called Juscelino Kubitschek (who was president of Brazil at the time) who actually managed to make it happen. There's a statue to him in the city – well, in fact there's more than one, but this is a very famous one, I've got a slide of it here. Here he is. Can everyone see? Martin? No? Sorry – look, if I show it like this, then everyone will be able to see, I hope. Better? Great. So, as I was saying, this is Juscelino Kubitschek.

Now, one of the things that you might not know about the city is that two guys designed it – their names were Lúcio Costa and Oscar Niemeyer. And by the way, Niemeyer is probably Brazil's most famous architect ever! Anyway, what they did was, they designed the city so that its basic shape is like an aeroplane.

Right – going back to Oscar Niemeyer, he designed a lot of the buildings in the city too. As I said before, Brasília's the capital now, erm, just as a matter of interest, it was Rio de Janeiro up until 1960. So a lot of the buildings are government ones, perhaps the most famous is this one, it's the congress building, two towers beside each other. And here is a photo I took at sunset, neat, isn't it? It's the building that's now sort of seen as the symbol of the country. Niemeyer did other kinds of buildings too – like the cathedral, it's pretty different because most of the building is actually underground, and above ground the roof is designed to look like a crown. Erm – what's next? Sorry, can you just bear with me for a moment? I know I should be able to do this without notes, but …! Oh, yes, well, there are some people who say Brasília isn't a very pretty place but I don't really agree. There are some beautiful lakes, and one of the bridges over the lake, this one, the newest one, it's also named after Kubitschek, remember, the guy who founded the city? I think this bridge with the white curved arches is really beautiful. My sister is an architect and she thinks it's really ugly, but I like it. So, that's about it. To sum up, I think Brasília's a really interesting place, and there are some nice things to do and see too.

Answers

a 3   b 1   c 2   d 4

b 🔊 Read through the expressions with students. If students are unclear of meaning, tell them they will hear the expressions in the listening and encourage them to try to understand the meaning from the context. Play the recording for students to tick the expressions when they hear them. If necessary, play the recording again, pausing at the expressions to clarify meaning.

c In pairs, students decide what each of the phrases in Exercise 6b is used for. With weaker classes, it might be a good idea to do this activity in open class and to play the recording again to see how Marco uses the phrases. If stronger students finish early, ask them to use the phrases and write examples of their own.

Answers

begin his talk 8
end his talk 6
to return to something he was saying before 1, 10
begin a new point 9
give himself time to think 4
add an extra point to what he is saying 3, 5, 7
emphasise something he was saying 2

(**d**) Tell students they are going to give a short talk on one of the subjects in the box. Make sure they spend a lot of time planning their presentation, but do not let them write down exactly what they are going to say. Emphasise the importance of organising basic ideas and having a framework for the presentation, which should include an introduction, main points with examples and a conclusion. Circulate and ensure students are planning to use phrases from Exercise 6b in their presentations.

(**e**) Students give their presentations to the class. If you have a large class, divide students into smaller groups. Encourage other students to ask questions at the end of each presentation. You may like to hold a vote to decide the best presentation.

7 Pronunciation
Linking sounds

(**a**) 🔊 Read through the phrases with students. Play the recording while students listen to how the underlined parts are said (they are linked without a pause between the words). Explain to students that when we speak, words are often joined together. This is especially true when a consonant at the end of one word is followed by a vowel at the beginning of the next. We also sometimes link words when two consonants meet (e.g. *just bear*, *first thing*) as full pronunciation of both consonants spoils flow and fluency.

(**b**) 🔊 Play the recording again, pausing after each sentence for students to repeat. Encourage them to link the sounds as on the recording.

(**c**) 🔊 Students read the phrases aloud, noting how the words are joined together and trying not to pause. Play the recording for students to compare their pronunciation.

8 Write

The planning for this exercise can be done in class and the writing can be set as homework.

Warm up

Ask students how they get reports on sporting events and concerts, plays and other events. Do they read newspapers and magazines? Do they watch television / listen to the radio / surf the Internet? Students discuss the best place to find reports and the type of things that reports include. What makes a good report? Listen to some of their ideas in open class.

(**a**) Tell students they are going to read a report on a match. Students read the report quickly and answer the questions. Tell students to concentrate on the task and not to worry about difficult vocabulary at this stage. Check answers.

Answers
1 football
2 Newhaven. They name some of the Newhaven players and a teacher, but refer to "the Shorthouse captain" and "the last Shorthouse player".

(**b**) Students read the text again to match the underlined words and phrases to their meanings 1–8. Allow students to compare answers with a partner before open class feedback.

Answers
2 coolly   3 few and far between   4 bitterly
5 sealed   6 put the ball over the bar   7 sizing up
8 smashed in

(**c**) In pairs, students discuss the effect of the underlined words in the text. Listen to some of their ideas in open class. (*The underlined words are more descriptive and colourful – they make the text much more interesting.*)

(**d**) Read through the instructions in open class. Ask students to take some time to think of an event, then make notes of the main points they want to include and plan the order in which to include them. Emphasise the importance of using verbs, adjectives and adverbs to make it more interesting. You may like to encourage students to do this activity as a speaking exercise in class and ask them to write the description as homework.

In a subsequent lesson, encourage students to read each other's descriptions and decide which they think is the best report.

11 Superheroes

Unit overview

TOPIC: Superheroes in graphic novels and comics

TEXTS
Reading and listening: an article about a reality show based on superheroes
Listening: an audition for a TV reality show
Reading: superheroes and graphic novels in other countries
Writing: a film review

SPEAKING AND FUNCTIONS
Designing a group of superheroes to save the world

LANGUAGE
Grammar: negative inversions
Vocabulary: from human to hero

1 Read and listen

If you set the background information as a homework research task, ask the students to tell the class what they found out.

BACKGROUND INFORMATION

Spider-Man: is a Marvel Comics superhero character also known in his everyday life as Peter Parker. He was created by Stan Lee and Steve Ditko and broke ground by featuring a hero who was a teenager. Since his incarnation and first appearance in *Amazing Fantasy* #15 (Aug.1962), he has become one of the world's most popular, enduring and recognisable superheroes.

The Incredible Hulk: is a fictional character created by Stan Lee and Jack Kirby. After nuclear physicist Dr Robert Bruce Banner was caught in the blast of a gamma bomb he created, he was transformed into the Hulk, a raging monstrosity. The character, both as Banner and the Hulk, is frequently pursued by the police or the armed forces, often as a result of the destruction he causes. The Hulk is usually depicted as green and first appeared in *Incredible Hulk* #1 in May 1962.

Superman: is a comic book superhero, originally created by writer Jerry Siegel and artist Joe Shuster and published by DC Comics. Created in 1932, the character first appeared in *Action Comics* #1 (June 1938). Superman is born Kal-El on the alien planet Krypton, before being rocketed to Earth as an infant by his scientist father moments before the planet's destruction.

Adopted and raised by a Kansas farmer and his wife, the child is raised as Clark Kent and, as an adult, the character develops superhuman abilities, resolving to use these for the benefit of humanity.

Wonder Woman: is a fictional DC Comics superhero created by William and Elizabeth Marston. Wonder Woman first appeared in *All Star Comics* #8 (Dec. 1941). She is the most famous female comic book superhero, and is written as a founding member of the Justice League. Marston designed Wonder Woman to reflect the concept of an empowered independent female character, with several subsequent writers also working this idea into the character. In addition to comic books, the character was featured in the popular 1975 to 1979 television adaptation starring Lynda Carter.

The Incredibles: are not comic book characters but a family of superheroes featured in a 2004 Academy Award-winning animated feature film. It was written and directed by Brad Bird, a former director of The Simpsons. The film was released in 2004 and according to the Internet Movie Database, it was the highest-selling DVD of 2005, with 17.18 million copies sold.

The X-Men: are a team of fictional comic book superheroes in the Marvel Comics universe. Created by Stan Lee and Jack Kirby, they first appeared in *The X-Men* #1, published in September 1963. The X-Men are fictitious mutants who, as a result of a sudden leap in evolution, are born with latent superhuman abilities. The X-Men comic book series was one of the earliest to adopt a multicultural cast.

Clark Kent: is a fictional character created by Joe Shuster and Jerry Siegel as the civilian secret identity of the superhero Superman.

Warm up

Books closed. In pairs, students make lists of superheroes. Set them a two-minute time limit to name as many as possible. Listen to some of their ideas in open class and make up a list on the board. Which superhero do they think is the most powerful and which the weakest? Can they think of any super-villains?

a Books open. Students look at the photos of superheroes and answer the questions. Encourage them to go into as much detail as possible when describing the superheroes. You may like to ask students to work in small groups and concentrate on answering the questions for just one of the characters, then ask each group to present their information to the rest of the class.

Answers
Spider-Man
The Incredible Hulk
Superman
Wonder Woman
The Incredibles
Wolverine and Storm from the X-Men

b Students read the text to check their answers. Before reading, pre-teach difficult vocabulary: *foe*, *arch-enemy*, *frailty*. Encourage them to look for the answers and not to spend time on new words.

c 🔊 Check understanding of questions 1–5. Elicit answers but do not comment at this stage. Play the recording, while students listen and read the text to answer the questions. Ask them to compare their answers in pairs before feedback. Play the recording again, pausing as necessary to clarify any problems.

TAPESCRIPT
See the reading text on page 74 of the Student's Book.

Answers
1 b   2 c   3 a   4 a   5 c

d Check students understand the definitions. Ask them to find phrases or expressions in the text which have the same meaning. Let them compare answers with a partner before feedback in open class.

Answers
1 life-threatening
2 on a daily basis
3 an instant hit
4 eliminated
5 foe
6 comes in handy
7 smash things up
8 can't find a way to
9 make-believe

Discussion box

Weaker classes: Students can choose one question to discuss.

Stronger classes: In pairs or small groups, students go through the questions in the box and discuss them.

Monitor and help as necessary, encouraging students to express themselves in English and to use any vocabulary they have learned from the text. Ask pairs or groups to feedback to the class and discuss any interesting points further.

---

2 Grammar
Negative inversions

a **Weaker classes:** Books closed. Write on the board:

Tom is very fit. He can run 100 metres in 11 seconds and he can swim 50 metres in 50 seconds.

Ask students how many examples there are of Tom's fitness (two). Tell students that if we want to emphasise both activities, we can use an adverb to start the sentence. Write on the board: *Not only can he run 100 metres in 11 seconds, but he can also swim 50 metres in 50 seconds.* Point out that after the adverbial *not only*, the subject and verb invert, as they do in question forms. Tell students that there are several negative adverbs which follow a similar pattern. Students open their books and follow the procedure for stronger classes.

Stronger classes: Read the examples to the class and ask students to complete the rule. Check answers and use the sample sentences as examples to show the inversion of subject and auxiliary. Ensure students are clear of the meaning of each adverbial phrase, giving example sentences as required.

Rule
negative; beginning; more; question; written

b Students complete the sentences using the correct form. Check answers and ask students to explain their choices, referring back to previous explanations.

Answers
2 You will
3 should you
4 had the opening credits
5 can I
6 It's
7 I have
8 did he direct

c Read through the example and elicit the answer to question 2. Students complete the sentences using the negative adverbial in brackets and compare their answers with a partner before feedback. If students are struggling with negative inversions, this exercise can be done in open class. Use the examples to explain the changes in word order.

Answers
2 Under no circumstances should you touch that.
3 Never before have I read such rubbish.
4 Not only can Superman see through walls, but he can also fly.
5 Rarely will you see such great special effects as in the new Superman film.
6 On no account must you say a word to anyone.
7 Not only does my friend look like Clark Kent, but he is also a journalist.
8 No sooner had I sat down to watch the film than the phone rang.

Language note
Common mistakes when using negative adverbials are to use a double negative, e.g. *On no account must you not say a word to anyone. *Never haven't I seen such a boring film*. Point out to students that as the adverb is negative, the use of *not* creates a double negative and it is therefore not used. Pay special attention to the use of *than* with *No sooner*, as students will often make the mistake of using *when* instead, e.g. *No sooner had I sat down when the phone rang*. This is grammatically incorrect, but is actually a common mistake made by native speakers.

Grammar notebook
Remind students to note down the rules for negative inversions and to write a few examples of their own.

┌─ OPTIONAL ACTIVITY ─────────────

For further practice of negative inversions, write the following sentence beginnings on the board and ask students to complete them in their own words.

Under no circumstances would I …
Never have I seen …
Not only can I … but I can also …
Rarely do I …

Divide the class into small groups and ask students to compare their sentences. Listen to some examples.

3 Vocabulary
From human to hero

Refer back to Exercise 1 and brainstorm the special powers of the superheroes. Look at the pictures with students and ask them to describe what they can see. Try to elicit words from the box. Go through the words in the box and clarify any difficulties. Students complete the gaps and compare answers with a partner before feedback.

Answers
1 short-sighted
2 squinted
3 puny
4 slouched
5 short of breath
6 panted
7 X-ray vision
8 superhuman strength
9 speed of light

┌─ OPTIONAL ACTIVITY ─────────────

Write the following questions on the board.

If you could become a superhero, what superpowers would you most like to have?
Would you like to become a superhero? What are the advantages and disadvantages of being a superhero?

In pairs, students discuss the questions. Listen to some of their ideas in open class.

Vocabulary notebook
Encourage students to start a new section *Physical abilities* in their notebook and add these words. They may find it useful to note down translations of the words too.

4 Listen

Warm up

Books closed. Ask students if they have seen any television programmes (such as *American Idol* or *The X Factor*) in which people audition to become singers or train to become dancers. In pairs, students discuss the format of these programmes. Listen to some of their ideas in open class.

(a) Books open. Students look at the pictures and decide on names for the superheroes.

(b) ◁)) Tell students they are going to listen to some auditions for a TV reality show based on superheroes. Play the recording, while students listen and complete the first two columns of the table. Tell them not to worry about understanding every word, but just to concentrate on the task. Let students compare their answers with a partner before feedback.

TAPESCRIPT
1
Man 1 Hello, my name is Captain Aquatic.
Interviewer Hello, Captain Aquatic. So can you tell us a little about your special powers?
Man 1 Sure. Well, as you can probably tell from my name, when it comes to water I have some very special powers. First of all I have lungs that can breathe equally as well on land as under water, which is pretty useful when chasing my arch enemy Shark Boy. What else? Ah yes. I can freeze water and I can use the frozen water to throw at people. I have superhuman strength so I can throw it pretty far. As well as all this, I have ultrasonic hearing, which is pretty handy under water too.
Interviewer Very impressive. Are there any less impressive things you should tell us about?
Man 1 Well, I do need special glasses to see underwater. If I lose these then I'm effectively blind and I can't see where I'm going. Luckily this has only happened once in my life so far and I always carry a spare pair with me just in case.
Interviewer That sounds like a good idea. And finally, what is your mission?
Man 1 My mission? My mission is to protect all the world's oceans, lakes and rivers and to keep them free from pollution. I also promise to hunt down all those who wish to harm the world's water supplies and make them pay for their crimes.
2
Man 2 Hi. Dynamico reporting for duty.
Interviewer Hello, Dynamico. So tell us. How can you help the world?

Man 2 Never has this world faced such dark and dangerous times. I am here to bring light wherever there is darkness and bring sunshine to everyone, everywhere on earth. This, I can only do by defeating the evil Rainmaker and his army of dark clouds.

Interviewer And how are you going to do this exactly?

Man 2 Well, I am a human battery, a source of great power and energy which gives me the ability to battle and defeat the masterminds of evil who would turn our world to darkness.

Interviewer Can you be a bit more specific?

Man 2 Well, I guess my greatest gift is that I can take the energy from other people simply by touching them. This extra energy gives me the ability to fly at the speed of light so I can be anywhere there's trouble in no time at all. Another by-product of my excess of energy is that I can actually turn myself invisible, which comes in handy when I don't want to be seen … erm, obviously.

Interviewer And weaknesses?

Man 2 I don't have any weaknesses.

Interviewer What? All great superheroes must have a weakness.

Man 2 My only weakness is that I care too much. My life is dedicated to my job and I have no time for friends and family. This makes me particularly lonely and sometimes I do get a bit depressed.

3

Interviewer Hello, come in and introduce yourself.

Woman Hi there. I'm Brainwave and I'm here to blow your minds.

Interviewer OK, go ahead.

Woman OK, well, first of all I can tell you that I've already passed my audition.

Interviewer And how do you know that?

Woman Because I can read minds and I've just read yours and I know that you like me.

Interviewer I'm impressed. What else can you do?

Woman Well, as you can probably tell from my name, my powers are more to do with the mind. That's not to say that I'm not strong or fast or things like that, but my real talents are more mental ones. For example, not only can I read minds, I can also move things by thinking about them. This is probably my best weapon and that's usually how I defeat my enemies. Finally I can also transfer things from my brain into the brains of other people so I'm really good at teaching people.

Interviewer Wow. So what's the downside to all this? I'm guessing there must be some price to pay.

Woman Yeah, well, obviously with all this intense mental activity I sometimes get incredibly bad headaches and these can make me powerless for days. It's a real pain but then I guess there has to be a price to pay.

Interviewer So who are you fighting?

Woman Well, it's not just one person, it's a group of them and they go by the name of The Man. The Man will do anything it can to make sure things never change. It is my aim to defeat The Man. My mission is to educate all the children of the world and open their eyes to the corruption that surrounds them so that together we can fight this evil and build a new society.

Answers
1 Name: Captain Aquatic
   Special powers: can freeze water; can throw things a long way; has ultrasonic hearing; has lungs that can breathe underwater
2 Name: Dynamico
   Special powers: can take the energy from people by touching them; can fly at the speed of light; can turn invisible
3 Name: Brainwave
   Special powers: can read people's minds; can move things by telekinesis; can transfer things from her brain into the brains of others

(c) 🔊 Play the recording again while students complete the remaining two columns of the table. Check the answers. Then play the recording again, pausing for clarification if necessary.

Answers
1 Weaknesses: needs special glasses to see underwater
   Mission: to protect the world's oceans, lakes and rivers and to keep them free from pollution
   Arch-enemy: Shark Boy
2 Weaknesses: cares too much and gets lonely and depressed
   Mission: to bring light to wherever there is darkness and to bring sunshine to everybody on Earth
   Arch-enemy: Rainmaker
3 Weaknesses: gets incredibly bad headaches
   Mission: to educate all the children of the world and open their eyes to the corruption that surrounds them
   Arch-enemy: The Man

(d) In pairs, students discuss which of the superheroes should get a part on the show. Circulate and help with difficult vocabulary. Encourage students to use the information from the recording. You may like to ask students to vote on the best superhero.

5 Speak
Saving the day

(a) Read through the task sheet in open class. Put students into groups of three and give them a few minutes to think of characters to save the world. Tell them that they are going to present these characters to the rest of the class and that they should be prepared to explain their superpowers and give examples of fantastic things they have done. Circulate and help with vocabulary as necessary.

(b) Give each group two minutes to present their superheroes. Organise a vote to decide on which group would be able to defeat the villains.

Culture in mind

6 Read

If you set the background information as a homework research task, ask the students to tell the class what they found out.

BACKGROUND INFORMATION

AK Comics: is an Egypt-based superhero comic publishing venture, and the first example of the genre produced in the Middle East. The company first began publishing monthly titles in February 2004, and its comics are produced in both Arabic and English. AK Comics was founded by Ayman Kandeel. Their mission is to fill the cultural and social gap that was created over the years between the West and East, by providing essentially needed role models.

Jalila: is the superhero name of female scientist Dr Asam F Dajani who at the age of 16 survived an explosion at the Dimodona nuclear plant and gained superpowers from the radiation. She protects the City of All Faiths from the warring Zios Army and the United Liberation Force. Besides excellent vision and hearing, her superpowers include the ability to travel at near-light speed, to harness and control powerful amounts of energy and the power to revitalise life and heal the wounded.

Nagraj: ("Snakeman") is an Indian comic book character from Raj Comics and is considered to be their flagship character. Created in the late 1980s, Nagraj was originally conceived as an enemy of international terrorism.

Rakan: is a fictional medieval warrior who was abandoned by his tribe as a child after a Mongol invasion. Weak and asthmatic, with a debilitating limp, he had little chance of survival until a saber-tooth tiger rescued him and raised him with her own cub Arameh. He is mortal and can get injured or killed but his superpowers include powerful animal-like instincts, tracking skills and Sheba martial art. Through the techniques of "sheba" (wisdom and peace) he is an invincible warrior.

Captain Canuck: is a superhero, one of comic books' most popular Canadian-owned heroes. Created by writer Ron Leishman and artist / co-writer Richard Comely, he first appeared in *Captain Canuck* #1 (July 1975).

(a) Look at the pictures and ask students what superpowers they think the superheroes might possess. Where do they think the superheroes come from? Listen to some of their ideas in open class. Ask students to skim through the text quickly and match the names with the pictures. During feedback, ask students to give reasons for their choices.

Answers
1 a   2 c   3 b   4 d

(b) Read through the questions with students and explain the meaning of *brought to life*, *extinct*, *patriotic*. Let students compare their answers with a partner before feedback.

Answers
1   Captain Canuck
2   Rakan
3   Zein
4   Aya
5   Nagraj
6   Captain Canuck

Discussion box
Weaker classes: Students can choose one question to discuss.

Stronger classes: In pairs or small groups, students go through the questions in the box and discuss them.

Monitor and help as necessary, encouraging students to express themselves in English and to use any vocabulary they have learned from the text. Ask pairs or groups to feedback to the class and discuss any interesting points further.

7 Write

The planning for this exercise can be done in class and the writing can be set as homework.

(a) Write the words from the box on the board and ask students to write a description of each of the words. After feedback, ask students to work in pairs and think of three examples of each. Listen to some of their ideas in open class.

(b) Ask students if they have seen any of the *X-Men* films and discuss the contents. Tell students they are going to read a review of the third *X-Men* film. Students read the review and fill the gaps with the words from the box.

Answers
1 sequel   2 plot   3 series   4 star   5 scene
6 special effects   7 characters   8 action

Example of negative inversion: *Rarely are part twos as good as the original film.*

(c) Students read the review again to answer the questions. They then discuss their answers in pairs before open class feedback.

Answers

1 disappointing/uninspiring
2 Hugh Jackman, Jean Gray returning from a watery grave
3 Halle Berry as Storm, Kelsey Grammer and the young actors. The action skips through events too quickly and you don't get to know any of the characters.
4 Information on previous *X-Men* films, the comic books and a possible series of Wolverine films.

d Students may be able to do this exercise without looking back at the text, but it's a good idea for them to look back at the text and see the expressions used in context. Let students compare answers with a partner before feedback. If stronger students finish quickly, ask them to write their own sentences using the expressions.

Answers

1 negative	2 negative	3 positive	4 positive
5 negative	6 negative	7 positive	8 negative

e Tell students they are going to write a review of a film that they found disappointing. Read through the table with them and give them some time to plan what information they are going to include. Encourage them to use some of the expressions from Exercise 7d. In a subsequent lesson, ask students to read and discuss each other's reviews.

12 On your own

Unit overview

TOPIC: Being alone

TEXTS
Reading and listening: extracts from the diary of a man on a desert island
Listening: three teenagers talking about things they like doing on their own
Listening: a song called *Message in a Bottle*
Writing: a leaflet to explain a project

SPEAKING AND FUNCTIONS
A discussion about how to spend time on a desert island
Discussing which things are best done alone and which are best done with others

LANGUAGE
Grammar: mixed conditionals (review); alternatives to *if*
Vocabulary: expressions with *time*

1 Read and listen

If you set the background information as a homework research task, ask the students to tell the class what they found out.

BACKGROUND INFORMATION

Bob Kull: Frank Robert (Bob) Kull was born on 24 July 1946, in Ventura, California, USA and holds both Canadian and American citizenship. He dropped out of the University of California at Berkeley in the 1970s, did a photography course at the Northern Alberta Institute of Technology in the 1980s and went on to complete a BSc (Psychology, Biology, Environmental Studies) at McGill University. In October 2005 he completed his PhD (Interdisciplinary Studies) at the University of British Columbia. In 2001–2002, he lived in wilderness solitude on a small island off the coast of southern Chile.

Warm up

Books closed. Ask students if they have heard of the book *Robinson Crusoe* by Daniel Defoe, or the film *Cast Away* starring Tom Hanks. Discuss what students would miss if they had to live on a desert island for a year. If they could take three things with them, what would they take? Students discuss their answers in pairs or in small groups. Listen to some of their ideas in open class.

a Books open. Ask students to describe what they can see in the photo and answer the questions. Pre-teach *wilderness* and *settlement*. Students read the introduction to check their ideas.

b In pairs, students discuss how they think Bob Kull spent his time on the island. You may like to give them some ideas of your own to get them started. Monitor and help students with any new vocabulary.

c Students read the extract quickly to see which of their ideas it mentions. Remind them not to worry about every word, but simply to concentrate on the task. Check answers in open class.

Answers
He built a shelter, he went fishing, he walked along the beach. He spent some time reading and writing, but now he spends most of his time contemplating his existence.

d 🔊 Check that students understand the phrases, checking new vocabulary: *wind generator, hummingbird, patch*. Play the recording while students read. You could pause as necessary to check comprehension and clarify any difficulties. Students match phrases 1–8 with spaces A–H. They can compare answers with a partner before feedback in open class.

TAPESCRIPT
See the reading text on page 80 of the Student's Book.

Answers
1 E   2 B   3 G   4 A   5 H   6 D   7 F   8 C

e Ask students to read the sentences and help with any difficulties. Students read the text again and answer the questions. Check answers.

Answers
1 February   2 June   3 November   4 February

f Check students understand the definitions. Ask them to find the words in the text and choose the correct definition. Let them compare answers with a partner before feedback in open class.

Answers
2 is responsible for
3 made an informal visit
4 living arrangements
5 untouched by humans
6 walk casually
7 thick
8 confusing

OPTIONAL ACTIVITY

If your students are interested in music, tell them that there is a popular radio programme in England called *Desert Island Discs*. On the show, celebrities choose the eight records they would take with them if they had to go alone to a desert island. Give students some time to think of the three songs they would take with them. In pairs, students compare their lists and explain the reasons for their choices. Listen to some of the most interesting choices in open class.

Discussion box

Weaker classes: Students can choose one question to discuss.

Stronger classes: In pairs or small groups, students go through the questions in the box and discuss them.

Monitor and help as necessary, encouraging students to express themselves in English and to use any vocabulary they have learned from the text. Ask pairs or groups to feedback to the class and discuss any interesting points further.

2 Speak

Read through the instructions with students. In pairs, students work together to decide how they will fulfil each of the rules. Monitor to help with any difficult vocabulary as they discuss their ideas. You may like to give them some examples for the project they should complete.

Ask different groups to present their ideas to the class and encourage others to comment and ask questions. Try to get the class to come to agreement about the best way to survive on a desert island.

Weaker classes: Weaker students can write their sentences before speaking. Encourage them to look at their notes as little as possible.

3 Grammar
Mixed conditionals (review)

Students covered mixed conditionals in SB4, Unit 9.

a **Weaker classes:** Students should now be quite familiar with conditional sentences, but if you feel they need to be reminded, write the following sentences on the board and ask students which time they refer to:

If I had millions of pounds, I would give it all to charity. (hypothetical present/future)
If I hadn't eaten all that chocolate, I wouldn't have been sick. (hypothetical past)
If you smile at my sister, she goes red. (general fact – past, present and future)
If he doesn't come soon, I will telephone him. (future)

Tell students that sometimes we link past and present with conditionals and write the following examples on the board:

If I hadn't eaten all that chocolate (past), *I wouldn't feel sick now.* (present)
If I had millions of pounds (present), *I wouldn't have had to work.* (past)

Follow procedure for stronger classes.

Stronger classes: Ask students to look at the examples from the text and match the examples with definitions i and ii. Use the examples to point out the present consequence and the general truth. Ask check questions to ensure students understand: *Is the rainforest thick?* (yes); *Has he explored a lot of it?* (no); *Does he know how valuable solitude is?* (yes).

Answers
i 2   ii 1

b Read through the example with students and ask them to tell you the present consequence (*he is feeling lonely*) and the past action (*he didn't speak to anyone last night*). Students rewrite the sentences using one of the mixed conditional patterns and compare answers with a partner before feedback.

Answers
2 If I had caught some fish yesterday, I wouldn't be feeling hungry today.
3 If I was a big reader, I would have brought some books with me.
4 If my camera wasn't broken, I would have taken some pictures today.
5 I wouldn't know it was my birthday if I hadn't brought a calendar with me.
6 My mouth wouldn't be hurting if I hadn't pulled my tooth out yesterday.
7 If my fishing rod wasn't broken, I would have gone fishing this morning.
8 I wouldn't be tired today if I had slept well last night.

Language note
Students may have the impression that there are only four types of conditional (zero, first, second, third). Point out that there are a lot of different types of mixed conditional and write the following examples on the board:

If my friends weren't coming to stay on Saturday (future), *I would have bought some tickets to Paris this weekend* (past).

If Mark had got the job (past), *he would be moving to Berlin next week* (future).

OPTIONAL ACTIVITY

If students need further practice with mixed conditionals, ask them to do the following matching exercise. Students match a beginning from column A with an ending from column B. Let students compare answers with a partner before feedback.

You may like to write each clause on a piece of card, give each student a piece of card and ask them to mingle and find the rest of their sentence. Students must say their clause to other students and not read other cards. As feedback, ask individual students to read their sentence and pay attention to intonation.

A	B
1 *If I had won the lottery*	a *I would have gone out yesterday*
2 *If I had passed all my exams*	b *I would be able to play tennis tonight*
3 *If I spoke Spanish*	c *I would be able to get a job*
4 *If I didn't have an exam this afternoon*	d *I wouldn't have got lost in Madrid*
5 *If I hadn't broken my arm*	e *I would be rich*

Answers

1 e   2 c   3 d   4 a   5 b

Grammar notebook

Remind students to note down the rules for mixed conditionals and to write a few examples of their own.

4 Listen

(a) In small groups, students look at the pictures and discuss the advantages and disadvantages of doing each activity on your own. Encourage them to talk about their own experiences. Ask some students to give examples to the rest of the class.

(b) 🔊 Tell students they are going to listen to three teenagers talk about things they like doing on their own and things they like doing with other people. Play the recording. Students listen and tick the activities in Exercise 4a they talk about. Ask them to compare answers with a partner before checking in class.

TAPESCRIPT

Interviewer   For teenagers nowadays being with a group of friends is even more important than it is for adults. But inevitably, there will always be times when they're on their own, whether they want to be or not. And perhaps one of the most important things of being a teenager is developing an ability to be alone, comfortably and without feeling lonely. We're talking to some teenagers about 'being on your own'. First, Alex. Alex, how do you feel about being on your own?

Boy 1   Well, I really don't mind it, as long as it isn't for an extended period of time, you know? I don't like being alone for long periods of time ...

Interviewer   And what for you would be a 'long period' of time?

Boy 1   Oh, hard to say. I mean, suppose I got home after lunch and there was no one there, that'd be OK until about eight o'clock, I guess – then I'd just have to phone someone, otherwise I'd go crazy!

Interviewer   And what do you do to fill the time when you're alone?

Boy 1   Easy. There's always stuff to do. I can listen to music, read, go for a walk, anything.

Interviewer   All nice things to do.

Boy 1   Yeah, I think so. I mean, it's important to make time to be on your own for a while – it gives you time and space to sort things out a bit and make those decisions that can be difficult.

Interviewer   Do you agree, Judy?

Girl   No, I have to say I don't. I hate being on my own. I always feel like I'm just killing time – it doesn't matter what I'm doing, I'm just killing time until I see some of my friends again, or get together with my sister or something, just to be able to talk and have a laugh. So my mobile is an absolute must for me at all times so that I can keep in touch with people, you know.

Interviewer   So imagine you had to spend a day without seeing anyone, how would you survive?

Girl   Oh, I'd survive, of course. I mean, I wouldn't fall apart or anything like that, you know, I wouldn't start screaming and pulling my hair out but when I'm on my own, it doesn't matter where I am, at home or in town or anywhere, you know, in no time at all I want to be with another person.

Interviewer   So, if you do ever find yourself on your own and with time on your hands, how do you cope – I mean, what kinds of things do you like to do?

Girl   I like to just sit down somewhere by myself and think, think about things that are going on in my life, things I'd like to do in the future – day-dream, I suppose!

Interviewer   Now Harry. Harry, do you think it's important, though, to be able to be alone sometimes?

Boy 2   I do, yes. I mean, everyone needs a bit of privacy now and again, and time to think a bit as well. And there are some things that, you know, you can really only do when you're on your own.

Interviewer   Such as?

Boy 2   Read. Study. Things like that. I reckon being alone is never really a bad thing, provided you've got something positive to do. Like reading, or painting, or practising a musical instrument or something. For me a great way to be alone is to pick up my guitar and just strum a bit – I can happily spend hours doing that.

Interviewer   You wouldn't prefer to play with someone else?

Boy 2   No, that's OK too, just different.

Interviewer   OK, now for all of you – are there any things you couldn't possibly imagine doing alone? Apart from the obvious things like playing tennis, of course!

Boy 2   Watching football on TV – especially if England are playing, you know, got to have someone else there to commiserate with when England lose!

Boy 1   I'd agree with that!

Girl Going to the cinema. On my own? Never!

Boy 1 No, I couldn't go to the cinema on my own unless it was a film I really wanted to see and no one wanted to go with me. Another thing for me would be going on holiday – I'd really want someone to go with.

Interviewer Well, thanks to all of you but I'm afraid our time's up for this week, so goodbye to everyone and thanks very much again.

Answers

Playing the guitar, watching TV

c 🔊 Students read through the sentences and try to fill the gaps, using a pencil so that they can change answers later if necessary. Play the recording again, pausing if necessary to help students complete the sentences. Check answers.

Answers

1 Judy   2 Alex   3 Harry   4 Alex   5 Alex
6 Judy   7 Harry   8 Alex

d In pairs, students talk about their own feelings about being alone. Discuss any interesting answers in class.

5 Vocabulary

More expressions with *time*

Students studied some different expressions with *time* in SB 4, Unit 4.

Warm up

Books closed. Ask students if they know of any expressions with *time*. Write any examples on the board.

a Books open. Read through the sentences with students and ask them to circle the correct answer. If the phrases are unknown, tell them to guess and to use a dictionary to check, if they have time. Let them compare answers with a partner before feedback.

Answers

2 gives   3 killing   4 at   5 no   6 hands   7 up

b Check understanding of *homeless*. Ask students to look at the notices and decide where they might find them. Students discuss answers with a partner before feedback in open class.

Weaker classes: You might like to write the answers on the board in random order for students to choose from.

Answers

1 a launderette
2 a job adverts board
3 a hospital / blood donor service
4 a charity for the homeless
5 a language school

c Ask students to replace the underlined expressions in Exercise 5b with a phrase from the box. Check answers.

Answers

1 make it possible for you   2 find something to do
3 find the time   4 have you got nothing to do?
5 very quickly

Vocabulary notebook

Encourage students to start a new section *Expressions with time* in their notebook and add these words. They may find it useful to note down translations of the words too.

┌─ OPTIONAL ACTIVITY ─────────────
In pairs, students write a short dialogue which contains one or more of the expressions with time. You could ask pairs to act out the dialogue to the class, leaving a gap when they come to the expression with time for the rest of the class to complete.

6 Grammar

Alternatives to *if*

a **Weaker classes:** As an introduction to this topic, ask students to write down an example of each of the four types of conditional sentence using the following prompts:

zero:
first:
second:
third:

Circulate and check students are using the correct forms. Take four examples and write them on the board. Use the sentences to explain the grammatical structures. Ask students if they know of any alternatives to *if*. Follow the procedure for stronger classes.

Stronger classes: Look at sentences 1–6 and focus on the words in bold print. Ask students to work in pairs and go through questions i–iii for each sentence. Point out that for question iii, students may need to change the word order of the sentences to include *if*. As feedback, discuss the answers in open class and use the sentences to clarify answers.

Answers

i   Sentences 1 and 3 are first conditional, 2, 4, 5 and 6 are second conditional
ii Sentences 1, 3 and 4
iii I'd just have to phone someone. If I didn't, I would go crazy.
    If you were spending a day without seeing anyone, how would you survive?
    I couldn't go to the cinema on my own if it wasn't a film I really wanted to see.

b To clarify the meaning of each of the alternatives to *if*, write the following definitions on the board. Ask students to match the definition to the *if* alternative.

on condition that (two answers): (provided that; as long as)
if things had been different: (otherwise)

put yourself in this situation (two answers): **(suppose; imagine)**

except under the circumstances that: **(unless)**

Students read through the sentences and decide which is the correct option. They could work on this in pairs. During feedback, refer back to the definitions on the board and the sample sentences in Exercise 6a to clarify any difficulties.

Answers

2 Suppose   3 unless   4 otherwise   5 Imagine
6 as long as

(c) Look at the example with the class. Point out that we do not need to use *that* when using *provided*. You might want to go through the whole exercise with the class before students write their answers. With weaker classes, give students the first word of each sentence to guide them.

Answers

2 I must get some time to myself, otherwise I'll never finish this book.

3 I don't mind being alone as long as I've got a good book to read.

4 Suppose you got abandoned on a desert island, what would you do?

5 Imagine you had a week of holidays now, what would you do?

6 I would never go on holiday alone unless I had to.

(d) Students rewrite sentences 1, 2 and 3 using *unless*. Point out that the word order and meaning of the sentence may change. Let students compare answers with a partner before feedback.

Answers

1 I won't go to the cinema with you unless you promise to help me with my homework afterwards.

2 Unless I get some time to myself, I'll never finish this book.

3 I don't like being alone unless I've got a good book to read.

(e) Students rewrite sentences 1 and 2 using *as long as*.

Answers

1 I'll go to the cinema with you as long as you promise to help me with my homework afterwards.

2 As long as I get some time to myself, I'll finish this book.

Language note

Students may make the mistake of thinking *unless* always has the same meaning as *if … not*.
This is often true, e.g. *Unless you study, you won't pass the exam* has the same meaning as *If you don't study, you won't pass the exam*.
However, we use *if … not* but not *unless*:
• when we say in the main clause that an action is unexpected

I'll be very surprised if Sally doesn't win.
• in questions
  If Bob doesn't come, what are we going to do?

Grammar notebook

Remind students to note down the rules for alternatives to *if* and to write a few examples of their own.

OPTIONAL ACTIVITY

Ask students to work in pairs and to ask each other questions 2 and 5 from Exercise 6b. Students could also create dialogues starting with one of the other sentences. Listen to some of the dialogues in class.

7 Speak

(a) Students write the numbers of the activities on the grid according to whether they think it is best done alone or with others. Give an example on the board if students are unclear.

(b) Students compare their grids and take it in turns to talk about their reasons. Encourage them to use conditional sentences as much as possible. Circulate and check they are using the language correctly. Ask some students to give examples of conditional sentences to the rest of the class.

8 Song

If you set the background information as a homework research task, ask the students to tell the class what they found out.

BACKGROUND INFORMATION

The Police: Sting (bass and vocals), Andy Summers (guitar) and Stewart Copeland (drums) were the members of this three-piece British new wave band which was strongly influenced by reggae. The group released five albums between 1978 and 1983, all of which gained platinum status. They had five UK number one hit singles including *Walking on the Moon, Message in a Bottle* and *Every Breath You Take*. Their singer Sting went on to become a very popular solo artist.

Message in a Bottle: is a 1979 song by The Police, from their second album, *Regatta de Blanc*. The song can be understood to be about dealing with isolation and loneliness caused by the loss of a loved one, suggesting that everyone has to deal with loss and loneliness as part of the human experience. The island and the bottle are metaphors. The single was The Police's first number one hit in the United Kingdom, but only reached number 74 in the United States.

(a) Ask students to look at the picture and discuss the questions in pairs. Listen to some of their answers in open class.

(b) Read through the words with students, paying attention to pronunciation. Tell them that they are going to hear a song called *Message in a Bottle*, which contains the words, and ask them to discuss how the words might be connected to the title. Allow them to use dictionaries if they are unclear of the meaning of any of the words. Monitor to check students are pronouncing the words correctly and using them in the right context. Listen to some of their ideas in open class.

(c) 🔊 Play the recording. Students listen and complete the sentences with the words from Exercise 8b. Then ask them to read through the lyrics and see if their predictions in Exercise 8a were correct. Let students compare answers in pairs before checking the answers. Play the recording again if necessary, pausing at the answers.

TAPESCRIPT
See the song on page 84 of the Student's Book.

Answers
1 castaway   2 island   3 lonely   4 loneliness
5 rescue   6 SOS   7 SOS   8 note   9 hope
10 washed up   11 shore   12 alone   13 alone
14 castaways   15 home

(d) Students discuss the questions in pairs. Listen to their ideas in open class.

Did you know …?

Read the information in the box with students. Ask students if they know any other songs by The Police or any other songs which are about loneliness.

9 Write

The planning for this exercise can be done in class and the writing can be set as homework.

Warm up

Write *gap year* on the board and elicit the meaning. Ask students what they would like to do in their gap year. Listen to some of their ideas in open class.

(a) Ask students to read through the leaflet and work with a partner to answer the questions. During feedback, write on the board some of the phrases and expressions used in the text to attract the reader. Encourage students to write these in their notebooks.

Answer
The leaflet is advertising an open day for a company which organises projects for gap year students. It attracts readers' interest by having an interesting heading, asking questions, using positive comments from other students, personalisation (it is addressed directly to the reader), inviting the reader to the open day, using imperatives and exclamation marks, offering extra information, making the whole process sound simple, saying "See you soon".

(b) Read through 1–10 with students and explain the meaning of new vocabulary: *rhetorical*, *catchy*, *encouragement*. Ask students to read the leaflet again and decide which occur in a well-written leaflet.

Answers
2, 3, 5, 6, 8, 9, 10 all occur in the example.

(c) Tell students that they are going to write a leaflet and read the instructions. In the planning stage, encourage them to:

- brainstorm ideas and take notes
- experiment with different ways of putting their ideas together to make the leaflet interesting
- ask rhetorical questions
- use catchy slogans
- make the leaflet dynamic by including titles, adjectives and imperatives

OPTIONAL ACTIVITY
Leaflets and brochures are an effective source of authentic English. You may have access to leaflets in English at your local tourist information office. It is a good idea to collect a variety of brochures for use in class. Brochures can be analysed following a similar procedure to Exercise 9 or you can prepare a reading race, in which students have to use the leaflets to find information, e.g. on opening times, price, type of activities and events on offer. The brochures and leaflets can be placed randomly around the room for students to circulate and find the answers.

Module 3 Check your progress

1 Grammar

a 2 I appear to have lost my wallet.
3 He seems to be a bit disappointed with my decision.
4 It was unquestionably a terrible decision.
5 This discovery is undoubtedly the most important for a century.
6 They appear to be very happy about something.
7 It seems we have no chance of winning any more.
8 This has been unquestionably the best day of my life.

b 2 We were tired but we still managed to finish the race.
3 both correct
4 We looked for half an hour but eventually we were able to find a parking space.
5 both correct
6 We had a school uniform but on Fridays we could wear anything.
7 Sorry I wasn't able to come to your party but I was busy.
8 I wasn't able to remember anything.

c 2 Under no circumstances must you tell him where I am.
3 Never have I heard such rubbish.
4 Not only was he late to my party but he forgot to bring any music too.
5 Rarely do I get up before midday on a Sunday.
6 On no account were we allowed to go into the woods.
7 Not only will we get free tickets, we'll get to meet the band too.
8 No sooner had they arrived home than the police car arrived.

d 2 If he didn't know first aid, he wouldn't have saved my life.
3 If I didn't speak Spanish, I wouldn't have understood the film.
4 If I hadn't missed the plane, I would be in Hawaii now.
5 If she wasn't a vegetarian, she would have been able to eat something.
6 If I didn't like children, I wouldn't have enjoyed the party.
7 If I hadn't forgotten to take an aspirin, I wouldn't have a terrible headache.
8 If I hadn't stayed up until 2am, I wouldn't be really tired today.

e 2 I'll tell you everything provided you promise not to say who told you.
3 Suppose it happened to you, what would you do?
4 She must take this antidote, otherwise she'll die before we get to the hospital.
5 Don't use this unless you really have to.
6 If we don't leave now, we'll miss the train.
7 I'll go to the party with you as long as you promise to give me a lift home.
8 I'll never speak to him again if he doesn't apologise.

2 Vocabulary

a 1 yawns
2 bites
3 rub
4 cough
5 blink
6 fiddle
7 stroke

b 2 false
3 true
4 false
5 true
6 true
7 false
8 true

c 2 strength
3 squint
4 breath
5 slouching
6 puny
7 vision
8 short-sighted
9 speed of light

d 2 gives
3 killing
4 at
5 no
6 hands
7 up

How did you do?
Students work out their scores. Check how they have done and follow up any problem areas with revision work for students.

Module 4
Youth and old age

YOU WILL LEARN ABOUT ...

Ask students to look at the pictures on the page. Ask them to read through the topics in the box and check that they understand each item. You can ask them the following questions, in L1 if appropriate:

1 What type of animal is this?
2 When did people wear shoes like these?
3 How do you think the mother and daughter are feeling?
4 How old do you think the man is?
5 Would you recommend anyone to have cosmetic surgery? Why (not)?
6 What are these people performing?

In pairs or small groups, students discuss which topic area they think each picture matches. Check the answers.

Answers
1 Bagpuss, a famous old TV character
2 The Bata Shoe Museum
3 The generation gap between parents and children
4 How old we will live to be in the future
5 The world of cosmetic surgery
6 A trip to the opera

YOU WILL LEARN HOW TO ...

Use grammar

Students read through the grammar points and the examples. Go through the first item with students as an example. In pairs, students now match the grammar items in their book. Check answers.

Answers
Future perfect: She'll probably be sixty before she'll have saved enough money to buy a house!
Future continuous: He certainly won't be voting for that man in the coming elections.
Alternative ways of referring to the future: My brother's off to Australia next month.
Past tenses with hypothetical meaning: It's time we learned to accept new technologies.
Substitution: Viewers were asked to vote and thousands did so.

Use vocabulary

Write the headings on the board. Go through the items in the Student's Book and check understanding. Now ask students if they can think of one more item for the *Life choices* heading. Elicit some responses and add them to the list on the board. Students now do the same for the other headings. Some possibilities are:

Life choices: *settle down, start a family*
Commonly confused words: *advise/advice, raise/rise*
Old and new: *out-of-date, obsolete*
Teenspeak: *totally, busted*

13 The age wars

TOPIC: Differences between young people and old people

TEXTS
Reading and listening: an article about the generation gap
Listening: six people talking about the article about the generation gap
Reading: two poems by D. H. Lawrence and William Shakespeare
Writing: a letter in response to a letter in a magazine

SPEAKING AND FUNCTIONS
A discussion about plans for the future

LANGUAGE
Grammar: future perfect and future continuous (review); alternative ways of referring to the future
Vocabulary: life choices

1 Read and listen

If you set the background information as a homework research task, ask the students to tell the class what they found out.

BACKGROUND INFORMATION

Marbella: is a city in Spain, by the Mediterranean Sea. It is an important beach resort on the Costa del Sol, famous for being the playground of the very wealthy.

Warm up

Books closed. Ask students to choose three members of their family or friends and to think of an adjective to describe each person. In pairs, students describe their families. Listen to some of their examples in open class.

(a) Books open. Look at the photo and title of the article and ask students what they understand by it. Do they think *war* and *battle* are the right words to describe differences between generations?

(b) 🔊 Play the recording while students listen and read the text to order the paragraphs. Ask them to underline the words and phrases which helped them decide on the sequence. Students compare answers with a partner before listening to the recording to check answers. Ask students to explain which words and phrases act as links between the paragraphs.

TAPESCRIPT
See the reading text on page 90 of the Student's Book.

Answers
The paragraphs appear in this order: 1 8 3 7 2 5 4 6

(c) Read through the paragraph with students and ask them to spot four factual mistakes. This can be done as a whole class activity from memory or you may like to let students refer back to the text and compare answers with a partner before feedback.

Answers
Gerry's in his late fifties. He's been working for the company for nearly forty years. He wants to buy a villa in Spain. He wishes his daughter would take her future seriously.

(d) Ask students to write a similar paragraph about Josephine. Encourage them to make notes first and decide on the order in which to present information before writing the final version. If you have an imaginative class, you could ask them to include four factual mistakes and read their profile to a partner for them to spot the mistakes. Monitor and help with vocabulary as required. Listen to a few examples in open class.

If there is not enough time in class, this activity can be done as homework.

(e) Check students understand the definitions. Ask them to find phrases or expressions in the text which have the same meaning. Let them compare answers with a partner before feedback in open class.

Answers
1   read at leisure
2   outside the city centre
3   dirty and in bad condition
4   the smoke that comes out of a car
5   worry about
6   stop working
7   get lost in a world of thoughts
8   in a bad condition

Discussion box
Weaker classes: Students can choose one question to discuss.

Stronger classes: In pairs or small groups, students go through the questions in the box and discuss them.

Monitor and help as necessary, encouraging students to express themselves in English and to use any vocabulary they have learned from the text. Ask pairs or groups to feedback to the class and discuss any interesting points further.

2 Grammar

Future perfect / future continuous (review)

(a) **Weaker classes:** To remind students of the use of the future continuous and future perfect, ask them to imagine where they will be and what they will be doing next Saturday at 7pm. Listen to a few of their ideas and encourage/elicit the use of the future continuous. Write an example on the board and explain to students that we use this tense to express an activity in progress at a particular point in the future.

Ask students to make a list of things they will have achieved in twenty years' time. You may like to give some examples of your own, e.g. *I will have written a book*; *I will have got married*. Encourage students to use the future perfect in their answers. Write an example on the board and explain that we use this tense to express an activity which takes place at some time before a point in the future.

If students have difficulty with these tenses, ask them to write three sentences in each tense, using the examples on the board as a guide. Circulate and ensure students are using tenses correctly. Continue with the procedure for stronger classes.

Stronger classes: Students read the sentences and decide which are examples of the future continuous and which are examples of the future perfect. Check answers and draw attention to the structure of the tenses: *will + be + –ing* (future continuous) and *will + have* + past participle (future perfect).

Answers
1 and 4 are future continuous
2 and 3 are future perfect

(b) Students complete the sentences with the correct tense. Check their answers in open class.

Answers
2 will have finished; will be travelling
3 won't be going
4 will have had; will be trying
5 won't have seen
6 will have moved; will be living
7 will have arrived; will be sleeping
8 will be driving; won't have passed

> **Language note**
> Another use of the future continuous and future perfect is to say what we believe or imagine is happening around now.
> *Bob won't be using his car today – he took the bus to work.*
> *He has such a bad memory – I'm sure he will have forgotten it's my birthday tomorrow.*

Grammar notebook
Remind students to note down the rules for the future perfect and the future continuous and to write a few examples of their own.

3 Listen

(a) In pairs, students discuss the problems mentioned in Exercise 1. Students should use language from the text if possible. Allow students to look back and check if they can't remember the problems or language used.

(b) Tell students they are going to hear six people giving their opinions on the article. Play the recording while students tick the boxes. Ask them to compare answers with a partner before checking in open class.

TAPESCRIPT

1

Speaker 1   I'm 55 and I'm about to lose my job. The reason why? The industrial design company I work for are keen to adopt a younger and more dynamic image. In other words, I'm too old. The truth is, I suspect, that young people are cheaper to employ, which in turn means better profits for the company directors.

There's little chance that I'll find another job in my area at my age, so unlike the Gerry in your story, I'm not looking forward to a comfortable retirement at all. It's true that I was lucky enough to be able to buy a house when I was younger and it's also true that this house is now worth a lot more than I paid for it but that doesn't mean much as where will I live if I sell it? It's not just my house that has risen in value. So please be careful when you write about the age wars. Not all fifty to sixty year-olds are like Gerry. Oh, and I do care about the environment, passionately.

2

Speaker 2   I've just finished my first year at university and I'm thinking of changing courses. I started a degree in business, mainly because it was what my dad wanted me to do. He wants me to be a businessman like him but I've decided that I've got no interest in it at all. I want to do philosophy. The problem is that it's going to be really expensive for me to study. It's going to put at least another £10,000 on my student loans. It'll mean that I have to work part-time, which is something I never wanted to do at university. I think the problem for young people today is that we have to make all our life decisions so early and there's no room for mistakes. I'm 19 and I'm already having to think about things like how I'm going to be able to buy a house and raise a family. It's too early. I just want to enjoy life for a while.

3

Speaker 3 Like all other kinds of war, the age war is just stupid. It's not a war, it's just that we are facing a couple of social problems and it seems easier to blame old people than to sit down and find the solutions. In fact, if people keep on describing this situation as a war, things are bound to get worse.

Firstly, house prices are too high for young people to buy. Next, young people have to pay to go to university. Easy, stop spending taxpayers' money on going to war and start investing in free education again. Finally, old people don't care about the environment. Well, many of us older people do. And it's not as if all young people take it so seriously either. This is the problem that worries me most and we need to unite young and old and middle-aged, all of us, to fight this problem.

4

Speaker 4 I don't know what all the fuss is about. Why's Josephine so worried? Who's going to inherit her father's houses and savings when he dies? She is, of course. She's just lucky to have a father who's able to provide for his family. As for the problem of the environment, well, each generation needs something to complain about, doesn't it? Back then for us in the 60s it was nuclear weapons. It's no different.

5

Speaker 5 In response to what your last caller said, I think he represents exactly the kind of older person who is responsible for all these problems. I can't believe he dismisses global warming as a problem that will just go away if we close our eyes and ignore it. If his generation had thought more carefully about how much energy they were using, they wouldn't be leaving the planet in such a mess for us.

And yes, like Josephine, I am supposed to inherit the family house when my parents pass on but since they are both in excellent health and the average lifespan is getting longer, I could well be in my 60s before this happens. That's more than forty years away. I hope to have finished university, found a job and a husband and had children by then. I don't want to wait around for the family money.

6

Speaker 6 My brother's off to Australia next month. The reason why? He can't afford to buy a house in the UK. He's a computer programmer. It's a good job but he doesn't earn enough to be able to buy somewhere to live. They say that house prices are due to fall but he can't wait any more. It's crazy. He's only 24. I haven't even finished school yet but I'm already thinking about joining him there when I do.

Answers
Speakers 1, 3 and 4 are from Gerry's generation.
Speakers 2, 5 and 6 are from Josephine's generation.

c ◁)) Read through the statements with the class. Students listen to the recording again to decide if statements are true or false. Remind them to correct the false statements.

Answers
1 F (it's because young people are cheaper to employ)
2 F (he would not be able to afford to buy another house and everything is very expensive)
3 F (he has no interest in his business degree)
4 T
5 F (old people are blamed, but they are not the cause)
6 T
7 T
8 F (they are both serious problems)
9 T
10 T
11 F (he can't afford a house)
12 T

4 Grammar
Alternative ways of referring to the future

a Books closed. Tell students that there are various other ways of referring to the future and ask them if they know of any. Write any good examples on the board.

Books open. Read through the examples with students. Ask them to work in pairs and decide which definition best explains the use of the words in bold.

Answers
a Sentences 3 and 5
b Sentence 2
c Sentence 4
d Sentence 1
e Sentence 6

b Students choose the correct option to complete the sentences. Ask them to compare answers with a partner before feedback. During feedback discuss why the other options cannot be correct in these sentences, referring back to the sample sentences and explanations in Exercise 4a.

Answers
2 due to
3 thinking of
4 bound to
5 supposed to
6 about to
7 supposed to
8 about to

Language note
Refer back to Unit 2 and the examples of the future in the past. Point out that the alternative future expressions can all be used to refer to the future in the past by using *was/were*, e.g.
We were due to leave at seven o'clock.
I was about to call John when I remembered he was away.

OPTIONAL ACTIVITY

At the beginning of Exercise 4, write the following instructions on the board:

Think of:
Something you are going to do soon
Somewhere you are going soon
Something that is going to happen
Something you think will definitely happen

Ask students to write a sentence for each of the above using a future tense. They should be able to write sentences with *will* and *going to*. Listen to a few answers but don't comment at this stage. After Exercises 4a and 4b, ask students to rewrite their sentences using some of the alternatives to the future.

Grammar notebook
Remind students to note down the rules for alternative ways of referring to the future and to write a few examples of their own.

5 Vocabulary
Life choices

Warm up

Books closed. To introduce the topic of life choices, write *The River of Life* at the top of the board and a wavy line (to represent a river) below it. Draw several points on the line and tell students that the line represents your life (or the life of a friend) and the points are important events in that life. Describe the important events to the students and either write words or draw a picture at each point on the line to represent them. Ask students to do the same in their notebooks and describe their own "river of life" to a partner. Monitor and help with vocabulary as necessary.

(a) Books open. Students match the verbs 1–8 with the words a–h. Point out that the expressions cannot always be translated literally into other languages and that the words should be learnt together as they have a different meaning from when they are used separately.

Answers
2 c   3 c   4 b, d   5 e, f, g   6 a, f, g   7 f, g
8 f, g

OPTIONAL ACTIVITY

Ask students to work in pairs and order the eight expressions according to when they normally take place in someone's life. Ask them if they think this is the best order to do things and if they know anyone who has done the things in a different order and listen to some of their information in open class.

(b) Students complete the gaps in the text with the expressions. Let them compare their answers with a partner before feedback. With stronger classes, you may like to ask them to try to complete the text without looking back at Exercise 5a before looking back to check answers.

Answers
2 settle down   3 start a family   4 left school
5 changed careers   6 take early retirement

OPTIONAL ACTIVITY

Ask students to predict when they will do each of the activities and to write sentences using the future continuous and future perfect, e.g. *By 2020 I will have started a family; I will be paying off my student loan until I am 30.* In pairs, students compare sentences. Listen to some of their ideas in open class and encourage comment.

Vocabulary notebook
Encourage students to start a new section *Life choices* in their notebook and add these words. They may find it useful to note down translations of the words too.

6 Speak

(a) Students discuss who they think is asking each question, who to and why.

(b) Students discuss how their grandparents would have answered the questions differently. After discussion in pairs, hold a class discussion about how life choices have changed since their grandparents' time.

Literature in mind

7 Read

If you set the background information as a homework research task, ask the students to tell the class what they found out.

BACKGROUND INFORMATION

D. H. Lawrence: born on 11 September 1885, David Herbert Lawrence was an important and controversial English writer of the 20th century, whose prolific and diverse output included novels, short stories, poems, plays, essays, travel books, paintings, translations, literary criticism and personal letters. Lawrence's unsettling opinions earned him many enemies and he endured official persecution and censorship. He is now generally valued as a visionary thinker and a significant representative of modernism in English literature, although some feminists often object to the attitudes toward women found in his works. He died on 2 March 1930.

William Shakespeare: was an English poet and playwright widely regarded as the greatest writer of the English language. He wrote approximately 38 plays and 154 sonnets, as well as a variety of other poems, and it is generally believed that Shakespeare produced most of his work between 1586 and 1612. Shakespeare is the most quoted writer in the literature and history of the English-speaking world, and many of his quotations and words have passed into everyday usage in English and other languages. He died on 23 April 1616.

Beautiful Old Age: is a poem by D. H. Lawrence published in 1929 in a collection of poems entitled *Pansies*.

Warm up

Write *D. H. Lawrence* and *William Shakespeare* on the board and ask students what they know about them. Listen to some of their ideas in open class.

(a) Tell students they are going to read two poems and decide if the writer is positive or negative about growing old. Tell them not to worry about difficult vocabulary at this stage.

Answers
Poem a is positive. Poem b is negative.

(b) Students read poem a again and find words to match the meanings. Let them use dictionaries for help if necessary and to compare answers with a partner before feedback.

Answers
1 wrinkled   2 undaunted   3 soothing   4 fragrant
5 dim

(c) Read through the poem with the class, pausing to help with difficult vocabulary: *ripe, fulfilment, unsoured*. In pairs, students find the parts of the poem with a strong link between people and nature, and discuss why the poet does this. Listen to some of their ideas in open class.

Answers
Links: *ripe, ripen like apples, scented like pippins, like apples, fragrant like yellowing leaves, stillness and satisfaction of autumn, faced all weathers.*
The poet is saying that everything in the natural world grows old and that some things are at their best when they have ripened.

(d) Tell students that poem b was written over 400 years ago and includes some language which is very rare in modern English. Ask students to read poem b again but not to worry about the unknown words. With a partner, students discuss what they understand by the poem. Can they understand it despite the old-fashioned language? Listen to some of their ideas, before asking them to match the words 1–8 with their meanings. Check answers.

Answers
2 g   3 f   4 e   5 h   6 d   7 a   8 b

(e) Read through the poem with students to check comprehension and deal with difficult vocabulary: *morn, bare, nimble, lame, defy, stay'st*. In pairs, students discuss why the poem talks about age and youth as if they were people. Listen to some of their answers.

Answers
Students' own answers

(f) In pairs, students discuss the questions. Encourage them to use language from the poems to support their ideas. This task could be extended into a class discussion or a debate on the importance of poetry and whether it is a good way of expressing feelings.

8 Write

The planning for this exercise can be done in class and the writing can be set as homework.

(a) Tell students they are going to read a letter to a newspaper which is a response to the article in Exercise 1. Pre-teach *smug, prohibitive, struggling*. Ask students to read the letter quickly and answer the questions and compare answers with a partner before checking answers in open class.

Answers
1   She is a younger person.
2   By increasing taxation on second homes.
3   She says a lot of the money raised through taxation is spent on the military and it should be spent on education.
4   The environment.

(b) Read through the first sentence of the letter with students and ask them to underline grammar points 1 and 2.

Answers
1 I was intrigued   2 entitled

(c) Students read the letter again and find further examples of the grammar points. Let them compare answers with a partner before feedback in open class.

Answers
passive voice: are denied, is suggested
past participle used as adjective after a noun:
included, concerned

(d) Tell students they are going to write a letter in response to a letter they have read in a magazine. Read through the three letters with students. Ask them to choose one of the letters and write a reply. They can choose whether to agree or disagree. Encourage students to plan their letters carefully and

- use the letter in Exercise 8a as an example
- include an introduction and a conclusion
- include several examples to support their point of view
- start with *Dear Sir* and end with *Yours faithfully*

14 The beauty hunters

Unit overview

TOPIC: Ways of becoming and staying young and beautiful

TEXTS
Reading and listening: an article about the advantages and disadvantages of cosmetic surgery
Listening: a scientist talking about biogerentology
Speaking and listening: a group of musicians discussing an album cover
Writing: differences between a report and an article

SPEAKING AND FUNCTIONS
A discussion about whether it's better to look beautiful or not
A discussion about biogerentology

LANGUAGE
Grammar: past tenses with hypothetical meaning
Vocabulary: commonly confused words
Pronunciation: stress and intonation

1 Read and listen

If you set the background information as a homework research task, ask the students to tell the class what they found out.

BACKGROUND INFORMATION

Cosmetic surgery: dates back to the ancient world where doctors in ancient India were utilising skin grafts for reconstructive work as early as the 8th century BC. The Romans were able to perform simple techniques such as repairing damaged ears from around the 1st century BC. The New Zealander Sir Harold Gillies developed many of the techniques of modern plastic surgery in caring for those who suffered facial injuries in World War I. He is considered to be the father of modern plastic surgery.

Warm up

Books closed. Ask students to name any famous people who have had cosmetic surgery. Do students think it looks good? Would they consider having cosmetic surgery done? What would they have done? Listen to some of their ideas in open class.

(a) Books open. In pairs, students make a list of the advantages and disadvantages of cosmetic surgery. Write some of their ideas on the board.

(b) Tell students they are going to read a magazine article about cosmetic surgery. Read through titles 1–6 to check understanding. Students skim through the article quickly and match the titles with the paragraphs. Tell them not to worry about difficult words, but to concentrate on the task. Check answers.

Answers
1 E   2 F   3 D   4 C   5 A   Title B is not used.

Did you know …?

Read through the information in the box with students. Invite comments. You may like to do a survey to find out how many students would consider having cosmetic surgery and to find out which operations are thought to be most acceptable.

(c) 🔊 Students read the text again and find out who mentions sentences 1–8. Let students compare their answers with a partner before playing the recording to check answers, pausing for clarification where necessary. During feedback, ask students to point out the part of the text that led them to choose their answer.

TAPESCRIPT
See the reading text on pages 96 and 97 of the Student's Book.

Answers
1 Sue Kennedy
2 Dr Ken Berrick / Debbie Caron
3 Sue Kennedy
4 Danny Glass
5 Dr Elisabeth McKenna
6 Dr Ken Berrick
7 Dr Elisabeth McKenna
8 Danny Glass

(d) Read through the words and the definitions with the class. Ask students to look back at the text and match the words to their definitions. Students compare answers with a partner before feedback in open class.

Answers
2 a   3 h   4 f   5 g   6 b   7 c   8 e

OPTIONAL ACTIVITY

If you would like your students to do some further work on the vocabulary in the text, you can use the following exercise. Write the following definitions on the board and ask students to find words and expressions with the same meaning in the text. The words are in the order of the text. To make the exercise more challenging, you could write them on the board in a different order.

1 *to summarise*
2 *it makes me very happy to say*
3 *nearly all*
4 *improved how they think about themselves*
5 *to get old*
6 *I'm glad I spent my money*
7 *I haven't changed*
8 *just after*
9 *despite the fact that*
10 *it upsets me*

Answers
1 in short
2 I can say with great satisfaction
3 the overwhelming majority
4 raised their self-esteem
5 to age
6 I don't regret a penny of it
7 it's the same old me underneath
8 immediately following
9 even though
10 it makes me really angry

Discussion box

Weaker classes: Students can choose one question to discuss.

Stronger classes: In pairs or small groups, students go through the questions in the box and discuss them.

Monitor and help as necessary, encouraging students to express themselves in English and to use any vocabulary they have learned from the text. Ask pairs or groups to feedback to the class and discuss any interesting points further.

---

2 Grammar

Past tenses with hypothetical meaning

Warm up

Books closed. Write the word *hypothetical* on the board and ask students what they understand by the term (theoretical, imaginary, unreal). Ask students to work in pairs and think of three hypothetical situations. Encourage them to be as imaginative as they like! Listen to some of their ideas in open class and ask the other students if they would like to be in the situation and why / why not. Try to elicit some of the hypothetical language from Exercise 2.

(a) Books open. Read through the sentences from the text and answer the questions. Point out the use of the past tenses and *would*. Students work in pairs to answer the questions. Check answers.

Answers
1 Sentence d
2 Present

(b) Read through the rules with students. You may like to complete the rule in open class and deal with any problems of understanding.

Rule

desire, annoyance, change, emphasise, preference

If students are confident with the structures, ask them to think of their own examples in each case.

(c) Look at the example with the class. Ask students to rewrite the sentences using the words in brackets. Students compare answers with a partner before feedback.

Answers
2 I'd rather you didn't interrupt me while I was speaking.
3 I wish you would listen to what I say!
4 If only we knew his name.
5 It's time we made a decision.
6 I wish I had enough time.
7 I'd rather you didn't drive so fast.
8 If only I could make her understand.

(d) Divide the class into pairs and give each partner a letter, A or B. Read through the instructions and the sample dialogue. Elicit further possible answers, encouraging students to use different hypothetical structures. Students create their own dialogues using sentences 1–5 and then change roles. Circulate and ensure students are using the structures correctly. Ask a few pairs to give some examples as feedback.

Language note

In unreal hypothetical sentences, after *I'd rather / I wish / If only* we can use *were* after any subject, including *I*, *he*, *she* and *it*. This use of *were* is sometimes called the past subjunctive and is generally used only in formal contexts. In spoken English we normally use *was* instead of *were*. The only case when *were* is preferred to *was* is with *If I were you, I would …*

OPTIONAL ACTIVITY

Ask students to imagine they have committed a crime and been put in prison for twenty years. They now regret their crime. Ask students to work in pairs and think of things that they might say. Give them examples to get them started: *I wish I hadn't robbed that bank; If only I was at home with my wife; I'd rather be lying on a beach than in this prison*. Circulate and help with vocabulary as necessary. Listen to a few examples in open class as feedback.

Grammar notebook

Remind students to note down the rules for past tenses with hypothetical meaning and to write a few examples of their own.

3 Listen and speak

(a) Students look at the photos. Ask students to discuss the questions in pairs. Also ask them how older people keep looking and feeling young, and how they will do so in the future. Discuss answers in open class, but do not comment at this stage.

(b) 🔊 Tell students they are going to listen to a biogerentologist. Before listening, ask students to say what they think a biogerentologist is. Play the recording while students listen and make a note of the most surprising things he says. Students compare answers with a partner before feedback.

TAPESCRIPT

Interviewer Professor Elliott, you are among the leading experts in the field of biogerentology. A rather complicated name for a scientific area that should surely interest us all, and has recently been the focus of a lot of controversy. Could you briefly explain to our listeners first what you actually do?

Guest Certainly. Biogerentology is about extending the happiness of a healthy life to as many people as possible, for as long as possible.

Interviewer Right. Living long and being able to fully enjoy life – I assume that's what everyone wants. But why has there been so much controversy about it recently?

Guest Well, to cut a long story short we can say that the big battle of the 21st century will probably be the battle over life and death. The question isn't about whether we will be able to live longer any more. The question is: will scientists be given permission to develop measures that can significantly extend human lives? Will we, for example, be allowed to continue research in the area of therapeutic cloning to produce stem cells, or will mankind decide that there are moral boundaries which should not be transgressed?

Interviewer Certainly very important questions which we can't answer here and now. But could you elaborate on how feasible this all is? I mean, we would all like to live longer, and look 10, 20 or 30 years younger than we are. And we want to enjoy life, and not have any illnesses – will all these wishes remain illusions forever, or will there be a day when they actually come true?

Guest Most certainly, and probably very soon.

Interviewer You sound very sure! Can you give some concrete examples, please?

Guest Well, imagine a typical scenario of a family reunion in the year 2090. Think of a big family of five generations coming together.

Interviewer Five generations. You must be joking!

Guest That's exactly the point. I'm not joking at all. Let's imagine that they're meeting for a weekend in a beautiful hotel near the sea somewhere. Imagine great-great-great-grandma going swimming with her great-great-great-grandson who's celebrating his 25th birthday, the reason for the family reunion.

Interviewer A 25-year-old and his great-great-great-grandma. That's a bit unlikely, isn't it?

Guest Not at all. The great-great-great-grandma is 164, and her great-great-great-grandson has just turned 25. That's a very realistic scenario – but what's fascinating about it is that they are going swimming in the sea together, and the 'old' lady is as fit as the 25-year-old, her skin as elastic and glowing, her muscle tone as firm and supple.

Interviewer What about her cognitive skills? At the age of 164, would she still be able even to recognise her relatives? Wouldn't she be totally senile?

Guest Not at all. After the swim the two of them sit down for a meal, and they have a conversation about an academic subject she has recently started to study, and her memory is as acute as the 25-year-old she's talking to.

Interviewer A fascinating scenario – so what do we need to do to make it all come true?

Guest What I've suggested is more than realistic. We can actually expect major breakthroughs in human, plant and animal biology within the next two decades, and they'll all work together to support the aim of giving humans the chance to live considerably longer.

Interviewer Will we all have to eat pills instead of food? And what kind of society will we live in? Won't there be lots of social conflicts between the haves and the have-nots, the ones who will never be able to afford the idyllic scenario you are talking about?

Guest Very good questions. Let's look at nutrition first: we'll eat as well as we always have, better, in fact. Our food will contain all kinds of nutrients, but it will also contain medication the elderly people need on a daily basis to repair damage to their ageing cells.

Interviewer What about illnesses?

Guest Well, thanks to new discoveries in genetic sciences people will have stronger immune systems, more athletic bodies and cleverer brains. And what is most important, genetic diseases such as Alzheimer's will be a thing of the past. Another example: scientists have recently managed to basically 'turn off' the genes for producing bad cholesterol in monkeys. If this works for humans, and there seems to be every reason to believe it will, then it could significantly reduce the rate of heart disease.

But let me come back to a question of yours that I haven't had a chance to answer yet, and that is the kind of society we'll live in. To put it in a nutshell, the world will be cleaner and greener, and a more peaceful place. Individuals will have a lot more choice through biotechnical pharmaceuticals and we'll finally overcome the limitations imposed on us by our genes, our evolution and our environment.

Answers
Students' own answers

c 🔊 Read through the sentences with the class and check any difficult vocabulary: *prolonging* and *acute*. Play the recording and ask students to choose the correct answers. Let them compare answers in pairs before checking in open class. If necessary, play the recording again with pauses during feedback.

Answers
1 a 2 b 3 b 4 c 5 a

d Read through the questions and divide the class into pairs or small groups. Students discuss the questions. Circulate and help with vocabulary as necessary. Ask different groups to report back to the class and invite others to comment.

Weaker classes: Before the discussion, you may like to go through the questions briefly and make sure that students have understood the main points of the recording before discussing in pairs.

OPTIONAL ACTIVITY

If students are interested in this area, write the following sentence on the board:
In order to prolong life, scientists should be allowed to do research into cloning and develop ways of extending human life.

Divide the class into two groups, one in favour of the statement, the other against. Give each group a set amount of time to organise their arguments, then ask them to debate the topic. Encourage as many people as possible to give their opinions.

---

4 Vocabulary
Commonly confused words

a Tell students that all the words in this exercise are commonly confused. Ask them to read the sentences and choose the correct word to complete them. If they aren't sure of some answers, ask them to guess or check in a dictionary if they have time. During feedback, explain the meaning of the incorrect option in each case. You may like to ask students to write sentences including the incorrect options.

Answers
2 affect 3 sensitive 4 sensible 5 advise
6 advice 7 raised 8 risen

b Check that students understand the words in the box. Ask them to complete the sentences and to check their answers with a partner before feedback in open class.

Answers
2 lose 3 lie 4 lay 5 insure 6 ensure
7 persecuted 8 prosecute

c Ask students if there are any other English words that they regularly confuse. Give an example of your own, e.g. *kitchen* and *chicken*, *cook* and *cooker* are commonly confused. Listen to any examples in open class. Recommend to students that they type 'commonly confused words' into an Internet search engine for help and advice on words that they may confuse.

Vocabulary notebook
Encourage students to start a new section *Commonly confused words* in their notebook and add these words. They may find it useful to note down translations of the words too.

5 Speak and listen
Warm up

Books closed. Ask students to work in pairs and discuss their favourite CD covers. Ask some students to describe their favourite covers to the class.

a Books open. Students look at the three possible covers and decide which one they like best. In open class, ask some students to describe the covers and explain the reasons for their choice. You may like to hold a class vote on the best cover.

b 🔊 Tell students they are going to listen to three members of the band discussing the covers. Students listen and answer the question. Tell students not to worry about understanding every word, but just to focus on the task.

TAPESCRIPT
Girl 1 ... so these are the three options they've given us, and we need to let them know what we think by about the end of the week so they can ...
Boy I haven't really had much of a chance to look at them yet ...
Girl 2 No, nor me.
Girl 1 Well, none of us have really. Tell you what, let's just kind of spread them out – like ... this ... and then we can ...
Girl 2 OK. Wow, they're all right, aren't they?
Boy Not bad. I really don't like this one, though.
Girl 1 What – the one with the lake and everything?
Boy Yeah.
Girl 2 I thought it was quite nice – I mean, it's not my favourite but it's not too bad.
Boy But it's too pretty, isn't it? I mean, you know, we're called Liverpool Hotel and this picture's got nothing to do with hotels or Liverpool or anything.
Girl 2 True. But on the other hand, is it so important to have a picture that's got something to do with the band name?
Boy I'd have thought it was vital. It's our first CD, after all, so we need to ...
Girl 1 No, I don't think it's so important really.
Boy The thing is, we've got to choose the one that really says something about us as a band, don't you reckon?

Girl 2 Well, yeah, you might be right.

Girl 1 OK, well, to be honest, I don't think any of these say much about us.

Boy No? Not even the one in the room?

Girl 2 This one? It's a bit gloomy, isn't it? Look at it, brown and grey and dark ...

Boy Exactly – just like our songs! That's what's so good about it!

Girl 1 He's got a point, I suppose.

Girl 2 Hmm. Yeah, OK, I can see where you're coming from. So you think the mountain one's too pretty?

Boy Yes! Look at this writing in the water here, I mean what's that got to do ...

Girl 1 I think we're going round in circles a bit here, aren't we?

Girl 2 Hang on, Colin hasn't finished yet.

Boy No, it's OK.

Girl 1 Well, are we saying then that this one's the best – the one outside the hotel?

Boy What do you think, Trace?

Girl 2 I like it. It's cool. I really like the way they've put 'Liverpool' next to the hotel sign.

Boy I can live with it.

Girl 2 Is it really our decision anyway?

Girl 1 Well, to tell you the truth, no, I don't think it is entirely. I mean, the record company's bound to use the one they want, but I think we can influence them – they certainly said they wanted to know how we feel, anyway.

Boy OK – so let's tell them we go for the second one, the one outside the hotel.

Girl 2 Yeah? Everyone OK with that?

Girl 1 OK.

Boy Yeah, all right ...

Answer

The second one – the one outside the hotel

c 📢 Read through the phrases in the box with students and check understanding. Play the recording again. Students listen and complete the sentences with the expressions in the box. If necessary play the recording again during feedback, pausing for clarification. Pay particular attention to the intonation used with these expressions.

Answers

1 tell you what
2 I mean
3 on the other hand
4 the thing is
5 to be honest
6 to tell you the truth
7 we're going round in circles
8 I'd have thought
9 exactly
10 though

d In pairs, students match the phrases to their uses. Check answers in open class.

Answers

2 to introduce a contrasting idea *on the other hand*
3 to try to get the conversation back to the main topic *we're going round in circles*
4 to give an opinion *I'd have thought, the thing is, I mean*
5 to add the idea of contrast after stating a fact or opinion *though*
6 to introduce and soften a negative fact or opinion *to tell you the truth, to be honest*
7 to agree with what someone has said *exactly*

e Divide the class into small groups. Tell them to imagine that they are going to start a new school magazine and that they have to choose one of the three covers. Circulate to ensure students are using the phrases from Exercise 5c in the correct context and with suitable intonation.

f Tell students to imagine they are organising a charity event. In small groups, they discuss which of the three prizes would be best. Ask some of the groups to explain their choices in open class and invite other students to comment.

6 Pronunciation

Stress and intonation

a 📢 Students turn to page 122 and read the sentences. Ask them to say the sentences and mark where the stress should be. Play the recording to check answers.

TAPESCRIPT / ANSWERS

1 The <u>thing</u> is, ...
2 On the <u>other</u> hand, ...
3 <u>Tell</u> you <u>what</u>, ...
4 To be <u>honest</u>, ...
5 To <u>tell</u> you the <u>truth</u>, ...
6 We're going <u>round</u> in <u>circles</u>.

b 📢 Play the recording, pausing after each sentence for students to repeat. Encourage them to produce the same intonation patterns as on the recording. Pay particular attention to whether the speaker's voice goes up or down at the end of the phrase.

7 Write

The planning for this exercise can be done in class and the writing can be set as homework.

If you set the background information as a homework research task, ask the students to tell the class what they found out.

BACKGROUND INFORMATION

Tate Britain: is the national gallery of British art and works actively to promote interest in British art internationally. Located in London, it is one of the family of four Tate galleries which display selections from the Tate Collection. The displays at Tate Britain show the development of art in Britain from the time of the Tudor monarchs in the sixteenth century, to the present day.

Tate Modern: is the national gallery of international modern art and was created in 2000 from a disused power station in the heart of London. The Tate Modern displays the national collection of international modern art. This is defined as art since 1900. Tate Modern includes modern British art where it contributes to the story of modern art, so major modern British artists may be found at both Tate Modern and Tate Britain.

The National Gallery: is an art gallery in London, located on the north side of Trafalgar Square. It houses Western European paintings from 1250 to 1900. The collection of 2,300 paintings belongs to the British public, and entry to the main collection is free, although there are charges for entry to special exhibitions.

Warm up

Write *report* and *article* on the board. In pairs, students discuss what each of the pieces of writing is. What is the purpose of each? What do they look like? What type of language do they contain? Listen to some of their ideas, but do not comment at this stage.

(**a**) Read through the descriptions of reports and articles with the class and check the understanding of *judge*, *sub-titles*, *unambiguous*. Ask students to write numbers 1–8 in the table and check answers in open class, giving examples where necessary to clarify.

Answers

	report	article
What is it?	7	1
What is its main purpose?	4	2
What is its layout / visual appearance?	5	6
What is its style?	8	3

(**b**) Tell students they are going to write a report or an article based on a project called *Art in London*.

Read through the notes with students and check any difficult vocabulary: *accessible*, *principal*, *in principle*, *outcomes*, *deadline*. Students choose whether to write a report or an article. Give students some time in class to plan their writing and to make sure they have included all the points from Exercise 7a.

In a subsequent lesson, ask students to look at each other's pieces of writing to see if all the points in Exercise 7a have been included. If you take the work to mark, you could make a note of any particularly good work and point this out to the class.

15 Days gone by

Unit overview

TOPIC: Unusual museums

TEXTS
Reading and listening: an article about the People's Museum
Listening: a radio programme called *Our Heritage*
Reading: an article about three unusual museums
Writing: notes

SPEAKING AND FUNCTIONS
Discussing the best place for a school trip
Choosing three items to represent *Our Heritage*

LANGUAGE
Grammar: substitution; ellipsis
Vocabulary: old and new

1 Read and listen

If you set the background information as a homework research task, ask the students to tell the class what they found out.

BACKGROUND INFORMATION

The People's Museum: is a unique programme from the BBC, for which members of the public searched through the nation's museums, galleries, churches and stately homes to find a selection of the most treasured items. The series re-ignited interest in local museums and galleries, and gave the public a chance to see and learn about hidden treasures they never knew existed. Added to this was the interactive element where viewers voted each week for their favourite item to go into the virtual museum.

Bagpuss: was a children's television programme, first shown in 1974. Although only 13 episodes were made, the programme was so popular that the series was repeated 27 times to successive generations. Bagpuss is a toy cat who spends his time sleeping in a shop owned by a little girl called Emily. The shop itself doesn't sell anything – each week Emily brings in objects that people have lost. Bagpuss will wake up and examine them, in the company of his friends. In 1999 *Bagpuss* was named the country's favourite BBC children's programme of all time, beating off the challenge of modern TV programmes such as the *Teletubbies*.

Suffragettes: from the middle of the 19th century many women campaigned to obtain the right to vote. These women were known as Suffragettes and carried out direct action such as chaining themselves to railings, setting fire to the contents of mailboxes, smashing windows and on occasions setting off bombs. They organised themselves into groups, held meetings, sent petitions to Parliament and tried to persuade MPs to change the law to enable them to vote. Many Suffragettes were imprisoned and went on hunger strikes. Women in the United Kingdom were finally given the vote on the same terms as men in 1928.

The Supermarine Spitfire: was an iconic British single-seat fighter used primarily by the Royal Air Force and many Allied countries through World War II and into the 1950s. Its design allowed a higher top speed than the other contemporary designs. It remains one of the classic fighter aircraft of all time, and certainly one of the most instantly recognisable. In the United Kingdom it has become known as the aeroplane that saved the country in the Battle of Britain.

Warm up

Books closed. Ask students to work in pairs and make a list of museums that they have visited and to discuss what they saw there. Listen to some of their answers in open class. Ask students to think of adjectives to describe museums and write some of their ideas on the board.

a Books open. Students look at the items in the photos and decide in which type of museum they would find them and why they would be there. Look at the example sentence and ask students to write similar sentences about the other objects. Listen to some of their ideas and elicit anything they know about the objects.

b Tell students they are going to read a description of a museum called the People's Museum. Students read the text quickly and match the pictures to a paragraph. Remind them not to worry about every word, but to concentrate on the task. Let them compare answers with a partner before feedback.

Answers
a 4   b 6   c 6   d 7   e 4   f 5

c 🔊 Read through sentences 1–8 and check understanding. Play the recording, while students listen and find sentences or phrases with the same meaning as sentences 1–8.

See the reading text on pages 102 and 103 of the Student's Book.

Answers

1 Unfortunately all too often these remain unappreciated, gathering dust, unnoticed by the wider public.
2 Furthermore – no admission charges.
3 the majority of artefacts were chosen from small, regional museums
4 Other objects put forward were from a less distant past.
5 perhaps last century's biggest brain
6 stands head and shoulders above the rest
7 My colleagues did not really expect the plane to win, and frankly neither did I.
8 there are rumours of a part two

— OPTIONAL ACTIVITY —————————

If you would like students to do further comprehension work on the text, write the following questions on the board:

1 *What does the text suggest are two possible views of museums?*
2 *How did they decide what to put in the museum?*
3 *Which item should always be found in a British museum?*
4 *Why did the Spitfire win?*
5 *Why do they want to make a new series?*

Students read the text again and write their answers using their own words. Students compare answers with a partner before open class feedback.

Answers

1 Dull and depressing and full of boring objects / places full of treasures, where we can contrast past and present.
2 Reporters chose items that should go in. Viewers then voted for their favourites.
3 The works of Shakespeare.
4 It is a sign of Britain's spirit that we should never forget.
5 To show the importance of remembering what has gone before.

Discussion box

Weaker classes: Students can choose one question to discuss.

Stronger classes: In pairs or small groups, students go through the questions in the box and discuss them.

Monitor and help as necessary, encouraging students to express themselves in English and to use any vocabulary they have learned from the text.
Ask pairs or groups to feedback to the class and discuss any interesting points further. If students are interested in the idea of a People's Museum for their country, you could develop this into a project.
Divide the class into small groups and give students time to research the objects they have chosen. In a

subsequent lesson, each group gives a presentation to the rest of the class. Hold a vote to find out which are the most popular objects.

2 **Grammar**

Substitution: *the ones / so*

(a) **Weaker classes:** Explain to students that, in order to make written English less repetitive, we substitute words or ideas with other words. Write the following groups of sentences on the board:

I like all types of films. I like films with happy endings. I like films where the hero is killed.
I asked my students to do their homework.
My students did their homework.
My brother wore a red hat. I wore a red hat.

Ask students to work in pairs and turn each group of sentences into one sentence, avoiding repetition as much as possible. Listen to some of their ideas and elicit the following:

I like all types of films, both the ones with happy endings and those where the hero is killed.
I asked my students to do their homework and they did so.
My brother wore a red hat and so did I.

Point out that *the ones* can also be singular (*the one*) and *those* becomes *that* to refer to one thing. Explain that we say *neither did I* to refer to a negative.

Follow the procedure for stronger classes.

Stronger classes: Read through the examples with students and ask them to decide what the words in bold refer to. Students discuss in pairs. Check answers.

Answers

2 small regional museums
3 an important function
4 voted
5 restoring interest
6 there will be another series
7 didn't expect the plane to win
8 voted for the Spitfire

(b) Rule a: 4, 5 + 6
Rule b: 7 + 8
Rule c: 2
Rule d: 1 + 3

(c) Students rephrase the underlined parts of the sentences. Ask them to compare answers with a partner before feedback.

Answers

2 I don't think the museums in London are as interesting as those / the ones in Rome.
3 The museum's collection of medals isn't as good as that of coins.
4 I want to go there and no one is going to prevent me from doing so.

5 I had always wanted to visit the Science Museum, and last week I did so.
6 'Will James come with us?' 'No, I don't think so / I think not.'

> **Language note**
> The opposite of *I think so* is *I don't think so* or, formally, *I think not*.
>
> Students may make the mistake of thinking the opposite of *I hope so* is **I don't hope so*. Point out that this is not correct and that the opposite of *I hope so* is *I hope not*.

Grammar notebook
Remind students to note down the rules for substitution and to write a few examples of their own.

OPTIONAL ACTIVITY
If students find substitution difficult, you may like to give them some further examples. Write the following sentences on the board. Ask students to decide on the correct answer. Students compare answers with a partner before feedback in open class. During feedback, pay close attention to structures and deal with any questions.

1 *The mountains in Spain are not as high as that / those in Switzerland.* (those)
2 *Will it take a long time to finish? Well, it might do / do so.* (do)
3 *He doesn't like swimming and neither do I / don't I.* (do I)
4 *Is John coming on Tuesday? I hope not / I don't hope so.* (I hope not.)
5 *I didn't want to go to France and so / neither did my sister.* (neither)
6 *I really like cows. I especially like the one / the ones with big brown eyes.* (the ones)

3 Speak

Warm up

In open class, ask students what they think a good day out should include. Elicit ideas and write them on the board. The list should include the following: *things to look at, things to do, educational, fun, exciting, memories, photos, shopping.*

Divide the class into groups of five and tell them that they are going to plan a school trip. Each student chooses one of the activities and argues why this should be chosen. You may like to give students some thinking time before starting the discussion. Encourage students to refer to the list on the board for ideas. Circulate and help with vocabulary as necessary. After a few minutes, hold a class discussion and a vote to decide which trip would be best.

4 Listen

If you set the background information as a homework research task, ask the students to tell the class what they found out.

BACKGROUND INFORMATION
Titanic: in 1997, James Cameron directed this film, which was based on the sinking of the *Titanic* in 1912. It starred Kate Winslet and Leonardo DiCaprio. The film won 11 Oscars including best film and best director and is the most successful film of all time, grossing an incredible $1,835,300,000 at the box office.

a Look at the photos with students and ask which of them they think should be in a museum. Pre-teach *heritage*. Tell students they are going to listen to a programme called *Our Heritage*. Play the recording while students listen and answer the questions. Let them compare answers with a partner before feedback.

TAPESCRIPT
Presenter Good evening, and welcome to *Our Heritage*. It's the programme where we invite ordinary people like you and me to talk about artefacts that they have in their own homes – or that can be found in the town or city where they live – and explain why they think the artefact should go into the 'Our Heritage' collection. Now, remember, the 'Our Heritage' collection is intended to be a collection of items that tell us something about who we are as a society, and how we live now, but also how we got to where we are – how we became this society. So the items suggested can be more or less contemporary, or they can be a little old-fashioned too. Right – so let's move straight on and ask Belinda Hope to join us. Hello, Belinda.

Woman 1 Hi, Eddie. Thanks for having me on the programme.

Presenter Good to have you here, Belinda. Right – can you tell us what you've got here, please?

Woman 1 Yes, I'd love to. It's a video of the film *Titanic*.

Presenter From when?

Woman 1 From about 1998. The film was made in 1997, I know that for sure, and I think the video came out the following year, so I'm going to say 1998.

Presenter OK. So tell us your reasons.

Woman 1 Lots. First of all, just the fact that it's a video – a physical object. I know it's obsolete technology now, but videos changed so many things, didn't they, when they first came out – I mean, people could record things from TV for the first time, you could get your favourite films and watch them again and again in your own home, all that stuff. Plus, of course, the sinking of the *Titanic* is a bit of history in itself. Plus ...

Presenter Wow, lots of reasons!

Woman 1 Yeah, right. But this is the last one, promise! Erm. What was I saying? Oh yes – this particular film set new standards of computer graphics, at that time anyway, so the video also tells us a lot about that kind of technology at that time. Put this in the 'Our Heritage' collection, and I think there's lots to be said about the times we live in.

Presenter OK, Belinda – thanks so much for that, as ever it'll be down to our listeners and viewers to decide whether or not the video of *Titanic* makes it into the collection. Now, next up we've got Mike Dickinson from nearby Reading. Hi, Mike.

Man Hi, Eddie.

Presenter All yours, Mike.

Man Right. OK, well, what I've brought along, as you can see, is a tin of tomatoes. I really wanted to bring fresh tomatoes but I thought they wouldn't last in the collection!

Presenter OK, Mike!

Man Anyway, I got these in 2006, would you believe? Look, there's the date and the sell-by date on the side of the can.

Presenter Right. But why choose a tin of tomatoes, Mike?

Man Thought you'd never ask, Eddie. Here we go, then. Right. First of all, it's food – the most important thing on the planet, unless I'm much mistaken. And it seems to me that fresh food – that's why I wanted fresh tomatoes – is getting harder and harder to find. Next reason is that since it's a tin, it tells us something about the food technology we've got these days, and it could change radically in the near future, I reckon.

Presenter Interesting. But tell me – just out of interest – when's the sell-by date?

Man End of next year, Eddie. So it's not out-of-date yet!

Presenter Even so – we'd better put a warning on if it goes in the collection – do not open! Otherwise the tomatoes will be off!

Man Yes, they might be!

Presenter OK, Mike, thanks a lot – let's see what viewers think about a tin of tomatoes in the collection. It's certainly a novel idea! OK – and our third guest tonight is Yvonne, Yvonne Morgan, right?

Woman 2 That's right, Eddie. Hi.

Presenter Hello. And let's see – hmm, now that's really interesting. Tell us what've you got there, Yvonne.

Woman 2 Well, it's an electric guitar. Actually this one belonged to my dad, he was in a band back in the 1970s.

Presenter A famous one, by any chance?

Woman 2 Not really – they made one record but it didn't get anywhere, and then he went back to being a family man and working in the bank.

Presenter Could be worse.

Woman 2 Yes, that's right. Well, anyway, I decided to suggest the guitar for the collection because without the electric guitar, you know, music just wouldn't be what it is now, and it's easy to forget that, I think.

Presenter Absolutely. And it's incredible, really, because ... you say the guitar's over 30 years old?

Woman 2 Roughly, yes, I can't tell you exactly when it was made but I'm sure an expert could.

Presenter Yes, but it doesn't really look outdated, does it? I mean, someone playing this in a band now, you'd hardly notice, would you?

Woman 2 No, maybe not. Actually it was falling to pieces until a couple of years ago, in really bad condition, the lacquer and everything was falling off and the strings were broken as well, so I had it restored.

Presenter Looks great, I must say. So – do you want to say anything else about it?

Woman 2 Erm, well, not a lot, I suppose. Like I said, I think music's a very important aspect of the times we live in, and this guitar for me represents that. Erm, so having this in the collection would, you know, be a recognition of music in modern society and things like that.

Presenter OK, Yvonne, thanks a lot. Now, before we go on, let me remind you viewers that it isn't us here on the programme who decide which item to pick each week, it's you – so phone us and vote. In case you've forgotten our number, we'll refresh your memory by putting it up on screen now, OK? There you go – 1625 double 3 double 3 double oh. And don't forget if you want all the up-to-date information on our show, don't forget to visit our website.

Answers

1 to talk about the artefacts people think should go into 'Our Heritage'

2 *Titanic* video; tin of tomatoes; electric guitar

b 🔊 Play the recording again and ask students to complete the table. Check answers. You may want to play the recording again, pausing if necessary for clarification.

Answers

	Object one	Object two	Object three
When was it made?	1998	2006	1970s
Name of object:	*Titanic* video	tin of tomatoes	electric guitar

Reason(s) for suggesting it:

Object one: video changed many things, the sinking of the *Titanic* is history, the film sets new standards of computer graphics.

Object two: it's food – the most important thing on the planet, it's fresh food, the tin tells us something about food technology.

Object three: without the electric guitar, music wouldn't be what it is today.

(c) In pairs, students decide which of the objects they would choose. Students compare their answers in class discussion.

5 Grammar
Ellipsis

(a) Explain to students that it is common to leave words out in English and give some simple examples: short answers *Yes, I will (go to the beach with you)*; omission of subject *He went to the shop and (he) bought a newspaper*; omission of auxiliary *I have been to Paris and (I have) seen the Eiffel Tower*.

Read through sentences 1–5 with students and ask them to choose the words which were left out. Check answers.

Answers

1 b   2 e   3 a   4 c   5 d

Look

Clarify to students that ellipsis is mostly used in informal conversations. Underline the fact that it is very common indeed, especially when speakers know each other very well.

(b) Look at the example and ask students to do the same with the other sentences. Ask them to compare answers with a partner before feedback.

Answers

2	a P	b B	c W
3	a W	b B	c P
4	a B	b W	c P
5	a W	b B	c P

(c) Look at the first dialogue with the class as an example. Elicit any possible answers (*Yes, I'd love to go out*; *Yes, I'd love to*) and decide which is the best. Ask students to work in pairs and do the same with the other dialogues. Ask individual pairs to say the dialogues in open class as feedback and discuss any other possible answers.

Answers

1 A: Do you want to go out tonight?
   B: Yes, I'd love to. (though this could even be shortened to *love to*)
2 A: Do you think John has arrived?
   B: I'm not sure, but he might have.
3 A: I don't want to go to the party.
   B: Why not?
   A: Sally might be there.
   B: I don't think she will.
4 A: Is this the right answer?
   B: It might be. Why not ask Phil?
   A: No, I don't want to.
   B: Why not?

Language note
Ellipsis is also used in formal written English. After an adjective, it is not necessary to repeat the noun, though we usually use *one* to substitute the noun:
What's the difference between an African elephant and an Indian (one)?

When using prepositional verbs, we can ellipt the first preposition if both prepositions are the same, but not if they are different:
I have heard (about) and read about your past.
I have listened to and thought about your ideas carefully.

─ OPTIONAL ACTIVITY ─

Write the following dialogue on the board:
Have a good time last night?
Not really. You?
Not bad. Went to the cinema.
The Odeon?
No, the Arts. Saw a film about zombies.
Good?
A bit boring.

Ask students to work in pairs and rewrite the dialogue in full sentences without ellipsis.

Answers
Did you have a good time last night?
No, I didn't have a good time really. Did you have a good time?
I had quite a good time. I went to the cinema.
Did you go to the Odeon?
No, I went to the Arts. I saw a film about zombies.
Was it good?
It was a bit boring.

Ask students to create a dialogue of their own consisting entirely of ellipted sentences and then act it out for another pair, who listen and then repeat the dialogue without the ellipsis. Circulate and help as necessary. Listen to a few examples in open class as feedback.

Grammar notebook
Remind students to note down the rules for this structure and to write a few examples of their own.

6 Vocabulary
Old and new

(a) Students read sentences 1–6 and match them to the things mentioned in Exercise 4a. Students compare answers with a partner before feedback.

Answers

2 video   3 tin of tomatoes   4 tin of tomatoes
5 electric guitar   6 the programme's website

(b) Students complete the definitions in the table with adjectives 1–6 from Exercise 6a. Allow them to use a dictionary if necessary.

Answers

old: old-fashioned; out-of-date; obsolete
new: contemporary; novel; up-to-date

(c) Read through the questions with the class and check understanding. You may like to discuss question 1 in open class as an example. Encourage students to use vocabulary from Exercise 6a in their answers and to give reasons for their opinions. Ask a few pairs to tell the class about their partner's answers.

(d) Students work in pairs to complete the sentences. Point out that they may need to use different forms of the verbs in the box and to include pronouns where necessary. Check answers in open class.

Answers

1 renovated   2 restored   3 update you   4 renew

(e) Read through sentences with the class and check difficult vocabulary: *falling to pieces* and *subscription*. Students choose the correct option to complete each sentence and compare answers with a partner before feedback. During feedback, use the sentences to clarify the meaning of the incorrect options in each sentence.

Answers

2 outdated   3 restore   4 novel   5 up-to-date
6 renovated   7 renew   8 update

Vocabulary notebook

Encourage students to start a new section *Old and new* in their notebook and add these words. They may find it useful to note down translations of the words too.

┌─ OPTIONAL ACTIVITY ─────────────

Students may like to learn some idioms with *old and new*. Write the following words on the board and ask students to match them to the definitions. Stronger classes may be able to guess the meaning of the idioms without seeing the definitions.

1	*the new kid on the block*	a	*someone who is similar in character to their father or mother*
2	*the good old days*	b	*an easy way of earning money*
3	*a chip off the old block*	c	*a time in the past when you believe life was better*
4	*a New Man*	d	*start something new*
5	*as old as the hills*	e	*someone who believes in equality of the sexes*
6	*be money for old rope*	f	*someone who is new in a place and has a lot to learn*
7	*turn over a new leaf*	g	*very, very old*

Answers

1 f   2 c   3 a   4 e   5 g   6 b   7 d

In pairs, students write a short dialogue which contains one or more of the expressions. Listen to some of the examples in open class.

7 Speak

(a) Give students a few minutes to work together in small groups and think of three items for *Our Heritage*. You may like to give them some ideas of your own to get them started. Circulate and help with vocabulary as necessary.

(b) Groups present their ideas to the rest of the class. Ask them to come to the front of the class and encourage them to use the board to help present their main arguments. You may like to set a time limit to ensure every group has the same opportunity to express their ideas.

(c) Hold a class vote to decide which are the best five objects to include in the collection.

Culture in mind

8 Read

If you set the background information as a homework research task, ask the students to tell the class what they found out.

BACKGROUND INFORMATION

The Museum of Bad Art: is the world's only museum dedicated to the collection, preservation, exhibition and celebration of bad art in all its forms. It was founded in 1993 and the pieces in the collection range from the work of talented artists that have gone awry to works of artists barely in control of the brush. What they all have in common is a special quality that sets them apart in one way or another from the merely incompetent. The exhibition can be viewed online.

The British Lawnmower Museum: restores machines for the collection. Since opening, the museum has drawn widespread interest and has captured the imagination of enthusiasts from as far afield as Australia, the USA, Europe and the Far East. It boasts a unique collection of restored garden machinery and memorabilia, dating before the invention of the lawnmower, and includes the largest toy lawnmower collection in the world.

The Bata Shoe Museum: celebrates the style and function of footwear and contains over 10,000 shoes. Artefacts on exhibit range from Chinese bound-foot shoes and ancient Egyptian sandals to chestnut-crushing clogs and glamorous platforms. Over 4,500 years of history and a collection of 20th-century celebrity shoes are reflected in the semi-permanent exhibition, All About Shoes.

(a) As an introduction to this exercise, ask students if they have visited any unusual museums. Listen to some of their ideas in open class. Tell students they are going to read about three unusual museums. Read through questions 1–6 and check understanding of *premises* and *houses*. Students read the text quickly to answer the questions. They can compare answers with a partner before feedback in open class.

Answers
1 B 2 C 3 B 4 A 5 B,C 6 A

(b) Check understanding of *life in the fast lane*. Students read the text again and answer questions. There is a fair amount of new vocabulary in the text, but encourage students to work without help from you or a dictionary at this stage. Ask them to underline any words and phrases they don't understand. Let students compare answers with a partner and discuss possible meanings of new words together before feedback. After feedback, you may want to read through the text with the students, pausing to check their comprehension and their grasp of vocabulary.

Answers
1 c 2 d 3 a 4 b 5 e

(c) In pairs, students think of a question for each of the five people in Exercise 8b. You may like to ask students to create dialogues and take it in turns to play the part of one of the people. Listen to some of the dialogues in open class.

OPTIONAL ACTIVITY

If you would like your students to do more close comprehension work on the text, you can use the following *true / false / don't know* exercise. The statements are in the order of the text. Ask students to explain the reason for their answers during feedback.

1 *The paintings at MOBA have all been found in people's rubbish.* **(false)**
2 *The museum is getting bigger.* **(true)**
3 *The MOBA website is very popular.* **(don't know)**
4 *Edwin Beard Budding first used his lawnmower in the dark.* **(true)**
5 *Brian Radam's best friend is a gardener.* **(don't know)**
6 *The Lawnmower Museum has the world's most expensive lawnmower.* **(don't know)**
7 *Sonja Bata's museum is in her house.* **(false)**
8 *Sonja Bata is over sixty years old.* **(true)**

Discussion box
Weaker classes: Students can choose one question to discuss.

Stronger classes: In pairs or small groups, students go through the questions in the box and discuss them.

Monitor and help as necessary, encouraging students to express themselves in English and to use any vocabulary they have learned from the text. Ask pairs or groups to feedback to the class and discuss any interesting points further.

9 Write

(a) Students look at the notes and decide where they might find each one. Tell them not to worry about any errors or exercises at this stage, just to skim through quickly and concentrate on the task. Listen to some of their ideas in open class.

(b) Read through questions 1–5 with students. In pairs, students answer the questions. Depending on the speed your class works, you may like to break up this exercise and do one question at a time and give feedback before continuing. Tell students that the exercises focus on areas of grammar and vocabulary from previous units and that they can look back if necessary.

Answers
1 advice (should be advise); there (their); insure (ensure); from (form)
2 What a great trip that was.
3 Possible answer: The use of cameras is forbidden. Visitors are requested not to touch the exhibits. Souvenirs can be purchased in the gift shop which can be found next to the exit.
4 called; are going; latest; provided; to call; didn't: a phone number is missing
5 Possible answer: If you really love dogs and want a Labrador, we're giving some away free. Call Sue 3433 3454.

(c) Read through the guidelines with students. Use the notes in Exercise 9a for clarification. Do all the notes follow the guidelines? How could they be improved? Discuss in open class.

Answer
4

(d) Tell students they are going to write some notes. Tell them to plan what information they are going to include and to follow the guidelines in Exercise 9c. In a subsequent lesson, students can deliver the notes to other members of the class or put them on the walls for students to read.

16 Swapping places

Unit overview

TOPIC: Experiencing other people's cultures and ways of life

TEXTS
Reading and listening: a magazine article about a father and son experiencing each other's taste in music
Listening: a radio review of the film *Freaky Friday*
Listening: a song called *My Generation*
Writing: proverbs and cinquains

SPEAKING AND FUNCTIONS
Discussing quotations about things people wish they'd known at 18

LANGUAGE
Grammar: revision of various structures
Vocabulary: teenspeak

1 Read and listen

Warm up

Books closed. Ask students if they have been to any concerts recently. In pairs, students discuss the type of concerts they have seen or would like to see. Listen to some of their ideas in open class.

a Books open. Look at the photos with the class. Students imagine they have been at the shows and write five adjectives to describe each one. Students compare adjectives with a partner before feedback.

b 🔊 Read through the sentences with students and check understanding of difficult vocabulary: *a sneaking suspicion, choreographed, high culture, disdained, transition*. Ask students if they have the same taste in music as their parents. Tell students they are going to read two texts from a newspaper article in which a father and son take each other to a concert of their choice. Students read the texts and write the number of the missing sentences in the spaces. Allow students to compare answers with a partner before playing the recording, pausing as necessary to check answers and for clarification.

TAPESCRIPT
See the reading text on pages 108 and 109 of the Student's Book.

Answers
A 7   B 2   C 6   D 5   E 8   F 1   G 4   H 3

c Read through the statements with students and ask them to read the text again to decide if they are true or false. If they are false, encourage students to explain why in their own words.

Stronger classes: Ask students to do the exercise without looking back at the text. Students read the text again to check answers.

Answers
1 T
2 T
3 F (He says it's an enthusiast's opera and he doesn't see why it should be made accessible to kids.)
4 T
5 F (He says it didn't feel like revival for the sake of revival.)
6 T
7 T
8 T

d Read through the words with the class. Ask students to work in pairs and find the words in the text, looking at the context of each one. Students explain them in their own words. Listen to some of their answers in open class and decide on the best definitions.

Possible answers
1 it hadn't changed for many years
2 the most important thing
3 formal and conventional
4 came in quickly
5 from a wide range
6 watching movies at home
7 make others share our opinions
8 what Ferdy likes doing

Discussion box
Weaker classes: Students can choose one question to discuss.

Stronger classes: In pairs or small groups, students go through the questions in the box and discuss them.

Monitor and help as necessary, encouraging students to express themselves in English and to use any vocabulary they have learned from the text. Ask pairs or groups to feedback to the class and discuss any interesting points further.

---

2 Grammar

Review

a Read through the sentences in Exercise 1b with the class. Students match descriptions a–h with sentences 1–8. Take this opportunity to go over any areas of grammar that you feel students need to revise. Stronger classes may be able to say which structures the sentences contain without looking at the descriptions. If students enjoy this activity, encourage them to think of their own questions to ask each other.

a like b rushing c to feel

11 (possible answers)

a I am having my garden redesigned.

b I have just had my camera repaired.

c I am going to have my car cleaned.

12

a Not only do the contestants have to camp in a different place each night, they also have to hunt for food.

b No sooner had Susie arrived at the party than she left.

c On no account must you eat or talk during this exam.

Answers

a 3 b 5 c 7 d 1 e 8 f 2 g 6 h 4

(b) Divide the classes into two groups. Groups take it in turns to choose a question for the other group to answer. This activity will be more successful if you act as referee and stick strictly to 30 seconds for each answer. Keep score on the board. Make a note of any questions which students find difficult to answer.

Answers

1

a We spent a long sunny Saturday morning on the beach.

b He drives around in an expensive red Italian sports car.

c How much is that small antique wooden coffee table under the window?

2

a They appear to be asleep.

b It's believed to be really good for you.

c He seems to be much older than the last time I saw him.

3

a I won't be able to make it to your party, I'm afraid.

b The fire spread fast but we managed to escape just in time.

c I might have been able to phone you if I knew your number.

4

a The window had been broken by the thief to escape.

b She didn't know that she had been seen.

c The whole town had been destroyed by the hurricane.

5

a 'D̶o̶ ̶y̶o̶u̶ want to come round for dinner tonight?'

b 'A̶r̶e̶ ̶y̶o̶u̶ happy now?'

c 'I̶t̶'̶s̶ ̶a̶ nice day, isn't it?'

6

a He denied saying / having said anything.

b She asked if he was ready to go.

c He admitted not really liking the film / He admitted that he hadn't really liked the film.

7

a It was Paul that told her, not me.

b What I didn't like was that he never said 'thank you'.

c What's embarrassing about my dad is that he sings in the shower.

8

a As long as we hurry, we won't miss the train.

b Unless we hurry, we'll miss the train.

c We'd better hurry, otherwise we'll miss the train.

9

a Anya knew by now that it **would** be too cold …

b I was convinced I **was** going to win the quiz.

c David was **going** to get a job in France …

3 Listen

(a) In pairs, students discuss the questions. Ask them to decide on the most common reasons for arguments between teenagers and parents. Listen to some of their ideas in open class.

(b) Look at the photo with the class and tell students it is taken from a film called *Freaky Friday* which tells the story of the conflicts between a mother and her teenage daughter. Divide the class into pairs and give each student a letter, A or B. Students write down complaints about their partner. Circulate and help with vocabulary as necessary. Students tell each other their complaints.

(c) Tell students they are going to listen to a review of *Freaky Friday*. Play the recording while students answer the question. Tell them not to worry about unknown vocabulary at this stage.

TAPESCRIPT

Now, I'm going to be honest. I really didn't think I was going to like *Freaky Friday*. I read the synopsis and thought 'yuck'. Mother and teenage daughter wake up one morning and find they've switched bodies. Then they have to find ways of surviving in their new identities and, of course, ultimately they come to a better understanding of what it really means to be the other one. I'm sure you get the idea. Furthermore it is a remake of a 1976 film starring Jodie Foster, and if you're a regular listener to this show, you'll know what I think about remakes. If you're not, then I'm sure you can imagine.

But then I catch an interview with Jamie Lee Curtis on breakfast TV. Well, I hate to admit it – she sold the film to me. I actually wanted to see the film. She was charming and talked so passionately about her role in the film that I thought it really can't be that bad.

So it was with renewed enthusiasm that I got to the cinema to finally start my day's work.

So, was Ms Curtis telling me the truth when she promised me that I'd have lots of laughs, or was I a victim of her well-refined marketing skills? Well, I'm happy to report that she was telling the truth and I did laugh. A lot actually. More than I could have ever imagined I would. And the main reason for most of this fun? Jamie Lee Curtis, herself. Now I've never really been sure what to make of Jamie Lee Curtis. I mean, as the complete horror fan, I'd loved her as the scream queen in the Halloween series, and then there were her classic comedy roles in *A Fish called Wanda* and *Trading Places*. But then how could she make a film so truly awful as *True Lies*? I'd never really forgiven her for that. Well, now I have.

Curtis plays a single mother trying to juggle her career as a psychoanalyst with bringing up her two children, a cheeky nine-year-old son and a typically rebellious guitar-playing 15-year-old daughter, Anna. Now Anna, played beautifully by Lindsay Lohan, is having trouble with the fact that her mum is getting married the next day, especially as she's still suffering from the death of her father a few years earlier. All this means that things aren't going too smoothly between mother and daughter. However, a meal out in a Chinese restaurant and some magical Chinese fortune cookies later and things start to get ... well ... Freaky. And this is where the real fun begins.

With their identities swapped, Curtis and Lohan really set off the fireworks. The mother, now in the body of a 15 year-old, has to deal with an over-attentive boyfriend and nasty teachers at school, while the daughter, now a 40-something woman, has to go on TV to promote her mother's new book *Through the Looking Glass*.

The results of this muddle are, at times, hilarious and both actresses do an exceptionally good job of convincing us that they are, in fact, the other one. Ms Curtis, rocking out with an electric guitar and coming out with cool teenspeak, is worth the admission price alone. OK, so I could have done without the slushy, over-sentimental ending but, for the sheer fun of the eighty minutes or so before this, I'll forgive all involved.

I'm even considering re-evaluating my opinion of remakes.

Answer
Yes

(d) 🔊 Ask students to read through the questions and then play the recording. Students listen and answer the questions. Allow them to compare answers with a partner before open class feedback. You may want to play the recording again, pausing as necessary.

Answers
1 He didn't like the synopsis; he hates remakes.
2 A TV interview with the actress Jamie Lee Curtis.
3 He liked some of her films, but not others.
4 She's a single mother with two children.

5 Because her mother is remarrying after the death of the daughter's father.
6 The mother has to deal with a boyfriend and nasty teachers; the daughter with a TV interview.
7 By convincing him that they are the other one.
8 He found the ending too sentimental.

4 Vocabulary
Teenspeak
Warm up

Books closed. Write the word *teenspeak* on the board and ask students what they think it means. Allow them to use L1 and think of any examples of teenspeak in their own language. In pairs, students discuss examples of teenspeak and try to translate it into English.

Open books. Tell students they are going to see some examples of English teenspeak. Ask students to cover the right-hand column and to try to guess the meaning of the teenspeak. Listen to their ideas but do not comment. Students uncover definitions and match a–h to sentences 1–8.

Answers
2 a   3 h   4 b   5 c   6 e   7 d   8 g

┌─ OPTIONAL ACTIVITY ─────────────
Ask students to create dialogues to include some of the examples of teenspeak. Listen to some of the dialogues in open class.

Vocabulary notebook
Encourage students to start a new section *Teenspeak* in their notebook and add these words. They may find it useful to note down translations of the words too.

5 Speak

Students read through the quotations and imagine what has happened to each of the people. In pairs, students discuss their opinions. Monitor and encourage students to answer in full sentences and to expand on their answers. Ask some pairs to report back and invite class discussion.

Weaker classes: Weaker students may benefit from writing their ideas down. Encourage them to look at their notes as little as possible during feedback.

6 Song
Warm up

Books closed. Ask students what they know about life in the 1960s. What do they think defines the sixties generation? Elicit ideas and write examples on the board. Explain that in the sixties, a lot of young people protested about war and politics and wanted to change the world through love and peace. Ask students if their generation want to do the same. Do people still write protest songs?

(a) Books open. Ask students to work individually and write down four adjectives to describe their generation. Students compare their lists with a partner. As feedback, listen to some of their ideas and create a list on the board. Students may be interested to compare their generation with the sixties. When would they prefer to live?

(b) 🔊 Tell students they are going to listen to a song called *My Generation* by The Who. Play the recording while students listen and write down four adjectives to describe how the singer feels.

(c) 🔊 Play the recording again. Students listen, read the lyrics and complete the sentences. Let students compare answers in pairs before checking the answers. Play the recording again if necessary, pausing at the answers.

TAPESCRIPT
See the song on page 112 of the Student's Book.

Answers
1 put … down   2 get … around   3 f-f-fade … away
4 dig   5 s-s-sensation

(d) Students match the missing words with definitions 1–5. Check answers.

Answers
1 fade away   2 get around   3 dig   4 put down
5 sensation

(e) Ask students to write a short paragraph about the message of the song and who it is directed at. Circulate and help with vocabulary as necessary. Let students compare ideas in pairs before asking some students to read their paragraphs in open class.

Did you know …?

Read through the information in the box with the class. Ask students if they know any of the artists or music mentioned and invite them to give any interesting information about them. Ask them who are the greatest rock bands of their generation.

7 Write

The planning for this exercise can be done in class and the writing set for homework.

Warm up

Write the following proverb on the board:

The early bird catches the worm.

Ask students what the proverb means and listen to some of their ideas. Ask them if they know any other proverbs in English.

(a) Read through the proverbs with students and check understanding of *blames* and *hesitates*. In pairs, students discuss the questions. Circulate and help with vocabulary. Listen to some ideas in open class and encourage further discussion. Ask students if they have any similar proverbs in their language.

Possible answers
1 Saying something is better than keeping quiet.
2 It's better to have something than have the chance of getting more.
3 If you get something wrong, it's your fault.
4 Some things take a long time.
5 Only innocent people tell the truth – it's better to lie.
6 The person who has control of a situation in the end is most successful.
7 Be brave and keep going or someone will get there before you.
8 Don't stay somewhere too long, or you won't be welcome.
9 Do things today.

(b) Read the meaningless proverb to students and ask them which two proverbs it is made up from.

Answer
A bad workman blames his tools.
Rome wasn't built in a day.

(c) Students work together to create their own meaningless proverbs. Listen to a few examples and ask the class to guess what the proverbs mean.

(d) **Weaker classes:** Before introducing the cinquain, you may like to check students' awareness of syllables. Write the following words on the board and ask students how many syllables they contain: *understand* (3), *interesting* (4), *children* (2) etc. Follow the procedure for stronger classes.

Stronger classes: Read through the cinquains with students and point out the number of syllables in each line. In pairs, students discuss the meaning of each cinquain. Encourage them to use their imagination and listen to some of their ideas in open class.

(e) Tell students they are going to write their own cinquain. Give them some time to think of a topic that interests them and to plan which words they would like to include. Remind them that their cinquain must consist of 22 syllables. In a subsequent class, students can place their cinquains around the room for others to read. They may like to vote on which was the best cinquain.

Module 4 Check your progress

1 Grammar

(a)
2 will be doing
3 will have read
4 will be fixing
5 will be leaving
6 will have found
7 will have visited
8 will be singing

(b)
2 off to
3 due to
4 bound to fail
5 supposed to
6 thinking of taking
7 supposed to
8 off to

(c)
2 I wish my sister wouldn't keep taking my clothes without asking.
3 I'd rather we gave our money to charity this year instead of going on holiday.
4 It's time you stopped complaining about it and did something.
5 If only I had enough money to buy a new car.
6 I wish I hadn't said that!
7 I'd rather you didn't tell her.
8 It's time we sat down and talked about it.

(d)
2 don't think so
3 the ones
4 neither did her brother
5 those
6 doing so
7 that of
8 so do I

(e)
2 He seems to be a bit shy.
3 ... we found the house had been broken into.
4 ... and neither did my friend.
5 He denied having lied to me.
6 It's the way she speaks to me that I find most annoying.
7 Unless he apologises, I won't talk to him again.
8 It was a difficult test but I managed to pass it.

2 Vocabulary

(a) 2 a 3 g 4 b 5 c 6 d 7 f 8 h

(b)
2 sensitive
3 effect
4 advice
5 lose
6 insure
7 lie
8 prosecuted

(c)
2 novel
3 renovated
4 out-of-date
5 restore
6 update
7 renew
8 old-fashioned

How did you do?
Students work out their scores. Check how they have done and follow up any problem areas with revision work for students.

Writing Bank 1
1 Model letter

(a) The courses sold through IQ language programmes are not as good as their publicity says they are – the writer feels that, after his bad experience with the company, people should think again before booking one of these courses.

(b) Student's own choice from the relevant boxes

Writing Bank 2
1 Model letter

(a) The writer plans to take a gap year off between school and university to work to earn money, in order to go to West Africa as a volunteer and then to travel around Europe.

(b) 1 How's life? 2 Sorry I haven't written for a while 3 I reckon 4 Keep in touch 5 Let me know how you are 6 Take care

Writing Bank 3
1 Model story

(a) They could hardly believe their eyes, they were really amazed and felt in awe.

(b) Student's own answers

Writing Bank 4
1 Model composition

(a) 'Stars' of reality TV enjoy media attention if it helps them in their careers so they shouldn't be surprised if the press then invades their lives more than they had expected.

(b) 1 first and foremost 2 since 3 on the other hand 4 whereas 5 furthermore 6 consequently 7 in other words 8 to sum up

Writing Bank 5
1 Model report

(a) Finnish men have won the competition 6 times.

(b) 1 after 2 and in doing so 3 by 4 which 5 to 6 When 7 in order 8 who 9 but 10 and

Writing Bank 6
1 Model notes and notices

(a) 1 Jake – Read this!!!!!! ...
2 Party this Friday ...
3 Wanted – Sales assistants ...
4 For sale – Dawes 10-speed mountain bike ...

(b) 1 I am interested in buying
2 I am selling
3 I am looking for
4 I have found
5 I am giving away
6 This is the final time I am going to say this
7 We want to advise you about a dangerous situation

(c) 1 pt 2 Ex cond 3 asap 4 obo 5 Mon – Sat 6 /hr 7 ft 8 BYOB 9 footie

Workbook key
(1) Animal instincts

1 **(a)** 2 link 3 revered 4 free 5 countless 6 erratic 7 harm's 8 leading 9 hit

(b) 2 worst 3 countless 4 leading 5 broken 6 erratic 7 way 8 bolted 9 link

2 2 had been making 3 had been erected 4 had been dug 5 had been following 6 had been alerted 7 had been lobbying

3 **(a)** 2 b 3 d 4 a 5 c

(b) 2 crowed 3 barking 4 roared 5 hisses 6 bleating 7 grunt

(c) 2 b 3 a 4 a 5 a 6 b 7 a

(d) 2 heroic 3 numerous 4 behaviour 5 unbelievable 6 safety 7 miraculous 8 difficulty

4 **(a)** suggested answers
clever careful patient strong

(b) 1 the hatred between Buck and Spitz
2 the cold wind 3 Buck's nest

(c) 1 T 2 F 3 T 4 T 5 F 6 T

(d) 1 poise 2 prone 3 divined 4 striving 5 unwonted 6 grope 7 loath

5 **(a)** Speaker 1 Speaker 2 Speaker 3 Speaker 4 Speaker 5

(b) 1 Because it brought the world of wildlife and conservation to a much wider audience.

2 Because he enjoyed seeing Steve work with crocodiles.

3 She thought he shouldn't have put his children in danger, and that it wasn't necessary in any case, as he was so popular anyway.

4 Because Steve was the same nationality as himself – Australian. It made him feel proud to be Australian as people all over the world respected Steve.

5 Steve's work rehabilitating injured wild animals.

TAPESCRIPT

Speaker 1 I'm going to really miss Steve, he was such an entertainer. I always looked forward to seeing him on TV. His own show, *Crocodile Hunter*, was great, but for me the best thing was his appearances on chat shows like the Jay Leno Show. He brought the world of wildlife and conservation to a much wider audience. He really loved animals and that always came across.

Speaker 2 Steve will always be 'Crocodile Hunter' for me. I loved seeing him on his show, wrestling crocodiles and doing all sorts of dangerous stuff. You know he was actually totally against crocodile hunting and worked with a Crocodile Relocation Programme which captured crocodiles that were in danger and moved them to safer locations. For me he was a hero.

Speaker 3 Steve worked a lot with his wife. He seemed to be a real family man. I didn't really like it when he used his children on his TV shows. He didn't need to do that as he was really popular without them. I remember there was huge controversy when he was filmed holding his baby son as he was feeding a crocodile. Irwin had been criticised before for his sensational behaviour but he was really slammed this time as people said that the baby had been put in danger by his dad's behaviour. I think Irwin was in control of the situation but I don't think he should have done it.

Speaker 4 Steve was a real ambassador for Australia. He made me proud to be Australian. His commitment and passion to conservation was amazing and everyone respected him. He was an ordinary man who everyone looked up to. The Prime Minister John Howard described him as 'one of Australia's great conservation icons' and even invited him to meet George Bush when he came to Australia in 2003.

Speaker 5 I know everyone associates Steve Irwin with crocodiles but he worked with lots of other animals too. He ran the Australia Zoo which looked after wild animal cubs that had been injured. He helped rehabilitate them so they could go back to live in the wild. His dad opened the Zoo and Steve took it over when he retired. I know everyone thinks of Steve as a showman and television star but he also did lots of work that no one knew about, saving animals that would have died if it hadn't been for him.

Unit check

1 2 wild 3 revered 4 buried 5 pet 6 instincts
7 survival 8 countless 9 been 10 starvation

2 2 c 3 a 4 c 5 b 6 c 7 c 8 b 9 b

3 2 The car ~~had parked~~ *had been parked* there for three days before anyone noticed.

3 His request had already been ~~refusing~~ *refused* twice.

4 I ~~was been~~ *had been* ready for hours before they came.

5 He heard that Jane ~~has been~~ *had been* promoted the week before.

6 My eyes were sore because I ~~have been~~ *had been* working at the computer all day.

7 The guitar ~~was already sold~~ *had already been sold* by the time Mike made his offer.

8 The company was closed because it ~~had been lost~~ *had been losing* money for years.

9 By the time we got to the station, the last bus ~~had been gone~~ *had gone*.

2 Snap decisions

1 **(a)** 2 pass with flying colours 3 unbiased
4 astounded 5 prejudices 6 opening
7 been demoted 8 screen 9 reinstated

(b) *Down*
1 reinstate 2 audition 3 astounded 4 screen
Across
5 unbiased 6 demote 7 opening

(c) 2 astounded 3 opening 4 screen 5 demote
6 audition 7 reinstate

2 **(a)** 2 PH 3 FP 4 FP 5 PH 6 PH 7 PH 8 FP

(b) 2 The professor was going to hand out the information sheets on lateral thinking, but he forgot them.

3 I wasn't going to join the debating society, but I changed my mind.

4 We were going to have snowboarding lessons, but our parents didn't let us.

5 Martha was going to buy a replacement MP3 player but she couldn't afford it.

6 I was going to start my new exercise regime last weekend, but I twisted my ankle on Friday.

(c) 2 a 3 c 4 b 5 c 6 c

3 **(a)** 2 a 3 e 4 f 5 b 6 c

(b) 2 jump to conclusions 3 mulls ... over
4 made your mind up 5 informed decision
6 snap decision

4 **(a)** 1 b 2 c 3 a

(b) 1 picture on the right
2 picture on the left
3 picture on the left

(c) 1 Could you perhaps tell us …
2 Let me think a moment.
3 It's a bit of a long story …
4 I think I'd have to say …
5 I don't really know what to tell you …
6 Tell us a bit about yourself …
7 Let's talk a bit, if we may …
8 Would you mind if I asked you …
9 Sure, fire away.
10 Just give me a moment.

TAPESCRIPT

Interview 1

Man 1   Hi there! We're doing a survey about library services in the town. Would you mind if I asked you a few questions?

Woman 1   Sure, fire away. What would you like to know?

Man 1   How often do you use the library?

Woman 1   I use it a lot, at least twice a month.

Man 1   And how would you rate the service?

Woman 1   I think I'd have to say it's good.

Man 1   That's good. And do you think the service could be improved?

Woman 1   Well, erm, they could have a wider selection of historical fiction.

Man 1   And maybe they could let me off the fines when I forget to take my books back!

Interview 2

Man 2   So, tell us a bit about yourself, David.

Teenager   Erm, well, I'm David Mould. I'm 18. I live in Chester…er. Sorry, just a moment.

Woman 2   That's OK. Don't worry. Perhaps you could tell us why you want to work here?

Teenager   Well, I've always wanted to be a journalist, and erm … when I finish school, erm … I … erm want to go to university and study journalism.

Man 2   I see.

Teenager   I thought it would be erm good to get some erm experience in my holidays. Erm, then I erm saw your advert.

Woman 2   Any favourite directors?

Interview 3

Man 3   Let's talk a bit, if we may, about your childhood. Your father was a musician, wasn't he?

Woman 3   Yes.

Man 3   Was he an influence?

Woman 3   Maybe.

Man 3   And your mother?

Woman 3   I don't really know what to tell you. I hardly ever saw my mother.

Man 3   Oh, and why was that?

Woman 3   It's a bit of a long story. I don't think your audience would be very interested.

5 (a) 1 d 2 a 3 e 4 c 5 b

TAPESCRIPT

1 **Speaker 1**   I can't imagine what came over you. (polite)
   Response   I know, I'm really sorry. (polite)

2 **Speaker 2**   Could you wait for a moment, please? (polite)
   Response   Of course. No problem. (polite)

3 **Speaker 3**   I wonder if you could explain what this is. (polite)
   Response   I'm sorry, I can't … because I don't know. (polite)

4 **Speaker 4**   Is there some problem you're not telling me about? (angry)
   Response   Yes, of course there is! (angry)

5 **Speaker 5**   I really think this is the end of our friendship. (angry)
   Response   I couldn't agree more! (angry)

6 (a) A Para 5   B Para 6   C Para 4   D Para 2
   E Para 1   F Para 3

(b) 1 His writing was not easy to understand by the general public.
2 Because he couldn't find work during the Great Depression.
3 He found them exciting and influential.
4 He travelled to remote areas in the Far East where people were not influenced in any way by cultural and social conventions.

(c) Students' own answers.

Unit check

1 2 dither   3 minds   4 snap   5 jump   6 mulls
7 informed   8 conclusion   9 over   10 decisions

2 2 a 3 b 4 a 5 b 6 c 7 b 8 a 9 a

3 2 Ashley wasn't ~~going talk~~ going to talk to Anna, but he changed his mind.
3 They knew it ~~would to be~~ would be a tough decision to make.
4 The researchers believed they ~~would to make~~ would make a major scientific breakthrough.
5 Ekman believed that showing Tomkins the pictures ~~prove~~ would prove his theory.
6 The players knew that if they lost, the manager ~~was being~~ would be less than happy!
7 The police insisted they ~~go to~~ were going to or would catch the escaped convict within days.
8 Last week, I met the girl Steve ~~going to~~ was going to marry before he met me.
9 I thought it ~~would~~ would be a bad decision not to invite my relatives to the wedding.

(3) Advertising

1 **(a)** 2 out 3 a 4 c 5 a 6 c

(b) 2 back 3 go 4 figure 5 shed 6 are

2 **(a)** 2 David's often late for class.
3 Are you working hard on your marketing course?
4 CD prices have fallen dramatically in the last few years.
5 She thought it over carefully.
6 He talks in a persuasive manner.

(b) 2 The marketing course was very interesting.
3 The shoppers queued up enthusiastically for the sales to start.
4 The restaurant was surprisingly empty.
5 In the case of an emergency make your way quickly to the exits. *Or* In the case of an emergency make your way to the exits quickly.
6 Please answer the next question honestly.

3 **(a)** *Down*
1 hoarding 2 slogan
Across
3 logo 4 commercial 5 sandwich board
6 jingle

(b) 2 adverts 3 logo 4 hoarding 5 slogan
6 sandwich board

4 **(a)** **Quality** cheerful young beautiful durable casual elegant unusual old
Size long big small
Shape square
Colour black red colourful dark brown bright
Place of origin English Italian
Material wooden leather metal plastic canvas

(b) Suggested answers
1 An old brown Italian leather briefcase.
2 A large colourful canvas backpack.
3 An elegant leather handbag.

(c) 1 durable, large, dark brown, Italian
2 beautiful, bright red, canvas
3 gorgeous, delicate, pearl
4 expensive, big, dark silver, German

5 **(a)** 1 f 2 h 3 e 4 a 5 d

(b) 1 Newspaper and magazine advertising
2 Because cars became popular.
3 Because not many people knew about it.
4 It made advertising fun.
5 Because cars got faster, and highways got bigger.

6 **(a)** 1 To provide information about Frenton Sixth Form College.
2 Students

(b) 1 Paragraph 1 2 Paragraph 3 3 students
4 Students' own answers.

(c) Students' own answers.

Unit check

1 2 slogan 3 hoardings 4 perfectly 5 logically
6 fit 7 advertisement 8 commercial 9 logo
10 advertising

2 2 c 3 b 4 a 5 a 6 c 7 c 8 b 9 c

3 2 They ~~didn't hardly understand~~ anything.
They understood hardly anything.
3 He changed ~~quickly~~ his mind as soon as he saw her.
He quickly changed his mind as soon as he saw her.
4 His ~~surprisingly~~ voice was calm. *His voice was surprisingly calm.*
5 ~~Desperately~~ she wanted to go to the party.
She desperately wanted to go to the party.
6 You don't seem very ~~enthusiastically~~ about the party.
You don't seem very enthusiastic about the party.
7 She misunderstood what he was ~~completely~~ saying.
She completely misunderstood what he was saying.
8 She found ~~incredible~~ him boring. *She found him incredibly boring.*
9 He ~~proud~~ presented his new advertising campaign to the team. *He proudly presented his new advertising campaign to the team.*

(4) Fight or flight?

1 **(a)** 1 mind 2 forehead 3 brain 4 mouth
5 heart 6 blood 7 hand

(b) 2 blood 3 forehead 4 mouth 5 hands
6 head 7 mind

(c) 2 racing 3 explode 4 pound 5 feel
6 pouring 7 dried

2 **(a)** 2 a S b T 3 a S b T 4 a S b T

(b) 2 always 3 tend 4 is 5 to 6 will

(c) 2 I tend to say the wrong thing.
3 When he's in the house alone he will often feel like phoning his friends.
4 Stephen's always complaining about his family.
5 When people start talking about politics I will walk away.
6 If I see people arguing I tend to step in and sort them out!

3 **(a)** 2 break 3 some 4 overdo 5 put 6 out
7 on top of 8 hard

(b) 2 on 3 out 4 try 5 breath 6 rest
7 take 8 up

4 **(a)** Suggested answers
Positive
polished   symphonic   lush keyboards
lush orchestrations   Sharon's gorgeous voice
Negative
Too much focus on Sharon's voice

(b) 1 bonus track   2 in stark contrast to
3 orchestrated number   4 band's trademark
5 pigeon-holed   6 maturing in composition

(c) 1 d   2 f   3 a   4 e   5 b   6 c

(d) Students' own answers.

5 **(a)** 1 Because she is afraid of Harley.
2 She had caught her leg on a fisherman's hook.
3 No, she isn't.

(b) 1 a   2 a   3 b   4 b   5 c   6 b

Unit check

1 2 mind   3 blood   4 soar   5 sweat   6 forehead
7 heart   8 cold   9 mouth   10 dried

2 2 c   3 a   4 c   5 b   6 c   7 b   8 c   9 a

3 2 Overwork tends ~~cause~~ *to cause* some degree of stress
in us all.
3 If you're really pressured, you'll often ~~to feel like~~
feel like crying.
4 She's the sort of boss who ~~isn't tending~~ *doesn't tend*
to give her staff a lot of support.
5 I don't know why Scott's ~~always is sitting~~ *always sitting*
there with his feet on his desk!
6 If you work out three times a week, you will ~~feeling~~
feel the benefits very quickly.
7 My personal trainer always ~~making~~ *makes* me do
things I didn't know I was capable of.
8 Do you think your workload ~~will it reduce~~
will be reduced over time?
9 Too much stress ~~tend~~ *tends to* lead to illnesses of
other kinds.

(5) Double lives

1 **(a)** 2 b   3 b   4 a   5 b   6 a

(b) 2 deception   3 outsmart   4 fake   5 defrauding
6 deny   7 slip   8 pass   9 scam

(c) 2 c   3 a   4 b   5 c   6 b   7 a   8 b   9 c

2 **(a)** 2 apologise   3 claim   4 advise   5 offer   6 deny

(b) 2 denied   3 offered   4 apologised   5 advised
6 confess

(c) 2 The lawyer claimed that Wilkins had defrauded
hundreds of pensioners out of their savings.
3 He advised us not to buy things from people
who stop us in the street.
4 The prisoner denied that he had conned anyone.
5 Peter confessed that he had forged his signature
to write the cheques.
6 The Chief Inspector offered to drop the charges
if we/I collaborated.
7 Mr McClean admitted that he had passed himself
off as a financial adviser in order to get his clients
to make bogus investments.
8 The journalist asked if he planned to give the
money back to the people he had conned.

(d) 2 offer   3 Offer   4 advise   5 apologise
6 deny   7 admit   8 ask

3 **(a)** 2 invasion   3 organise   4 resist   5 occupation
6 recruitment   7 transformation   8 identify
9 protection   10 transmit   11 survive
12 interrogate   13 signature

(b) 2 surrender   3 fought   4 sign   5 battles
6 declared   7 casualties   8 negotiations
9 recruits

Vocabulary Tip

Suggested answers
1 protector   protection   protective
2 claimant   claimable
3 captive   captivity   captor   capturer
4 player   playable   playful   playfully

4 **(a)** The text mentions agents and a conspiracy.
Eva is asked to watch everything carefully and
report back.

(b) 1 head of the security operation (he gives Eva orders
and tells her to report back to him)
2 was (the text says 'this was new, more to the point,
this was real')
3 she wants to look like a normal customer (it says
'though she wasn't in the least hungry')
4 doesn't know (text says 'she wondered if this was
Lt. Joos – if she knew, she would recognise him')

(c) 1 She is asked to watch carefully and report back
to Romer.
2 Because she's excited and her brain is very active.
3 Two young men and Lt. Joos.

(d) 2 h   3 f   4 a   5 g   6 b   7 e   8 d

(e) Students' own answers.

5 **(a)** 2

(b) 1 T   2 T   3 F   4 F   5 T   6 T   7 F   8 T

(c) 1 It was designed to make the Germans think that
Britain would attack France through the Pas de
Calais and not via Normandy.

2 They wanted the opposition to be weak.
3 It sent out false radio reports.
4 They gave a false picture of Britain's invasion preparations.
5 To make the Germans think that the main invasion would take place in Calais, and weaken forces in the Normandy area.

TAPESCRIPT

My father played a key role in Operation Fortitude. Operation Fortitude was the codename for the deception operations used by the Allied forces during World War II. It was divided into Fortitude North, a threat to invade Norway, and Fortitude South, designed to make the Germans believe that the main invasion of France would occur in the Pas de Calais rather than Normandy. Fortitude South was one of the most successful deception operations of the war, and arguably the most important.

The principal objective of Operation Fortitude was to make sure that the opposition faced by the troops invading Normandy would be weak enough to ensure its success. Equally important was to delay the movement of German reserves to the Normandy beachhead, and prevent a potentially disastrous counterattack. The plan therefore aimed to persuade the Germans that other attacks were planned in Scandinavia and the Pas de Calais.

In order to do this the Allied forces created a series of false radio reports related to these bogus invasions which the Germans naturally intercepted, and through German double agents.

The Germans had about 50 agents in England at the time, but the MI5, that's the British Military Intelligence division, the place where my dad worked, had caught and recruited many of them as double agents. In fact, although they did not know it, MI5 controlled all of the German agents in Britain at the time. MI5 planned to feed German Intelligence a misleading picture of the invasion preparations via their own agents. Reports sent by these agents were carefully controlled in order to support the view of forces in the UK which the Allied deception planners wished to present.

Fortitude South's mission was to convince the Germans that the Allied forces were going to invade France at Pas de Calais – a logical strategic choice for an invasion since it was the closest part of France to England. By doing this they hoped to reduce the number of troops in the Normandy area when the real invasion took place, and let German Intelligence think that the main invasion would still be in Pas de Calais.

They managed to do this by constructing additional bases and buildings, and positioning bogus vehicles and landing craft around false embarkation points along the south-east coast of England.

Unit check

1 2 confessed 3 fake 4 dealers 5 cash 6 identity
7 denied 8 documents 9 claims 10 passing

2 2 a 3 c 4 b 5 b 6 b 7 c 8 c 9 a

3 2 They offered ~~helping~~ *to help* us paint the garage.
3 I confessed to ~~have~~ *having* forgotten to do my homework.
4 She apologised ~~to~~ *for* having caused such a fuss.
5 They're the first to admit that *they* were lucky.
6 She denied ~~have~~ *having* told lies about where she had gone.
7 He claims that it ~~be~~ *is* the only way to solve the problem.
8 He advised me *to* study hard for the exam.
9 He never apologised for ~~have~~ *having* told me lies.

6 Legend or truth?

1 **(a)** 2 crop up 3 largely irrelevant 4 led to
5 climate of fear 6 classic example
7 wide range 8 single case

(b) 2 wide range 3 word of mouth 4 crops up
5 climate of fear 6 led to 7 single case
8 largely irrelevant

2 **(a)** 2 future 3 present 4 present 5 future
6 past 7 past 8 present

(b) 2 can't 3 will have 4 might 5 will
6 must have 7 may have 8 can't have

(c) 2 can't 3 must 4 can't 5 may 6 will
7 might 8 might 9 must 10 can't 11 won't

3 **(a)** 2 that's a likely story
3 she made that story up
4 It's the story of my life.
5 to cut a long story short
6 she told me a real sob story
7 let's hear your side of the story
8 it's always the same old story with you

(b) 2 She told me a real sob story.
3 Let's hear your side of the story.
4 End of story.
5 It's always the same old story.
6 She made that story up.

4 **(a)** 1 F 2 F 3 T 4 F 5 T 6 T 7 F 8 T

(b) 1 when all of a sudden 2 off she went
3 lying there 4 kind of 5 again and again
6 you believe it 7 that was the amazing thing

TAPESCRIPT

Speaker 1 I heard the weirdest story the other day. A friend of a friend of mine was at the beach when suddenly she felt something crawling into her ear. She tried to get it out but she couldn't find anything, so she forgot about it. Anyway a few days later she started getting these really bad earaches. So off she went to see a doctor. He checked her ears, and put this long needle into her ear again and again but he couldn't find anything. So he decided she must have an earwig, a small bug, deep in her inner ear.

Speaker 2   Yeah, right.

Speaker 1   Honestly, I swear it's true. He said it was kind of too deep to remove. And, would you believe it, he said that she'd have to wait for it to come out the other side.

Speaker 2   You've got to be kidding.

Speaker 1   Well, you can imagine how she felt but what could she do? Anyway, a few weeks later she woke up and lying there on her pillow there was a nasty-looking bug.

Speaker 2   Do you really expect me to believe that?

Speaker 1   It's true, I promise. Anyway, she put the bug in a jar and took it to the doctor to check if it was the bug causing her earaches.

Speaker 2   What, she just put it in a jar?

Speaker 1   That was the amazing thing, she was so cool about the whole thing.

Speaker 2   So what did the doctor say?

Speaker 1   Well, he looked at it and said that it was definitely the bug that had been causing her earaches.

Speaker 2   So she was happy, right?

Speaker 1   Well, yeah, for a while, but then a few days later she started getting really bad earaches again. So she phoned the doctor and do you know what he said?

Speaker 2   No, what did he say?

Speaker 1   He said I should have told you that the bug that you found in your ear was a female and it's probably laid a load of eggs inside your head.

Speaker 2   OK. Now I really don't believe you.

5   2   A <u>friend</u> of a <u>friend</u> of <u>mine</u>.
3   You've <u>got</u> to be <u>kidding</u>.
4   <u>What</u> could she <u>do</u>?
5   Do you <u>really</u> ex<u>pect</u> me to be<u>lieve</u> that?
6   It's <u>true</u>, I <u>promise</u>.
7   <u>Now</u> I <u>really</u> don't be<u>lieve</u> you.

6   **(a)**   1 B   2 A

(b)   1 A   2 B   3 A   4 B   5 Students' own answer.

(c)   1   people who prey greedily on others
2   valuable articles
3   people who collect things discarded by someone else
4   aggressive loud people
5   something provided without charge

(d)   Students' own answers.

Unit check

1   2 tell   3 argue   4 classic   5 wide   6 might   7 lead
8 largely   9 getting   10 cut

2   2 c   3 b   4 c   5 c   6 a   7 b   8 b   9 c

3   2   That's my sister's voice. She ~~can't~~ *must* have come home early.
3   She looks terrible. Something terrible ~~will~~ *must* have happened.
4   They didn't send me a card. They must ~~forget~~ *have forgotten* it's my birthday today.
5   It's twenty past eight. They will ~~arrive~~ *have arrived* by now.
6   When he sees what you've done, ~~he must~~ *he'll* be angry.
7   He can't have ~~make~~ *made* up the story. It's too realistic.
8   If you're a fan of Bond films then I'm sure ~~you can't~~ *you'll* like the new one.
9   I'm sorry, he's not answering the phone. He must ~~have been~~ *be* in a meeting.

(7) Inspiration and creation

1   1 appalled   2 vivid   3 spurred on   4 arson
5 deliberately   6 referred to

2   **(a)**   2   They had their house decorated.
3   We had our website designed.
4   Ann had her hair cut.
5   Joe had all the food for the party delivered.
6   Sue had the garage built.

(b)   2   He'd had a designer suit made.
3   He'd had his photo taken for a newspaper.
4   He'd had his hair dyed.
5   He'd had his hair cut.
6   He'd had his ear pierced.
7   He'd had his house decorated.

3   **(a)**   1   I get butterflies in my stomach
2   It makes my blood boil
3   I didn't know where to put myself
4   I was really cut up
5   I'm feeling a bit down in the dumps
6   I feel like I'm banging my head against a brick wall

(b)   1–5 Students' own answers.

4   **(a)**   will also be put on display
any number of entries can be sent
mustn't have been altered
a stamped addressed envelope should be included
all entries must be received
the winner will be announced
more instructions can be found

(b)   2 be cancelled   3 have been planned
4 have been cleaned   5 be planned   6 be cleaned
7 have been cancelled   8 be taken

(c)   2   The referee might cancel the game because the weather forecast predicts fog for this afternoon.
3   Someone who works at the bank must have planned the robbery.

4 You should have cleaned your room before you went out this morning.
5 We must plan the whole evening well.
6 Only professionals should clean these machines.
7 They might have cancelled the flight.
8 You can't take photos inside the museum.

(d)
2 The form must be filled in with a black pen.
3 The film should be kept in a cool, dry place.
4 Their car can't have been sold for more than £500.
5 Some of the movie might be filmed in our town.
6 Their new CD can be bought online.
7 The meat should have been cooked longer.
8 The car window must have been broken by the storm.

5
(a) Salsa 3   Tango 2   Waltz 1
(b) 1 waltz   2 salsa   3 tango   4 salsa
5 tango   6 waltz

6
(a) jogging   nature
(b) 1 b   2 c   3 b   4 d

Unit check

1
2 dumps   3 be   4 vivid   5 given   6 up
7 deliberately   8 appalled   9 had   10 top

2
2 c   3 a   4 c   5 c   6 b   7 c   8 c   9 a

3
2 We've had the house ~~painting~~ *painted* by professionals.
3 The car must have ~~be~~ *been* stolen.
4 I'm on top of the ~~globe~~ *world*.
5 Did you ~~cut your hair~~ *have your hair cut* at the new hairdressers?
6 I went to the opticians and ~~checked my eyes~~ *had my eyes checked*.
7 The money can be ~~pay~~ *paid* into my bank account.
8 If you ask me, I think he's got a ~~wire~~ *screw* loose.
9 The game will be ~~playing~~ *played* on Tuesday.

8 Virtual worlds

1
(a) 2 purchases   3 living   4 economy   5 take
6 cash   7 economic   8 economical   9 interest
10 currency

(b) 1 economic   2 earn a living   3 economy
4 cash card   5 purchases   6 open an account
7 take out   8 interest rate   9 currency

2
(a)
2 What's so amazing is that people will actually pay money to watch a virtual egg hatch.
3 What I find interesting is the chance to live a virtual life.
4 What I'd do first is get some new virtual clothes.
5 What's so dangerous is that people could get into debt in the real world.
6 What I think people should do is stop hiding in virtual worlds and concentrate on making things better in the real world.

(b)
2 No, it was Jim who told us.
3 No, what confused me was the ending of the film.
4 No, it was after we bought the house that the problems started.
5 No, the things she didn't say were what upset me.
6 No, it was his brother who failed it.
7 No, what I found difficult was the written exam.
8 No, it was the piano that I used to play at school.

(c)
2 No, it was the cinema you took me to.
3 No, what we saw was 'The Wizard of Oz'.
4 No, it was me who bought you a coffee.
5 No, what we did was meet my parents.
6 No, he didn't. It was my mum who liked you.
7 No, it was a hat she knitted you.

3
2 possessions   3 access   4 responsible   5 theft
6 compensation   7 creators   8 argument
9 value   10 liable   11 faulty   12 system

Study help
2 a   3 g   4 b   5 c   6 d   7 h   8 f

4
(a) 2 influential   3 researchers   4 participants
5 unknowingly   6 rating   7 exactly
8 information   9 popularity   10 proof
11 choice

(b) 1 F   2 T   3 F   4 F   5 T   6 T

(c) Stan 1   Jane 2   Paul 3

(d) 1 Paul   2 Stan   3 Jane   4 Stan   5 Jane
6 Jane   7 Paul   8 Stan

TAPESCRIPT

Stan   I love music. I'm a real music fan. And I really love discovering new music on my own. I buy loads of music magazines, *Q, Uncut* and *Mojo*, every month and I read all the reviews. If it sounds like I might like a band then I'll check them out on the Internet. I don't download stuff illegally – I go onto sites like Myspace. There are lots of great artists on them and loads of songs to listen to. I also listen on the band's official site. So I'll try and find out more about a band and hear some stuff and if I like it then I'll go and buy a CD by them. I'd like to buy more but they're so expensive. I also see quite a few concerts, about three a month.

Paul   I'm not really into music. I mean I like it and I do buy CDs occasionally but I don't really know much about it. Mostly I just listen to the radio, Radio 1 usually, and if I really like a song, then I might go out and buy it. Sometimes my friends lend me CDs so I sometimes get into stuff that way. But that's about it. I'd never go out and buy a magazine about music and I've never been to a live concert in my life. I'd rather go and see a football match instead.

Jane   I think the biggest influence on my taste in music is my brother. Seeing how he plays it loud all day in his bedroom, it's difficult to ignore it. But that's OK because he's into some really cool stuff like The Editors, Elbow and Star Sailor. I download most of his CDs onto my MP3 player so I can listen to them on the way to school. It's not really the kind of stuff my friends are into. They like more commercial stuff like McFly and the Scissor Sisters. I try to play them some of my music but they're not interested. Actually, although I say my brother's my biggest influence, recently I've started listening to some of the stuff my dad listened to when he was in his twenties. He kept telling my brother that the bands he listens to are all influenced by the bands he was into, so eventually I checked some out, and he's right. Bands like Echo and the Bunnymen, The Waterboys and Joy Division. They're not bad at all!

5 **(b)** national anthem government citizens
constitution stamp currency king

(c) 1 presented 2 East London 3 Prime Minister
4 currency 5 own face 6 a name 7 36,000
8 lovely home 9 lovely

TAPESCRIPT

Last night's TV highlight was undoubtedly the conclusion to the BBC2 series 'How to Start Your Own Country'. This fascinating series, which started six weeks ago, followed the progress of presenter Danny Wallace as he tried to create the world's newest country. Over the weeks viewers have watched Danny crown himself King Danny and declare independence for his one-bedroom flat in East London. His incredible journey also took him to the home of the Prime Minister where he delivered a declaration of independence to 10 Downing Street.

Along the way Danny took advice from politicians, members of royal families, a cardinal at the Vatican and the chief cashier at the Bank of England, who helped him set up his own currency.

He has also designed a stamp, with his face on it, of course, written and recorded a national anthem, written a constitution and installed a government.

So what was left for last night's programme? Well, every country needs a name and last night thousands of people turned up in Leicester Square in London to see Danny reveal the name that was democratically chosen by the more than 36,000 citizens who now regard Danny as their leader.

Since the beginning of the show, Danny has always said that the name of the country should be decided upon by the people and he invited viewers to send in their suggestions which included names such as Spexico, Wallaceland, Flatland, Kingdan and Dantopia.

The final choice came down to two names, Lovely and Home, and on the night Lovely won. Now anyone can become a citizen of Lovely by registering themselves at www.citizensrequired.com. And considering the charm of its leader, it's something that I'm seriously considering.

Unit check

1 2 principality 3 currency 4 It 5 independence
6 Prince 7 what 8 economic 9 independent
10 earn

2 2 a 3 c 4 a 5 b 6 b 7 c 8 c 9 b

3 2 It's too modern to be of any ~~valuable~~ *value.*
3 It's the way she talked to me ~~what~~ *that* annoyed me most.
4 It was in Majorca ~~what~~ *that* we first met.
5 Make sure you take a ~~waterless~~ *waterproof* coat.
6 It ~~were~~ *was* in the middle of the night that my car was stolen.
7 He's ~~hopeful~~ *hopeless* in the kitchen.
8 She's not very ~~trustable~~ *trustworthy.*
9 What you need to do in a situation like this *is* stay calm.

9 Understanding others

1 2 replicate 3 driving force 4 neurons
5 empathise 6 social disorders 7 incorporate
8 subtle

2 **(a)** 2 blinking 3 cough 4 tilt 5 fiddling
6 yawning 7 rub 8 biting 9 fold

(b) 2 The girl is biting her nails.
3 The girl is fiddling with her hair.
4 The man is folding his arms.
5 The girl is tilting her head.
6 The boy is rubbing his eyes.

Study help

1 a noun b verb c noun d noun
2 a verb b verb c verb d noun
3 a verb b verb c verb d noun

3 **(a)** They don't seem to
It appears
Definitely

(b) 2 Understanding your teenage children seems to be one of modern parents' greatest challenges.
3 Your parents undoubtedly love you.
4 It's true that our parents often appear to forget what it's like to be young.
5 If you try to meet your parents half way things will definitely start to improve.
6 It is believed that this is a source of great conflict in a family.
7 Your parents unquestionably want a happier home environment too.
8 This seems to be a problem for many families all over the country.

(c) 2 It appears to be broken.
3 It is believed to be the rarest animal in the world.
4 This discovery is thought to be the most important for decades.
5 They don't seem to know where they are going.

6 It's unquestionably the biggest problem facing this government.

7 There will definitely be some questions to answer.

8 He undoubtedly needs to do something soon.

4

(a) 1 B   2 C   3 A

(b) 1 T   2 F   3 F   4 T   5 T   6 T   7 T   8 T

(c) 2 h   3 g   4 a   5 f   6 e   7 b   8 c

5

(a) 1 C   2 B   3 D   4 A

(b) Students' own answers.

Unit check

1

2 yawning   3 fiddling   4 seem   5 undoubtedly
6 subtle   7 blinks   8 appears   9 strokes
10 incorporate

2

2 c   3 b   4 c   5 b   6 c   7 a   8 b   9 b

3

2 Stop fiddling ~~on~~ *with* your hair.

3 Global warming is believed to ~~been~~ *be* the most important issue of our times.

4 She has ~~got definitely~~ *definitely got* the talent to win this competition.

5 That cat doesn't like it when you ~~fold~~ *stroke* it.

6 It now appears not ~~being~~ *to be* as simple as it first seemed.

7 It is a problem that ~~needs unquestionably~~ *unquestionably needs* an urgent solution.

8 Can you ~~rub~~ *tilt* your head back so I can take a look inside your mouth?

9 It ~~doesn't seem~~ *seems* that Ronaldo won't be playing today.

10 The sporting spirit

1

Down
1 ambition   3 tread   4 seen   6 rushed   7 stunned
Across
2 butted   5 inappropriate   7 suspended   8 standing

2

(a) 2 c   3 a   4 a   5 a   6 c   7 c   8 b

(b) The following words should be crossed out:
4 ~~can't~~   5 ~~didn't to~~   6 ~~managed to~~
7 ~~could~~   9 ~~could~~

(c) 2 The pilot was able to make an emergency landing and the disaster was avoided.

3 The party next door was so loud that I didn't manage to get to sleep all night.

4 I could do things like that when I was younger but I'm too old now.

5 I was so scared I couldn't move.

6 Were you able to speak to him?

7 Living off fish and rain-water, they managed to survive for three weeks at sea.

8 Are you able to borrow the car tomorrow?

3

(a) 2 S   3 F   4 F   5 S   6 S   7 F   8 F

(b) 1 made it   2 blown   3 fallen through
4 messed up   5 going wrong   6 overcame
7 pulled off   8 fulfilling

4

(a) 1 b   2 c   3 c   4 a   5 c   6 b

(b) 1 matter   2 Now   3 fact   4 bear   5 back
6 happens   7 way   8 sum

TAPESCRIPT

Now everyone knows that the Olympics in 2004 were held in Greece but did you know that the first Olympic games were also held in Athens back over a hundred years ago in 1896? I'm talking about the modern era of the Olympics, of course, not the games that took place thousands of years ago in Ancient Greece. When it was decided that the Olympic games should be revived to allow the greatest international competition in sport, it was originally decided that they would start in Paris in 1900. However, because of the Olympics' origins in Ancient Greece, it was agreed that the games should start four years earlier and be staged in Athens. Erm, just as a matter of interest the games nearly had to take place in Budapest in Hungary because the Greeks were having financial difficulties. However, the Crown Prince Constantine of Greece set up an organising committee which managed to raise the money and save the games.

These first Olympics were on a much smaller scale than the Games we're used to today. For example, just over 200 men – no women competed at all – from 14 countries took part in a total of 43 events. Let's put that into context. Can you just bear with me for a moment while I check my notes? In the last Games in 2004, 11,000 athletes from 201 countries took part in 301 events. And of course, women were invited too.

Right, going back to the 1896 games, quite a few other things were different too. For example, winners were given a silver medal, not a gold one. They also received a crown of olive leaves. The bronze medal was awarded to the second-place athlete. So what did you get for third place? As it happens, if you came in third you got nothing. By the way, the first Olympic champion was American James Brendan Connolly, whose triple jump of 13.71 metres was enough to win him that silver medal.

Most of the athletes in these first games were actually Greeks, so unsurprisingly they won a lot of medals. Some of the most popular early events were tennis, fencing, weightlifting, shooting, swimming and gymnastics. Unfortunately some events had to be cancelled. Both the cricket and football competitions were called off because they couldn't find enough teams to take part. The rowing and sailing competitions never took place because of bad weather and rough seas. However, despite these minor problems, the games were a great success and many people wanted the 1900 Games to go to Greece as well. Of course that never happened.

To sum up, although the Games have got bigger and bigger, the great competitive spirit of the Olympic Games is still the same, and was born more than a century ago in Greece.

5 **(a)** 1 the k and s sounds jump over and join the following word
2 the g and n sounds jump over and join the following word
3 the t sound disappears
4 f becomes v and r becomes schwa
5 s jumps over to the next word and t changes sound

6 **(a)** Britain's best medal hope B
Athletes beaten by the heat D
Obsessive preparations C
Olympic dream ends in tears A

(b) 1 T 2 F 3 T 4 T 5 F 6 F

Unit check

1 2 couldn't 3 wrong 4 butt 5 messed 6 on
7 manage 8 inappropriate 9 ovation 10 suspended

2 2 c 3 b 4 c 5 c 6 a 7 c 8 a 9 b

3 2 We were so close to winning but we blew ~~on~~ it in the last minute and they scored.
3 We were lucky because we ~~could~~ *were able to* break the window and escape from the fire.
4 He's got a lot of talent. I think he can ~~do~~ *make* it all the way to the top.
5 I won't be ~~managed~~ *able* to come tomorrow. I've got an appointment at the doctor's.
6 It rained all day so they ~~didn't~~ *weren't* able to play a single game.
7 It was difficult at first but we ~~came over~~ *overcame* our problems, and things soon got better.
8 I ~~was managed~~ *could* run 100 m in 11 seconds when I was younger.
9 It's really easy to make. If you follow the recipe, you can't ~~make~~ *go* wrong.

(11) Superheroes

1 **(a)** 2 life-threatening 3 on a daily basis 4 smashing
5 still comes in handy 6 foes 7 twists
8 make-believe 9 can't find a way

(b) 1 make-believe 2 smashing 3 life-threatening
4 can't find a way 5 instant hit 6 twists
7 still comes in handy 8 foes 9 on a daily basis

2 **(a)** 2 b 3 b 4 a 5 a

(b) 1 have I 2 I have 3 was I 4 I was 5 I was
6 was I 7 had I 8 I had

(c) 2 b 3 b 4 a 5 c 6 b

(d) 1 Never has she been so embarrassed.
2 Rarely will you see a better film.
3 Seldom do politicians tell the truth.
4 On no account can you go into that room.
5 Under no circumstances should you touch the red wire.
6 Not only was she late but she also forgot to bring me a present.
7 No sooner had we left the house than the rain started.
8 Rarely did we go on holiday when I was a child.

3 **(a)** 1 slouch 2 strength 3 squint 4 pant
5 short-sighted 6 X-ray vision 7 puny
8 speed of light 9 short of breath

(b) 1 puny 2 strength 3 short-sighted 4 squints
5 X-ray vision 6 short of breath 7 panting
8 speed of light 9 slouched

4 **(a)** 2 e 3 c 4 f 5 b 6 a

(b) 5 4 6 7 2 8 3 1

5 **(a)** 1 3 5 6 7

(b) 1 d 2 a 3 d 4 b 5 d

TAPESCRIPT
Presenter Captain Aquatic.
Aquatic Present.
Presenter Dynamico.
Dynamico Here.
Presenter Brainwave.
Brainwave Reporting for duty.
Presenter The children of the St Thomas Orphanage need your help. £200 will ensure their Christmas party can take place. Without it, the party will be cancelled. Your task today will take you to the city centre where you have eight hours to raise the money. Failure to do so will mean a lot of unhappy children and elimination of one of you from the show. You have five minutes to discuss your strategy. Here's a copy of the rules. Your time starts now.
Brainwave OK, so let's get thinking. £200. That shouldn't be too difficult, should it?
Aquatic No, let's go to a cashpoint machine and withdraw it. £66 each. I've even got my bank card with me.
Dynamico I'm pretty sure that's against the rules. It would be a bit too easy.
Brainwave Yeah, afraid so. It says here in the rules that we can't use our own money.
Aquatic OK. Let's think of something else.
Brainwave It seems obvious to me. We're going to have to design some sort of poster and stop people and ask them to make a donation for our cause. I think if we wear our costumes, we'll definitely get people's attention easily enough.
Aquatic You want us to beg.

Brainwave Not beg. Collect for charity, if you like. It's the most obvious way.

Aquatic No way. I'm a superhero, not a charity worker.

Brainwave Well, you think of something better.

Dynamico OK, um, if Aquatic wants to do something more superhero-ish, then maybe we should be thinking about how we can use our special powers to help us with this task.

Aquatic You're right. Let's just go and rob a bank.

Dynamico What!

Aquatic Just for fun. We can go in and threaten to use our superhuman strength unless they give us the money. And then later we can go back and explain.

Dynamico You're serious, aren't you?

Aquatic Of course I am. What's the problem?

Dynamico Er, well, OK, er, first it's illegal, secondly we'll probably get shot, um, thirdly, if we don't get shot we'll probably spend the rest of our lives in prison.

Brainwave Plus it's not exactly superhero behaviour. We're supposed to be stopping crime, not causing it.

Aquatic You two are such cowards.

Brainwave No, we're just not complete lunatics, that's all.

Aquatic OK, well, what about this for an idea? Dynamico, you can make yourself invisible, can't you?

Dynamico Yeah. What about it?

Aquatic Well, why don't you go into one of those big mega-stores and borrow £200 from one of their tills?

Brainwave What! That's as bad as robbing a bank. Sometimes I wonder which side of the law you're really on, Captain Aquatic.

Aquatic I'm not talking about some small shop. Let's hit a big department store. They're huge. They wouldn't miss £200. They can afford it.

Brainwave And what about the poor assistant who finds her till is £200 short at the end of the day? She's the one who'll end up paying.

Dynamico Forget it, it wouldn't work anyway.

Aquatic Why not?

Dynamico Well, um …

Aquatic What is it?

Dynamico I, er, I can only turn invisible if no one's looking.

Aquatic You mean if I close my eyes, then you're invisible. Brilliant. What kind of special power is that?

Brainwave Leave him alone. Let's just think of something else.

Aquatic Well, it's about time one of you two came up with an idea. I'm the only one who's doing any thinking here. All you two can do is rubbish all my ideas.

Dynamico I've got it.

Brainwave What?

Dynamico We can offer to do odd jobs for people. You know, um … need something doing? We'll do it now.

Brainwave You mean like washing windows?

Dynamico Exactly, or washing up in restaurants.

Brainwave Great idea. Let's get moving.

Aquatic Oh how exciting. I can hardly wait.

Brainwave Come on Aquatic, we've got some doing good to do.

Unit check

1 2 short 3 panting 4 daily 5 smash 6 light 7 life 8 superhuman 9 sooner 10 than

2 2 c 3 a 4 a 5 a 6 c 7 a 8 c 9 a

3 2 Under no circumstances ~~I will~~ *will I* ever speak to him again.
3 No sooner had we got into the car *than* it broke down.
4 ~~I've got short sight.~~ *I'm short-sighted.*
5 Not only is he rude, but ~~is he~~ *he is* also arrogant too.
6 When I asked him to help he was out of the kitchen at the ~~velocity~~ *speed* of light.
7 On no account ~~you should~~ *should you* go beyond this line.
8 I'm a bit short ~~in~~ *of* breath.
9 Rarely ~~go I~~ *do I go* to the cinema.

12 On your own

1 2 ambiguous 3 drop by 4 wandered 5 hummed 6 undisturbed 7 dense 8 set-up

2 **(a)** 2 PO 3 PO 4 PP 5 PP 6 PP 7 PO 8 PP

(b) 1 b 2 d 3 c 4 f 5 e 6 a

(c) 2 e 3 h 4 a 5 b 6 g 7 d 8 f

(d) 2 If the town wasn't so small we wouldn't have seen everything in a day.
3 If she didn't love Almodovar films she wouldn't have bought all his films on DVD.
4 If he hadn't gone on holiday with his friends, he would have some money left.
5 If I were fitter I'd have finished the race.
6 If they liked me they'd have invited me.
7 If you hadn't told him my secret, everyone wouldn't know about it.
8 If he hadn't lived alone for a long time, it wouldn't be hard for him to meet new people.

3 **(a)** 2 e 3 f 4 a 5 b 6 g 7 d

(b) 2 We have to stop now because time's up.
3 She's got time on her hands.
4 We'll be there in no time at all.
5 Pay attention at all times.
6 I'm killing time before the match begins.

(c) 1 Time's up!   2 in no time   3 at all times
4 time on your hands   5 time   6 killing time

4 **(a)** 2 otherwise   3 as long as   4 Unless   5 Imagine
6 as long as   7 Suppose   8 otherwise

(b) 2 You can go out now provided that you clean up your room when you come home.
3 I couldn't move to another country unless I already spoke the language.
4 Buy a ticket for the car park, otherwise the police will tow your car away.
5 We'll get there in no time unless the traffic is bad.
6 I always write a list, otherwise I never remember all the things I have to buy.

5 **(a)** 3 ✓   4 ✓   5 into   6 that   7 just   8 ✓
9 the   10 ✓   11 who

(b) 1 legible   2 execution   3 undertaken   4 sealed
5 ashore

(c) 1 That the Mediterranean Sea was formed by the inflowing Atlantic Ocean.
2 A report of his journey and a note.
3 He wanted people to know about the New World, so he sent a message in a bottle in case he didn't survive the journey.
4 Because they might contain confidential information from the navy.

(d) 1 T   2 F   3 F   4 T   5 T   6 T   7 T   8 F

TAPESCRIPT

Speaker ... and anyone else who opened the bottles could face execution. Now, you might think that the idea of messages in bottles is a thing of the past. Well, yes and no. Only recently, a message in a bottle helped to save the lives of eighty-eight people who were shipwrecked in a boat near the coast of Costa Rica on their way to the United States. They saw a fishing boat but couldn't attract the attention of the fishermen, so they wrote an SOS message and put it in a bottle, which they then tied to one of the long lines holding the fishermen's net. When the fishermen hauled the net in, they found the note and rescued the people.

And, while messages in bottles may not be so common nowadays, there are variations on the theme. For instance, balloon mail is a similar method of sending undirected messages. The advantage of balloon mail is that a balloon can be launched anywhere and can, in principle, reach any point on earth. A further advantage is that a balloon will always end up somewhere, whereas a bottle dropped from land could be washed back ashore by the tide and so it might never go anywhere.

And so, nowadays, with things like balloon mail, the phrase 'message in a bottle' has now really come to mean a message with no particular intended destination, as opposed to the original versions which were always cries for help. Other 'messages in

bottles' have been launched by NASA, the American space agency. A graphic message in the form of a 6 by 9-inch aluminium plaque, known as the Pioneer plaque, was bolted to the frames of the Pioneer 10 spacecraft that was launched in 1972, and also to Pioneer 11, launched in 1973. These are messages that say 'we exist, and this is where we are'.

In the summer of 1977, NASA launched two spacecraft together called the Voyager Project. The spacecraft each carry a 12-inch gold-plated copper disk, known as the Voyager Golden Record, containing recorded sounds and images representing human cultures and life on Earth. No replies as yet – but don't forget that it took 300 years for Columbus' message to be found, so who knows?

6 **(a)** 1 21   2 27   3 29   4 18   5 34   6 23

(b) 1 She / He is glad not to be able to see her / his own face.
2 She / He doesn't know what they are.
3 She / He has lost feeling in her / his legs, and has lost the sense of touch. He / She doesn't feel any pain.
4 The writer thinks she / he is going to die.

(c) Students' own answers.

Unit check

1 2 hum   3 hands   4 charge   5 wander   6 set
7 ambiguous   8 imagine   9 misunderstand   10 space

2 2 c   3 b   4 b   5 b   6 a   7 a   8 b   9 b

3 2 I won't go to the match ~~otherwise~~ *unless* you come with me.
3 If I had a better memory, I ~~hadn't forgotten~~ *wouldn't forget* his name.
4 We ~~were~~ *would be* there now if you hadn't taken so long to get ready.
5 If I ~~would have~~ *had* gone on holiday, I wouldn't have any money left.
6 If you really were my friend, you ~~had~~ *would have* helped me yesterday.
7 I won't lend it to you, ~~as long as~~ *unless* you promise to give it back.
8 I'm going to write it down, ~~provided~~ *otherwise* I'll forget it in no time.
9 ~~Suppose~~ *Imagine* living on a desert island – what would it be like?

(13) # The age wars

1 **(a)** *Down*
1 suburban   2 retire   4 grotty   6 browse
Across
3 legs   5 fumes   7 daydream   8 lose

(b) 1 browse 2 daydreaming 3 grotty 4 suburban
5 lose sleep 6 retire 7 last legs 8 fumes

2 **(a)** 2 will pick 3 I'll be doing 4 we'll get
5 he'll be working 6 you'll have 7 I'll help
8 will be using

(b) 1 will you be 2 have finished 3 'll have finished
4 won't 5 won't be 6 'll be 7 'll have been
8 'll have decided

(c) 2 'll have travelled
3 will be driving, will have passed
4 will have left, will be looking
5 will be working, won't have finished
6 will have tidied, will be sitting

3 **(a)** 2 thinking of 3 due to 4 bound to
5 thinking of 6 about to 7 about to
8 supposed to

(b) 2 I'm supposed to be at the airport at 5 o'clock
in the morning.
3 The plane is due to leave at 7am.
4 I'm thinking of not going to bed tonight.
5 I'm bound to fall asleep.
6 I'm about to pack my suitcase.
7 I'm bound to forget something.

4 **(a)** 1 started 2 change 3 take 4 took 5 left
6 dropped 7 paid 8 settled

(b) 1 left 2 took 3 dropped 4 settle 5 started
6 paid 7 changed 8 take

5 **(a)** 1 foolish 2 seriously 3 risks 4 beans
5 imaginary 6 sensibly 7 try 8 begin
9 dawns 10 children

(c) 1

(d) 1 T 2 F 3 T 4 T 5 F

(e) 1 anew 2 errors 3 hygienic 4 contemplate
5 prolifically 6 barefoot

6 **(a)** 1 a 2 c 3 a 4 d 5 c 6 a 7 d 8 c

(b) 1 music, clothing and hairstyles
2 Discipline is less authoritarian.
3 Parents and children have begun talking more,
and adults now acknowledge children's thoughts
and feelings.
4 Children have too much power, and parents spend
too much time trying to make their children happy
rather than behaving appropriately as parents.
5 Parents are able to relate better to their children
and share their interests.

Unit check

1 2 parents 3 suburban 4 retired 5 browse 6 leave
7 off 8 grotty 9 sleep 10 bound

2 2 b 3 a 4 b 5 a 6 b 7 b 8 c 9 a

3 2 We're supposed to *be* doing a test tomorrow.
3 By 2020, humans will ~~travelled~~ *travel* to Mars.
4 Don't phone me at eight, I'll ~~watch~~ *be watching* the
football match then.
5 I haven't studied much so I'm ~~due~~ *bound* to fail the exam.
6 Sorry, I can't talk now – I'm about *to* have an interview.
7 I'm thinking *of* buying a new computer next month.
8 By December next year, I'll ~~work~~ *have worked* here for
two months.
9 Sorry, I can't talk to you now – I'm ~~bound~~ *off* to the theatre!

14 The beauty hunters

1 **(a)** 1 d 2 g 3 a 4 b 5 h 6 c 7 e 8 f

(b) 1 immaculate 2 vanity 3 fake 4 enhance
5 wrinkles 6 consultation

2 **(a)** 1 rather 2 wish 3 time 4 time 5 only
6 wish

(b) 2 knew 3 stopped 4 weren't / wouldn't be
5 wasn't 6 took 7 went 8 were

(c) 2 was in the national team
3 did / would do their homework on time
4 didn't bring dogs in with them
5 gave the tests back
6 didn't play football on the grass
7 wouldn't feed the animals
8 built more car parks

(d) 2 I wish I had less homework to do.
3 If only my friends were here.
4 I'd rather you didn't make so much noise.
5 If only I could buy a new MP3 player.
6 I wish you wouldn't do that.
7 I'd sooner go to the cinema.
8 It's high time something were done about this.

3 **(a)** 2 effect 3 loose 4 raise 5 advise
6 persecuted 7 lie 8 ensure

(b) 1 lose 2 loose 3 sensitive 4 persecuted
5 affect 6 advise 7 sensible 8 effect
9 advice 10 ensured 11 prosecuted 12 insured

4 **(a)** 1 b 2 b 3 c 4 a 5 c

(b) 1 He thinks Sally is being rude.
2 He thinks it's a waste of money.
3 Because they have too much money to spend.
4 He's never seen the effects of cosmetic surgery
before.

(c) 1 honest 2 truth 3 thought 4 hand
5 though 6 mean 7 circles 8 what

Girl   Did you hear about Paula's mother?

Boy   No – what about her?

Girl   She's had a nose job.

Boy   A nose job? You mean, she had an operation, cosmetic surgery?

Girl   That's right. And to be honest, she needed it.

Boy   Well, that's not a very nice remark.

Girl   Oh, come on Philip. You and I both know her nose was really big. Paula knew it too, and her mum, that's why she had the operation. And I bet she's a lot happier now, as well.

Boy   What do you mean?

Girl   Well, it's obvious, isn't it? A lot of people have cosmetic surgery done so that they'll feel better about themselves. And they're happy to spend the money, because something they really don't like about themselves can be changed. They're not trying to be film-star look-alikes, you know.

Boy   Maybe – but to tell you the truth, I reckon it's a waste of money.

Girl   Well, maybe you do, but they don't. I'd have thought people have the right to do what they want with their own bodies – and their own money, if it comes to that.

Boy   Well, of course they do. On the other hand, I bet there are people all over the world who'd love to do it. They'd love to have a new nose or eyes or whatever, but they can't afford it.

Girl   Well, yes. That shouldn't stop people who can afford it, though.

Boy   Well, I just think it's wrong. I mean, it's such a western thing to do. All these rich people with too much money to spend ...

Girl   Hang on, hang on. Paula's mum saved up a long time, you know, she didn't just take the money out of the bank. She didn't have a holiday for a couple of years, she had to sell a few things – she's not rich.

Boy   Yeah, OK, sorry. Let's talk about something else.

Girl   OK. We're just going round in circles anyway.

Boy   Tell you what – why don't we go round and see her?

Girl   Who? Paula's mum? Why?

Boy   Well, the thing is, I've never seen the effects of cosmetic surgery.

Girl   Oh Philip, you're impossible ...

5 **(a)** That's right. And to be honest, she needed it.
To tell you the truth, I reckon it's a waste of money.
I'd have thought people have the right to do what they want with their own bodies.
On the other hand, I bet there are people all over the world who'd love to do it.
That shouldn't stop people who can afford it, though.
I mean, it's such a western thing to do.
We're just going round in circles anyway.
Tell you what – why don't we go round and see her?

6 **(a)** A 3   B 1   C 4

(b)   1   The growing obsession with the idea of celebrity.
2   They copy clothes and hairstyles.
3   The technology has changed.
4   That by offering plastic surgery as a prize, they are violating a code of medical ethics.

Unit check

1   2 sensible   3 ensure   4 immaculate   5 fake   6 affected
7 consultation   8 prosecute   9 hadn't   10 learned

2   2 b   3 a   4 a   5 c   6 a   7 c   8 c   9 b

3   2   It's time we ~~leave~~ *left* for the concert.
3   It's very valuable, so we've ~~ensured~~ *insured* it for a lot of money.
4   How many eggs does this chicken ~~lie~~ *lay* every day?
5   It's so hot! I'm going to wear some nice, ~~lose~~ *loose* clothes.
6   I'd rather your friends ~~wouldn't~~ *didn't* come this weekend.
7   Don't talk about his girlfriend – it's a very ~~sensible~~ *sensitive* topic for him.
8   They've ~~risen~~ *raised* over ten thousand pounds for charity.
9   I don't like this house – I wish we ~~wouldn't~~ *didn't* live here.

(15) Days gone by

1   **(a)**   2 f   3 g   4 d   5 e   6 h   7 b   8 a

(b)   1 gloomy   2 safeguard   3 gem   4 extraordinary
5 countless   6 quintessential   7 eventual
8 shrink

2   **(a)**   1 hope so   2 those   3 so did   4 that
5 neither did   6 did so

(b)   2 so am I   3 neither are museums in Italy   4 that
5 I hope so   6 do so   7 did so   8 so did my friends

3   **(a)**   2 It's   3 We're   4 I   5 It's   6 Go   7 Turn
8 Take the   9 That's   10 It's a

(b)   1   2 Have you got   3 Have you   4 Is it   5 It's
2   1 Did you have a   2 it was   3 Did you
4 Do you   5 I've

(c)   1   A: Want a drink?   B: Yes, I'd like one.
2   A: Have a nice weekend?
B: No! The worst weekend ever.
3   A: This OK to eat?   B: Not sure, it might be.
4   A: Mike – got a minute?
B: Sorry, busy at the moment.
5   A: Come on, please help.
B: I would if I could but I can't.

4   **(a)**   *Down*
1 contemporary   3 old fashioned   6 restore
7 novel
Across
2 renovate   4 outdated   5 update   8 obsolete
9 renew

(b) 1 novel 2 update 3 restored 4 contemporary
5 obsolete 6 outdated 7 renovated
8 renew 9 old fashioned

5 **(a)** 1 The woman has returned a piece of sculpted
marble to Athens.
2 She heard about Greece's Elgin Marbles campaign.
3 She thinks the Museum should return all the
original Elgin Marbles.
4 Heidelberg University
5 Because they were legally obtained.

(b) 1 B 2 E 3 A 4 D 6 C

(c) 1 T 2 F 3 T 4 T 5 F 6 T 7 F 8 T

6 **(a)** 1 1971 2 19 3 78,000 4 Spanish conquest 5 15th
6 calendar 7 wind, firestorms (or floods) 8 1011 AD

(b) 1 Mexican
2 a large area of the museum is in the open air
3 Room 7 on the ground floor
4 It has a diameter of about four metres
(or weighs around 25 tons)
5 The Aztec sun god

TAPESCRIPT

Tour Guide OK everyone, please listen up now.
Well, here we are. This is one of the really special
highlights of our trip here in Mexico City. We're
outside the National Museum of Anthropology,
which is one of the most wonderful museums in
the world. It's a fairly modern building, as you can
see – it was opened in 1971. Erm, it was designed
by the Mexican architect, Pedro Ramírez Vázquez,
and built over a period of 19 months. Um, as you
can see, it's a huge building – the museum covers in
total an area of about 78,000 square metres, and of
those, about 36,000 are in the open air, quite
unusual for a museum I'm sure you'll agree.

OK, well, inside there are two floors, the upper floor
shows more recent Mexican history and
development but the lower, ground floor focuses on
Mexico before the Spanish conquest – the Spanish
arrived, you'll remember, in 1519. Anyway, here
you'll find many wonderful artefacts from various
civilisations including the Aztecs.

Now, you won't have time to see everything, that
would take about three days or more but there is
one thing you cannot, must not miss on any
account, and that is the Aztec Sun Stone. It's
housed in Room 7, on the ground floor. Here's a
picture of it, but go see the real thing, OK?! This
stone was carved in the late fifteenth century, it has
a diameter of about 4 metres and weighs around
25 tons. Now, as far as we know, it appears that the
sun stone is a kind of cosmological calendar – but
from the Aztec world and times, not what we'd
understand today.

In the centre of the stone is the Aztec sun god. The
rest of the carvings illustrate Aztec cosmology – the

Aztecs believed that before they existed, the world
went through four periods of creation and
destruction, which the Aztecs referred to as four
worlds. Now, around the centre image there are four
square panels, and they represent these four worlds
and their destruction – they were destroyed by
jaguars, wind, firestorms and floods, in that order.
There's a ring around the panels that's filled with
symbols representing the 20 days of the Aztec
month. Finally, two snakes form an outer ring, and
they point to the date when the fifth sun, the Aztecs'
current world, was created. That date is 1011 AD.

Well, anyway, enough of me talking, let's go inside
and see some of the wonderful exhibits. Now, if
you'll all just follow me …

Unit check

1 2 that 3 those 4 restoring 5 replaced 6 restored
7 neither 8 Eventually 9 so 10 novel

2 2 a 3 b 4 a 5 c 6 a 7 b 8 c 9 b

3 2 They asked me to go with them, but I didn't want *to*.
3 He's not American, and neither ~~she is~~ *is she*.
4 I had always wanted to go there, and last year I ~~so did~~ *did so*.
5 I didn't ring her, but if I'd had her number I would *have*.
6 Museums have one main purpose: ~~it~~ *that* of recording the past.
7 My bike was in a terrible condition, but I ~~renewed~~ *restored* it and now it's fine.
8 **A:** Do you think he'll phone? **B:** I hope *so*.
9 My membership ran out and I had to pay £50 to ~~renovate~~ *renew* it.

16 # Swapping places

1 1 a 2 b 3 c 4 b 5 a 6 c

2 **(a)** 1 must 2 have your head examined 3 managed to
4 had been waiting 5 had we sat down
6 must have been 7 it was Mozart 8 to read
9 otherwise 10 big hairy German
11 you'll have seen 12 supposed

(b) 1 a He walked down a long, dark, narrow corridor.
b I bought an expensive brown leather jacket.
c We were met by a strange little old man.
2 a I liked the film very much.
b He clearly didn't mean to do it.
c Surprisingly I finished the examination quickly.
3 a I had my hair cut.
b We had our house broken into last Sunday.
c Many people had their homes destroyed by
the fire.

4 a I love Japanese food and so does my mother.
   b He does an important job – that of making sure everyone gets paid.
   c She couldn't come to the party and neither could her sister.
5 a You won't get to university unless you work hard.
   b You must work hard, otherwise you won't get to university.
   c You'll get to university provided you work hard.
6 a He apologised for losing my watch.
   b He admitted having lost my watch.
   c He confessed to having lost my watch.
7 a I wish she was here with me.
   b It's time you left.
   c If only I hadn't forgotten his birthday.

3
1 busted   2 dorky   3 da bomb   4 slacker
5 Whatever   6 totally   7 biter   8 411

4 **(a)**
1 They produced the rock opera, Tommy.
2 When Pete Townshend announced it in an interview with *Rolling Stone* magazine.
3 A rock opera is based on a story.
4 It wasn't quite as successful.
5 They were very influential on future bands.

(b)
a 4 stand-alone   b 8 in the works
c 3 considerable   d 5 acclaim   e 1 let slip
f 2 landmark   g 7 elaborate   h 6 primarily

(c)
1 The Detours
2 Because he felt the band weren't very good.
3 In 1964.
4 He was noted for swinging his microphone around his head.
5 He launched solo albums, and he had a few acting roles in cinema and on TV.
6 Music composer and bank robber.
7 He performed at Carnegie Hall.

TAPESCRIPT

Roger Daltrey started life as a rebel, and at school wasn't really interested in learning anything. From an early age he was a dedicated fan of rock 'n' roll and along with Pete Townshend he started a band while still at school – it was called The Detours. When he left school in 1960, Daltrey got a job as a factory worker while continuing to play with the band. Daltrey never really believed the band were much good, and thought he would be a factory worker for the rest of his life. But they slowly got more and more work and in 1964 came a crucial moment, when they decided to change the name of the band to The Who.

Shortly after this, a string of number 1 hits brought them success. As singer on stage for The Who, Daltrey's trademark was to swing his microphone around over his head and above the heads of the audience – in 1967, in the USA, Daltrey managed to break 18 microphones during nine shows.

The big turning point in Daltrey's professional life came with the rock opera *Tommy*, and especially the film version in which Daltrey played Tommy, the deaf, dumb and blind boy who in the words of the song, 'sure played a mean pinball'. Daltrey realised that he had other talents and that he wasn't just the singer in a rock 'n' roll band, and he began to develop his own career. In the early 1970s he launched solo albums which were very well received, and he also developed his acting career with a number of roles both in cinema and on TV – roles which varied from the classical music composer Franz Liszt to the bank robber John McVicar, and appearances which included a slot on *The Simpsons* and one on *That 70s Show*.

The Who officially disbanded in 1983 but there have been several reunion concerts through the 80s and 90s, and Daltrey has always been there – there was even a reunion tour in 1989. Daltrey celebrated his fiftieth birthday in 1994 by performing at Carnegie Hall in New York in a show called 'Daltrey Sings Townshend'. Later he had a short weekly series on BBC Radio 2, presenting a personal choice of rock 'n' roll favourites.

5 **(a)**
1 30 Days
2 Morgan Spurlock and Alexandra Jamieson
3 They had to live for a month on the national minimum wage in Columbus, Ohio ($5.15)

(b)
A 3   B 1   C 5   D 2   E 4

(c) Students' own answers.

Unit check

1
2 had   3 thing   4 totally   5 Whatever   6 stuffy
7 Like   8 did   9 couldn't   10 otherwise

2
2 c   3 b   4 b   5 b   6 a   7 b   8 b   9 c

3
2 They gave me a ~~big Spanish delicious~~ *delicious big Spanish* meal.
3 He's nice, but he tends ~~being~~ *to be* a bit too shy sometimes.
4 The phones we use now are really different from ~~them~~ *those* we used ten years ago.
5 When we got there, we saw that the house had *been* knocked down.
6 It was hard but I ~~could~~ *managed to* do it in the end.
7 It's about time you ~~go~~ *went* home.
8 She apologised ~~to have~~ *for having* caused so many problems.
9 No sooner had we got there *than* it started to rain.

Acknowledgements

The publishers are grateful to:
Pentacor**big** for text and layouts
Annie Cornford: Editorial work
Pat Chappell: Workbook key